Sentencing Canudos

ILLUMINATIONS: CULTURAL FORMATIONS OF THE AMERICAS

John Beverley and Sara Castro-Klarén, Editors

SENTENCING CANUDOS

Subalternity in the Backlands of Brazil

ADRIANA MICHÉLE CAMPOS JOHNSON

University of Pittsburgh Press

Published by the University of Pittsburgh Press, Pittsburgh, Pa., 15260
Copyright © 2010, University of Pittsburgh Press
Manufactured in the United States of America
Printed on acid-free paper
10 9 8 7 6 5 4 3 2 1

Library of Congress Cataloging-in-Publication Data

Johnson, Adriana Michéle Campos, 1972-
    Sentencing Canudos : subalternity in the backlands of Brazil / Adriana Michéle Campos Johnson.
      p.   cm. — (Illuminations: cultural formations of the Americas)
    Includes bibliographical references and index.
    ISBN-13: 978-0-8229-6123-9 (pbk. : alk. paper)
    ISBN-10: 0-8229-6123-7 (pbk. : alk. paper)
    1. Brazil—History—Canudos Campaign, 1893-1897—Historiography. 2. Cunha, Euclides da, 1866-
1909. Sertões. 3. Canudos (Euclides da Cunha, Brazil)—Historiography. 4. Canudos (Euclides da
Cunha, Brazil)—In literature. I. Title.
    F2537.J65 2010
    981'.05—dc22   2010031531

CONTENTS

ACKNOWLEDGMENTS

I want to thank, first, Alberto Moreiras for the rigor and generosity of his mentorship and for pushing me to take intellectual risks. Thank you to John French, who asked the tough questions that put my work on da Cunha on this track and for alerting me to the Quebra-Quilos revolts. This project would not be what it is if it were not for Antonio Olavo, who opened up a different vision of Canudos for me by pointing me in the direction of texts I needed to read and people I needed to talk to. I'm also extremely grateful to all those who took the time and trouble to talk to me in Salvador: José Carlos Pinheiros, Renato Ferraz, Oleone Coelho Fontes, Lizir Arcanjo Alves, and Manoel Neto, to whom I'm particularly indebted for showing me present-day Canudos. I want to thank the staff at the Núcleo Sertão (UFBA) for allowing me to access the material there, Duke's Romance studies department and UCI's Latin American studies program for funding research trips to Salvador, and my comparative literature colleagues for making UCI such a wonderful place to work. My thanks to the members of the Subaltern-Popular Workshop for an intellectual home for five years. Thank you to the two anonymous reviewers of the manuscript for invaluable critique and suggestions and to Devin Fromm and Joshua Shanholtzer at University of Pittsburgh Press. Thank you to my mother for everything and always. I am indebted, finally to Patricio, Diego, and now Anaís for bearing with me during the birthing of this book and to Horacio, without whom none of this would be possible.

This book is dedicated to the memory of my father, Walter Johnson, who was still here when I began this project many years ago.

Sentencing Canudos

INTRODUCTION

> Many questions were troubling the explorer, but at the sight of the prisoner he
> asked only: "Does he know his sentence?" "No," said the officer, eager to go
> on with his exposition, but the explorer interrupted him: "He doesn't know
> the sentence that has been passed on him?" "No," said the officer, again, paus-
> ing a moment as if to let the explorer elaborate his question, and then said:
> "There would be no point in telling him. He'll learn it on his body."
> —Franz Kafka, "In the Penal Colony"

The title of my book owes something to Homi Bhabha's suggestion that "it
is from those who have suffered the sentence of history—subjugation, domination, diaspora, displacement—that we learn our most enduring lessons for living and thinking."[1] The notion of "suffering the sentence of history" sounds a
double register. Legally, a sentence is the imposition of punishment following a
judgment of condemnation. One is sentenced never to happiness but rather to
jail, to death, or to oblivion. Suffering the judgment of history, then, suggests
material defeat of some kind: subjugation, domination, annihilation, disap-
pearance. It refers to those who, like the prisoner in Kafka's tale, have no choice
but to learn their sentences on their bodies. In the grammatical register, however, a sentence is paradigmatically a predicative syntax, a law of language. It is
a structure of representation, a unit of closure. The coincidence of the norma-
tive and the constative that the concept of the "sentence of history" metaphorically betrays is perhaps at the heart of the reason peasant rebels often want to
destroy the written record, burning books and papers, since the written record,
as John Beverley puts it, "is also the record of their legal conditions of property-

lessness and exploitation."[2] Of course, a peasant may want to destroy a paper that assigns ownership of a particular piece of land to someone else so as to then take possession of that land, but this urge transcends such particularities; it more broadly concerns destroying a representation of the world in which peasants exist only insofar as they do not own land and are exploited, a world in which their identities, to paraphrase Ranajit Guha, amount only to the sum of their subalternities.[3] Likewise, the written record we call history is not just a totalizing depository of information but a mechanism of classification and intelligibility. Insofar as it ""creates the borders between history and nonhistory, it operates, as Michel Foucault suggests, as a system of discursivity.[4] Mark Taylor, commenting on Kafka's story "In the Penal Colony," writes that "philosophical sentences are judgments. Judgment, which works by subjecting the particular to the universal, has as its goal the establishment of law and order. Before and/or apart from judgment, there is, as Foucault suggests, anarchy."[5] What is before or apart from the sentence of the law is anarchy: what is rebellious to rule but also what is outside the archive of history, pure noise.

In this book I will suggest how the people of the community of Canudos were *sentenced to history.* The name by which we remember this community already encapsulates the problematic at the heart of the book, for the inhabitants called it *Belo Monte,* not *Canudos.* Under the leadership of the lay prophet Antônio Conselheiro, Belo Monte/Canudos fought a war against the still-fledgling republican government in Brazil in the backlands of the state of Bahia in 1896–1897. After three failed government expeditions, the conflict finally ended with the destruction of the community and the deaths of most of its inhabitants. At the end of the "Canudos War" one man declared: "There on the mountain peaks and gorges, on the darkened walls of plunging rocks, the story of a resuscitated people was written with the blood of the men of the backlands. There the whistling of the wind or the bellow of the wild bulls forever utters the epic of Brazilian heroism."[6] The history of Canudos is, for this man, both eternal and fleeting, both written and unwritten: forever inscribed, but only in the blood on rocks, the whistling of the wind, or the hoarse bellowing of the wild bulls. Far from being remembered only by the backland's wild bulls, however, the Canudos campaign has had no lack of written testaments and detractions, from the letters, poetry, articles, and novels of those who lived through it to any number of historical and artistic interpretations up to the present day.[7] Indeed, not only is it an indelible referent in Brazilian history, but it has jumped national borders, becoming inscribed in a larger Latin American tradition (for Roberto González Echeverría, *Os sertões* is, along with Domingo Sarmiento's *Facundo*, paradigmatic of what he calls the second phase of Latin American literature) and even emerging as an example in contemporary works on political theory by writers including Ernesto Laclau, Mike Davis, Slavoj Žižek, and Antonio Negri.

This visibility of Canudos, the fact that it has acceded to the status of a memorable event in the historical archive, is one of its first enigmas, since it was in many ways not that unique. One could draw up a catalog of comparable rebellions and revolts in Brazil around the end of the nineteenth century and the beginning of the twentieth, all tied to the same hybrid and uneven processes of modernization that ushered in the republic in 1889. In contrast to Canudos, however, such conflicts have suffered a general obscurity, largely because Brazilian historiography and public memory tend to emphasize the peaceful evolution of history wherein changes are supposed to have been tranquilly and cordially resolved by the elites and the people. One could list, for example, the Federalist Revolution, which broke out in Rio Grande do Sul in 1893 between two local oligarchic factions, a vaguely monarchist faction that had held prestige during the empire and the new president of the state. That same year the Revolta da Armada, a naval revolt led by monarchist officers, took place in Rio de Janeiro. Both uprisings were crushed. Brazil also witnessed a number of other movements that, like Canudos, had an expressly religious content. One great influence on Antônio Conselheiro was another wandering preacher, Padre Ibiapiana (1807–1883), who drew a great following in the northeastern region. While attracting persecution from the Catholic hierarchy, Ibiapiana survived thanks to his institutional ties, which shows that millenarian religious movements produced a variety of outcomes and did not necessarily lead to state violence. The movement that Padre Cícero Romão Batista led in Juazeiro from 1872 to 1934, a movement that joined social revindications with religious content, is another example of survival by accommodation with local powers. The Contestado Rebellion, however, which broke out in the backlands of Santa Catarina and Paraná from 1912 to 1916, underwent a fate similar to that of Canudos. Like Canudos, the Contestado Rebellion was a peasant-based movement in which a prophet preached the evils of the Brazilian republic and called for a return to the monarchy. According to Todd Diacon, the rebellion was in large part a reaction to the construction of railroad tracks in the area and the accompanying penetration of international capital and changes in land tenure that threatened peasant subsistence.[8] The events at Canudos, then, were no more exceptional than—or perhaps just as exceptional as—any of these. And yet, Lizir Arcanjo Alves asks, "A century later, when so many other revolts that took place in the nineteenth century have been forgotten, why have we not yet forgotten all that happened in Canudos?"[9] The enigma is the memory of Canudos. Or perhaps Canudos is the memory of an enigma.

Part of the answer for the enduring afterlife of Canudos is *Os sertões* (1901), by Euclides da Cunha, which strives to account for the conflict's origins and ferociously denounces the government for the massacre. The young war correspondent's book was an immediate bestseller in a country where 85 percent of the population was illiterate. Between 1902 and 1909 *Os sertões* sold 10,000 copies in three successive editions published by Laemmert; it then passed to Francisco Alves, which published the fourth edition in 1911. Between 1911 and 1982 Francisco Alves alone published twenty-eight editions of *Os sertões*.[10] More than thirty-five editions have been produced, and total sales in Portuguese have reached 750,000.[11] Not surprisingly, then, in 1994, when *Veja* magazine published the results of a survey in which fifteen leading Brazilian intellectuals were asked to name the twenty most representative works of Brazilian culture, the first book listed was *Os sertões*.[12] Thus, one answer to my question is simply that Canudos has endured because of the success of da Cunha's book. One typical version of this answer is given by Edivaldo Boaventura when he writes, "It is the style that paints what endures. The great force of Euclides's grandiose expression immortalized Canudos. Let us take into consideration Canudos, the phenomenon, and Euclides, the expression, and ask: if it weren't for Euclides da Cunha, what would have been the fate of Canudos?"[13] But Boaventura's answer is also symptomatic of precisely what I want to put into question.

What does it mean to pose the relationship between Canudos and da Cunha's text as one between a "phenomenon" and "its expression"? And what does it mean to understand the *force* of this expression in largely aesthetic terms, as Boaventura does here? These two elements in his answer exemplify the naturalization of intellectual mediation that takes shape in Latin America under the narrative of the intellectual as the voice of the voiceless (in a continent of mostly voiceless people) but that subaltern studies has taught us to recognize as a "sentencing" essential to the establishment of modern forms of governmentality.

It is not a matter—or not only a matter—of revealing da Cunha's particular political interests in his rendering of the Canudos War. Rather, I mean to use the story of Canudos and its multiple inscriptions to question how we understand the "location of culture" as a place of naturalization in the construction of modern governmentality, particularly in the two extremes formed in the bifurcation between the "cultured" and the "anthropological" versions of culture: literature or aesthetics, on the one hand, and everyday life, on the other.

My analysis thus unfolds in the space bounded by the state, everyday life, and writing and poses questions such as the following: How do writing and culture function in the constitution of the modern nation-state? How is a construction of hegemony related to changes in the order and legibility of everyday life? How do certain genres and strategies of representation interface with different principles of sovereignty? While each of my chapters is organized around a particular theoretical angle, they unfold in close confrontation with the thick materiality of the discourse on Canudos, shuttling between practices of thinking and writing that are deemed abstract and others that are more recalcitrantly local. Theoretical debates are never neutral or universal, and though, in the present economy of theoretical capital, Latin America may be marginal to many of them, it is my conviction that it nevertheless provides a place not only to think *about* but to think *from*.

Chapter 1, "The Voice of Others," interrogates the problem of intellectual mediation by analyzing the form it takes in the Latin American tradition of the intellectual as the voice of the voiceless. Of the innumerable examples of this narrative at work, we can take Henrique Coelho Neto's comments in 1915 at the yearly commemoration at Euclides da Cunha's tomb: "Euclides was . . . the real interpreter of the ignored masses. He was the taciturn poet of solitary spaces, the harsh historian of the barbarians. He described the deserts and the tragic inhabitants of savage lands."[14] This formula is by now easy to recognize and repudiate, for most now acknowledge that the intellectual doesn't *really* speak for the people. Still, the stubborn staying power of da Cunha's Canudos reflects the fact that the formula "the voice of the voiceless" rests on a set of deeply naturalized assumptions that continue to govern our practices of reading. First, the formula is embedded within a genealogy of political thought in which "the people" are posed as the origin of sovereignty, and this chapter briefly lays out Brazil's participation in an emerging transatlantic discourse on popular sovereignty. Second, as David Lloyd and Paul Thomas argue in *Culture and the State*, nineteenth-century Europe saw a convergence of theories of the state and theories of culture, with culture brought into suture the gap between "the people" and the state. Brazil and the rest of Latin America participated in this theoretical development, too, but postcolonial conditions forced theories of culture there to differ from efforts in Europe, so that by the twentieth century "culture" acquired the function of compensating for the state's failure to produce a people.

Chapter 2, "The Prose of Counterinsurgency," develops a subalternist perspective on the ways in which Canudos has been sentenced to history. I track changes in the description of Antonio Conselheiro and his followers beginning some twenty years before the conflict and culminating in *Os sertões*. A careful perusal of letters, both private and public, and newspaper articles reveals the emergence of something that I, following Ranajit Guha, call a prose of counterinsurgency, with Canudos slowly becoming a surface of inscription onto which a variety of tensions and fears were projected. As a result, Canudos became intelligible almost exclusively through a discourse whose central problematic is the security of the state. By reconstructing this process in such thick detail, I mean to make visible the contingency of the process and thus divest it of its inevitability. In other words, the narrative that came to dominate—and da Cunha's text was not so much a repudiation of this narrative as a crystallization of it—was not the only way to conceptualize what was happening in Canudos. Other alternatives were slowly overshadowed and delegitimized as the conflict advanced. That is, the construction of this dense textual web about Canudos reveals the emergence of a hegemonic discursive formation. David Lloyd and Paul Thomas define hegemony in such a way as to resituate it within the multiplicity it occludes. It is a process "by which certain paradigms become so self-evident as to relegate alternatives to the spaces of the nonsensical and the unthinkable. It is not so much that hegemony represses as that the dominance of its 'forms' of conceptualization renders other forms, other imaginaries, unreadable, inaudible, and incomprehensible."[15] My project, then, is both to denaturalize what seems so self-evident as to be as invisible as the air we breathe and to mark out the contours of alternatives that are invisible and inaudible precisely because their ties to all forms of evidence have been mangled.

Chapter 3, "The Event and the Everyday," analyzes one of these alternatives. One of the places where revisionist historiography has attempted to push the boundaries of the audible and comprehensible concerning Canudos—to extract it from what one historian called the "golden cage" of *Os sertões*—is the level of "everydayness."[16] This is an attempt to rewrite the historical archive by challenging an image of Canudos as "extraordinary," as an exceptional space and time that broke or interrupted a normal, "everyday" time. The idea that the inhabitants of Canudos were monstrous or that they represented the irruption of religious barbarism in an enlightened and more modern age evokes the image of an other than ordinary Canudos at the heart of the prose of counterinsurgency. Revisionist historians have attempted to show how "ordinary" Canudos was by detailing, for example, the community's economic activities and showing its similarities to other communities in the Bahian backlands, so that it hovers on the edge of becoming just one more city in a continuum of cities. In this chapter I draw on my fieldwork and interviews with local Bahian historians, critics, and filmmakers who work with local oral history, as well as the testimony of a merchant who lived in Canudos, to interrogate how the categories of the everyday and the ordinary function in political projects and critical theory alike. Everydayness has proved to be an elusive concept in contemporary theory despite the efforts by authors such as Henri Lefebvre, Michel de Certeau, and Maurice Blanchot. My study of state hegemony's ambiguous relationship to everydayness attempts to illuminate an obscure area in the study of governmentality. How are general political directives incarnated in everyday life, and what happens when the realm of the everyday proves resistant to change? What does it mean if everydayness is erased in a process of subalternization, as happened with Canudos? What is it about the normal, ordinary life of a rebel, peasant community such as Canudos that needs to be excised in the process of nation-state formation? And what are the limits to conjuring up the ordinary, everyday life of Canudos?

Chapter 4, "*Os Sertões*: Nationalism by Elimination," confronts da Cunha's reading of the conflict, first by reading *Os sertões* in its performative, or prescriptive, dimension—as a sentence, in other words—rather than in a descriptive dimension, as an act of re-presentation or the "expression" of a referent. *Os sertões* did not just "electrif[y] the nation because it shattered the elite's comfortable myth about Brazilian reality."[17] It also produced a new myth. Building a representational field that traverses and exceeds any given representation, my reading of *Os sertões* confronts this text with an "other scene" that da Cunha himself produced in his on-the-scene articles written for a São Paulo newspaper and the field notes he jotted down (published in 1975 as *Caderneta de campo*). By confronting these three sets of texts, I argue that da Cunha solves the conceptual challenges Canudos posed by subsuming it to the regulating ideal of the modern state. In the process da Cunha constructs a particular "visibility" and "sayability" (to use Foucauldian terms) that still have purchase today.

While subaltern studies has done much to provincialize historiography and to highlight its limited operational territory, one bound by specific notions of agency, subjectivity, and temporality (among others), in my last chapter, "Another Canudos," I extend those analyses to the problem of literary form within the horizon of competing versions of sovereignty proper to the encounter between modernization and postcolonial structures of power and representation. Here I consider two novels published three years before *Os sertões* (Afonso Arinos's *Os jagunços* and Manoel Benício's *O rei dos jagunços*) that produce a barely recognizable Canudos. The mere existence of alternative interpretations of Canudos (and these texts do exhibit real differences from da Cunha's) prompts questions about an economy of representation and its place in the larger picture of nation and state formation in Latin America. The central goal here is to discover what about these two marginalized and largely forgotten texts seems nonsense to us. Or, put another way, how do they perform representations whose "sense" does not seem to "express" the phenomenon of Canudos? First, and continuing my analysis of everydayness, I contend that the difficulty in "recognizing" Canudos in their representations arises from their attempts to locate the truth of the community and its rebellion on the level of ordinary, daily life (although it is not the kind of ordinary Canudos imagined by the revisionist historiography). While there is clearly a disciplinary intent to such an enterprise (by "normalizing" Canudos), it produces the unexpected effect of denaturalizing the "norms" regulating the government's actions. Second, I argue that the lack of correspondence between "Canudos" and their "expressions" results from the generic options undertaken by each text. In other words, each of these texts uses particular formal strategies to achieve its goal of presenting an ordinary Canudos. The dominant cultural grammar of the time, however, did not recognize these forms as viable ways of representing the community. Arinos, who was a monarchist, used the national family romance as the genre best able to enact a different principle of sovereignty. Benício, though, was as much a republican as da Cunha was. The interest in his case lies in the way his text veers clumsily between a historical essay and a novel, which I argue reveals Benício's dissatisfaction with the inability of a neutral, scientific principle of knowledge to account for the conflict. While da Cunha's text is grounded in an idea of sovereignty that aims to correct but not to impugn the ethics of the modern state, furnishing images and enunciations for a new form of governmentality, Arinos's and Benício's texts exhibit textual strategies that fit uneasily with an emerging project for the cultural presentation and integration of internal differences.

My overall argument is of course deeply indebted to the historians in the Subaltern Studies Group, who taught us to be suspicious of the accounts of insurgency performed by a lettered elite. These historians often began with the observation that the archive through which events such as peasant insurgency are registered almost exclusively comprises documents that reflect the perspective of power, since most of them were produced by and for the regime to understand and suppress such an insurgency. Thus Ranajit Guha says that the "historical phenomenon of insurgency meets the eye for the first time as an image framed in the prose, hence the outlook, of counter-insurgency—an image caught in a distorting mirror. . . . Inscribed in elite discourse it had to be read as a writing in reverse."[18] Although Guha's project was to recover insurgency by reading elite discourse against the grain (by deducing it as negativity), subsequent theorists have since then developed the argument that the subaltern insurgency under study inescapably remains the one produced by the historical archive. The archive produces what it names, just as Robinson Crusoe conjures up "wildness" when he sees a footprint on the island's shore and assumes that it has to do with something "wild." Certeau, discussing this moment in *Robinson Crusoe*, writes, "Naming is not here the 'painting' of a reality; it is a performative act organizing what it enunciates. It does what it says and constitutes the savagery it declares. Just as one excommunicates by naming, the name 'wild' both creates and defines what the scriptural economy situates outside of itself."[19] Subalternity, then, is both created and defined by elite discourse and does not exist apart from it.

In Latin American studies the issue of the subaltern as an external, autonomous domain versus the subaltern as an effect of discourse was raised with particular clarity and force by the historian Florencia Mallon, who identifies this division "as the deepest, most irresolvable, and also the most fertile tension in the Subaltern Studies project"[20] and warns against either flattening out the tension or discarding one of its components.

The recovery of subaltern practices, beliefs, and actions necessitated the use of new documents and especially new methods for reading old documents. This laborious and methodologically complex task led many historians into semiotics, literary criticism, and other forms of textual analysis. Yet, by encouraging the deconstruction of texts along lines of power and hierarchy and by decentering all subjects that emerged in the documents, according to Mallon, these techniques have ultimately questioned two assumptions central to the Subaltern Studies Group's political purpose: that subaltern practices enjoy some autonomy from elite culture and that subaltern politics possesses a unity and solidarity of its own.[21]

As her remark shows, Mallon was then, in 1994, particularly critical of a tendency she saw within the Latin Americanist version of subaltern studies, visible particularly in the "Founding Statement" of the Latin American Subaltern Studies Group (constituted formally between 1992 and 2000), namely, a tendency to privilege what she called the Foucauldian and Derridean theoretical position over a Gramscian one.[22] According to Mallon, the problematic result was that "access to most subalterns . . . remains elusive" if one is simply reading existing documents against the grain. She instead advocated maintaining the tension between "a more narrowly postmodern literary interest in documents as 'constructed texts' and the historian's disciplinary interest in reading documents as 'windows,' however foggy and imperfect, on people's lives."[23]

My approach differs slightly to the extent that Mallon ascribes a certain positive, ontic determination to subalternity—there is a subaltern thing-in-itself (identity, consciousness, subjectivity) out there—and assumes that the written record is, however foggy and imperfect, a means of access to it. If the problem of optics is taken seriously, however, then the concept of subalternity cannot be equated with a pure exteriority on the other side of the documents, cannot but name a recalcitrant difference that arises inside elite discourse with no ontic determination of its own. One cannot, in this case, work on retrieving the consciousness or agency of the subaltern on its own terms.

At the same time, however, by choosing the moment of insurgency as the starting point for analysis, Guha and others understand subalterns as "exerting pressure" on the structures that subordinate them.[24] Insurgency is proof that subalterns have, as Mallon puts it, a certain autonomy from elite culture, a unity and solidarity of their own. One can therefore also read the way in which the particular structures of elite discourse are themselves constituted and shaped by the challenge to their rule posed by insurgency. In this sense, documents are not foggy windows onto the subaltern, not something to see through, but artifacts in themselves, disfigured in symptomatic ways by the actions of subalterns, much as the universe can be warped by the presence of black holes, which can never be "represented" as such but only be deduced. In these circumstances, the task is to make visible the structural distortions produced by the "failed translation and assimilation of that which they constitute as minor or outside."[25] This means both the way otherness or difference has been assimilated into versions of "the same" (e.g., translating various forms of power relations in India, such as the caste system, patriarchy, and ethnic oppression, into class relations) and the way "self-exceeding exteriority," a heterogeneous array of positive differences, is translated into a difference of polarity or negativity (precapitalist, nonpolitical, etc.). Indeed, part of the intractability that the subalternists work to identify is the resistance of a self-exceeding exteriority to being represented as what Prakash will name a "self-confirming other."

Like Mallon, then, I have found a tension at the heart of subaltern studies, but an immensely productive one: if on the one hand we come to peasant insurgencies that have always been written over and turned into a datum in a history not the insurgents' own—sentenced to history—we cannot forget, on the other hand, that the very fact of insurgency posits a challenge and intractability to this history, that it signals the failures and limits of power. The alternatives posed by the rebellion disappear as it becomes inscribed in the archive within another's history, so that they become a "night-time of love" rather than a "lifetime of love."[26] At the same time, the intractability revealed in the representation of the subaltern as an "autonomous and unintelligible domain exterior" to the functioning of the dominant system, "beyond rational understanding,"[27] cannot but mark the continued possibility of an outside. This is the reason my project is not to uncover what Canudos was "really like" but both to investigate how it was constituted through discourse and to ask what we can learn about the way it continues to exert pressure on our judgments.

CHAPTER ONE

THE VOICE OF OTHERS

> Men who are destroyed (destroyed without destruction) are as though inca-
> pable of appearing, and invisible even when one sees them. And if they speak,
> it is with the voice of others, a voice always other than theirs which somehow
> accuses them.
>
> —Maurice Blanchot, *Writing the Disaster*

If Canudos wasn't special,
why da Cunha's obsession?

Euclides da Cunha was perhaps the first to voice the kernel of what was
to be the canonical and largely celebratory interpretation of his relationship to
Canudos.[1] In a letter to his friend Francisco Escobar in early 1902, da Cunha
presented *Os sertões* as an "avenging book": "And yet, however it may be, I am
heartened by the ancient conviction that the future will read it [the book]. That
is what I want. I will be an avenger and will have played a great role in life—that
of advocate for the poor sertanejos assassinated by a . . . cowardly and bloody
society."[2]

Although da Cunha describes his relationship to the *sertanejos* in terms
of voice (speaking for them), the relationship also implies vision. To speak for
the inhabitants of Canudos is also to represent the truth of Canudos. The slide
between auditory and visual metaphors reveals the conjunction of two senses
of representation that Gayatri Spivak notes in her critique of intellectual mediation: representation as proxy (used in politics to mean "speaking for") and
representation as portrait (used in art or philosophy to mean staging or signification).[3] We can detect this second sense of representation in da Cunha's as-

sumption that his book reveals a truth—that the violence against the *sertanejos* (inhabitants of the *sertão,* or hinterlands) was unjust—that might be invisible to his contemporaries but would become readable in the future. Da Cunha thus foresaw a future that was diametrically opposite to the future imagined by the soldiers fighting at Canudos. If these soldiers slit the throats of their enemies, it was because "they had not to fear the formidable judgment of posterity: for History would not go as far as that."[4] Da Cunha's condemnation of the soldiers' actions is tied to the assumption that history would indeed go there. He was right. It seems difficult now to imagine defending works such as Dante de Mello's *A verdade sobre "Os sertões,"* written by a military man who took offense at da Cunha's critique of the government's campaign.

Da Cunha's vision is all the more a revelation given his conversion from outright condemning the Conselheiristas to condemning the government's violence against them. In March 1897, for instance, before going to Canudos, da Cunha wrote to his friend João Luís lamenting the defeat of the third government expedition: "Furthermore, in this terrifying picture of disasters it is necessary to seek out our brothers in belief, those that can understand us. I believe that, like me, you are still under the gloom of the deplorable upset of Canudos, where our heroic and strong Republic bowed before a chaotic horde of fanatic men in rags."[5] His three weeks in Canudos became his road to Damascus.

To a large extent, the canonical reading of *Os sertões* has not strayed far from da Cunha's interpretation.[6] It continues to be governed by an assumption that da Cunha's book represented Canudos as both proxy and portrait. Olimpio de Sousa Andrade's commentaries on da Cunha's field notes illustrate such articulations of da Cunha's foresight, subtended by his search for truth:

> Like a powerful, highly sensitive antenna, his intelligence and intuition already captured distant voices and sounds, lost in the air, unperceived by others, but which said everything. . . . Later, clearly distinguishing what remained indistinct and confused to him in that tumult of voices emanating from the centers of decision, his mastery and courage would speak to the bewildered present in which he lived, and also to the future which could not ignore the movements in that surprising game of chess. . . . He proceeded in the ceaseless search of an elusive truth.[7]

The combination of voice and sight is clear in Andrade's formulation: da Cunha is able to hear as voice ("which *said* everything") what others, if they hear it at all, perceive as sheer noise. The elusive truth to which the voice leads

him would be in part, of course, the injustice in the government's actions—
this is where both tropes coincide—but the vision ascribed to da Cunha has
since acquired greater range than this point alone, since da Cunha analyzed
the conflict at Canudos not as a solitary incident but as a symptom of greater
and deeper problems traversing the country: the existence of a population and
territory that were completely unknown to the Brazilian elites and the state apparatus in their power and the state's consequent inability to integrate and represent a Brazilian totality. As A. de A. Lima said in 1924, at the yearly tombside
commemoration of the writer, da Cunha "literally came to reveal the error of
the way the mass of Brazilians had been forgotten."[8] Da Cunha and his book
were thus etched in the Brazilian archive as the place where larger problems
of Brazilian social formation are said to reveal themselves. Thus Os sertões has
been called the Bible of Brazil because it has been accredited with representative power over the country itself, because in it, as Oswald de Andrade claimed,
one saw "the dense unfolding of an unknown and authentic Brazil."[9]

This nationalist horizon—the way in which the work had been read as a
book-monument, as a foundational text—must be central to any evaluation of
Os sertões. Perhaps it was this dimension, more than anything else, that was
responsible for its initial acclaim. Readers could perceive in it "the knowledge
and preoccupation with understanding the land, man, mass psychology, man's
place in society, races, that is, all the prerequisites that a text had to have in order to be the architect of a nationality."[10] In her overview of the text's reception,
Patrícia Cardoso Borges suggests that, in contrast, more recent interpretations
of da Cunha's text tend to place an increasing weight on its role as "proxy" (as
opposed to "portrait"), a characteristic she ties to the emergence of a specifically "modern" preoccupation for the defeated and the marginal.[11] She suggests
that Silviano Santiago was the first to praise da Cunha specifically as defending the vision of the defeated, an act now seen as valuable in its own right.[12]
Santiago writes, for example, that "the great lesson of . . . Euclides is that of
a knowledge which, detaching itself from the authoritarianism inherent to its
own social origins, turns its eyes to the defeated, seeing in them a truth that
escapes the exclusionary directives of modernization."[13] Yet Borges argues that
this later interpretation does not escape the presiding nationalist logic so obvious in earlier interpretations and that it remains bound by the parameters of
da Cunha's own vision: "The necessity for a nationalist text is still perceived—
from local descriptions to defeated heroes. It is necessary to read Os Sertões beyond the eyes of Euclides, to perceive his missteps and show that the author

tried to do more than he could. We can, through his text, better understand his attempts and limitations (his and those of his time)."[14]

Borges's own reading indicates exceptions to the canonical reading I have been outlining. There are attempts, in other words, to read da Cunha's text as limited in vision. Examples from the disciplines of history and sociology include Marco Antonio Villa's Canudos: O povo da terra, which states that Os sertões "is a barrier for the historical understanding of the community created by Antonio Conselheiro,"[15] and José Augusto Cabral Barreto Bastos's Incompreensível e bárbaro inimigo,[16] which argues that Brazilian intellectuals, including da Cunha, found themselves before an uncomfortable, unexpected presence that refuted not only their ideals but the conceptual schema used to apprehend a reality that resisted conceding a theoretical status to the insurgency of Canudos, a reality that emerged as a repressed and unthought "non-history."[17] For Bastos, this epistemological discomfort demarcating their theoretical visibility is summed up in da Cunha's phrase "incomprehensible and barbarous enemy!"[18] Ultimately he concludes that Os sertões is, rather than an exaltation of the sertanejo, more plausibly conceived as "a fatalistic condemnation of the man of the sertão draped in the social biology popular at the time."[19]

Exceptions can be found also in the fields of literature and literary criticism. Early on Mário de Andrade wrote, "I can guarantee that Os sertões is false. The environmental disgrace of the Northeast cannot be described. One needs to see what it is. It is horrible. Euclides da Cunha . . . turned the unbearable blindness of that enormous sun into sonorous and brilliant turns of phrase and elegant images; he transformed what is simply misery into heroism and epic." This passage is cited in Leopoldo Bernucci's work A imitação dos sentidos to support his argument that one needs to read da Cunha's text as a literary artifact intertextually related to other written works that preceded it rather than as a faithful representation of the reality the journalist witnessed.[20]

Nonetheless, the trope of a visionary da Cunha recurs remarkably often even in texts that attempt to avoid this interpretation. It rears its head, for example, in a chapter where Bernucci addresses the way da Cunha, in an early article on the conflict, draws on Victor Hugo's account of the Vendée peasant revolt against the postrevolutionary French republic in his novel Quatre-vingt-treize. Assessing this moment of intertextuality, Bernucci writes: "The real question . . . is to see how the simile or metaphor of Vendée, even when inserted in a rather Manichaean way of seeing reality, and even when it is a ready-made optics that is imported and applied to the case of Canudos, opened up a path toward richer and more comprehensive reflections. And, as in other places in his writings, here too Euclides articulates and liberates the contradictions of Canudos, repressed by other systems of interpretation."[21]

This unexpected resurgence of the model of vision appears in, for example, Roberto González Echevarría's *Myth and Archive* (1990) and Luiz Costa Lima's *Terra ignota: A construção de "Os sertões"* (1997). For González Echevarria, *Os sertões* exemplifies the treatment of science as the master discourse in the nineteenth century. Da Cunha's deploys a "fine net of scientific studies over the sertão"[22] to bring the upheaval to order and defend himself from the possibility of collapsing into that other reality through discourse. This mobilization of science correlates with the republic's use of instruments of war to tame the city. González Echevarria asserts that *Os sertões* ironically reenacts the republic's errors. Yet even as da Cunha attempts to reduce the odd to the familiar, he also appeals to the language of the sublime and astonishment to account for the moments when the reality he witnesses overwhelms his grid. Thus, much as Canudos absorbs the republic (because, for González Echevarría, the republic can defeat it only by becoming like it), da Cunha's discourse escapes the hegemony of scientific discourse by joining its elusive object in its moments of literature. This moment of escape from the model discourse is the text's moment of sight: the realization of its limits.

Costa Lima's reading in *Terra ignota* resembles González Echevarría's in fundamental ways, but with less triumphalism and more complexity. Costa Lima analyzes *Os sertões* as a text split by not two but three modes of expression: first, the scene or center ruled by da Cunha's scientific models and characterized by a mode of "description"; second, the text's ornamental and literary dimension; and finally, the text's "subscene," dominated by mimesis. This third mode of expression is formed by the quasi-igneous mass of material that is not legitimated by the orienting method's criteria. Produced by a beyond-the-subject, it fluctuates in and out of the text, appearing at moments of great pressure: "The subscene is less a scene of a phantasmal order than a condensation in which the ghostly acquires form."[23] It is an accumulation of detours, silenced impasses, epistemological denegations, and islands of nonexplanation that stands in tension with the science ruling the text and threatens it when it surfaces in certain descriptions of the *sertão*, those populated with words such as *mirages, illusions,* and *ruins.* In contrast to González Echevarría's reading, Costa Lima's allows the subscene only a sporadic, fleeting presence, one that is insufficient to contest the hegemonic discourses. In fact, Costa Lima undertakes a close reading of several writers who inspired da Cunha (the theorists of crowd psychology Gabriel Tarde, Gustave Le Bon, and Scipio Sighele, as well as the psychiatrist Henry Maudsley and the scholar and historian of religion Ernest Renan) to show that—contrary to the canonical reading that has Euclides da Cunha breaking free from the rigidity of European models by confronting the reality of Brazilian society[24]—they were more subtle and hesitant than he proved to be.[25]

In reversing the traditional reading of da Cunha as someone who *sees* to focus instead on the impasses, limits, and aporias of his project, both Costa Lima's and González Echeverría's readings redeem da Cunha and his text precisely for these aporias, which are both limits but also moments of excess. We see here a curious twist to the dialectics of seeing: he now sees because, either consciously or unconsciously, he is confronted with the problem of not seeing. Ultimately, *Os sertões* is once again reinscribed as the true expression of Canudos, precisely for the aporias in which da Cunha's attempt to dominate the historical event breaks down, short-circuits, or reaches a roadblock.

What should we make of the difficulty in transcending the structure of mediation that we see exemplified in da Cunha's reception? This issue lies at the heart of Spivak's critique of a conversation between Foucault and Deleuze (held in 1977 and published as "Intellectuals and Power"). In this conversation, Deleuze and Foucault seek (as Deleuze says) "to establish conditions where the prisoners themselves would be able to speak."[26] Spivak criticizes Foucault and Deleuze for saying that the masses know ("perfectly well") "that they know far better than [the intellectual] and they certainly say it well," because this sentiment conflates the two senses of representation (as proxy and as portrait), covering up the discontinuity between them. In so doing, she argues, they reinstall the intellectual as representing the people: the way in which they claim to speak for the masses mutates or slides into producing the image and identity of the masses. In other words, Foucault and Deleuze try to transmit what the masses know under the fiction that the masses are speaking for themselves and that the intellectual has withdrawn from the process, but in representing the politically canny subalterns, "the intellectuals represent themselves as transparent."[27] The reemergence of this structure in Foucault and Deleuze—precisely where they try to banish it—illustrates the difficulty of eluding patterns of intellectual mediation on which our assessment of the relationship between da Cunha and Canudos should focus. In other words, if "what governs the canonicity of culture's texts is their approximation not so much to reality as to a regulative idea,"[28] Euclides da Cunha has acquired canonical status because he acts out the "regulative idea" of intellectuals speaking for the people. Although both Costa Lima and González Echeverría undertake deconstructive readings, showcasing the moments *Os sertões* breaks down, the reinscription of Canudos in terms of these formal aporias does not take them outside the narrative of the intellectual mediation so much as reveal more nakedly the place of the aesthetic within this structure. We may think, like Foucault and Deleuze, that we have managed to transcend this structure, but the stubborn staying power of da Cunha's Canudos is symptomatic of the ways in which we have failed to do so.

These two faces to the narrative of intellectual mediation warrant a deeper consideration. First, asking whether the intellectual does or does not speak for the people is meaningless outside a genealogy of political thought that construes the people as the origin of sovereignty. I thus will briefly lay out Brazil's position within a larger transatlantic discursive and theoretical shift during the nineteenth century concerning the nature of sovereignty, the state, and its relationship to the people. This entails discussing representation as proxy: when and how it emerged, what its consequences are, and what form it took in Brazil. For the second face of intellectual mediation, representation as portrait, I follow the argument about the rise of a particular concept of culture, and within it of aesthetic education, as central to configuring the relationship between people and state. In both cases, I emphasize the particular postcolonial conditions under which these concepts took shape in Brazil and elsewhere in Latin America.

The Idea of the State

The notion that the people are the origin of sovereignty is commonly connected to the rise of the early modern state in Europe in the seventeenth century and given its modern incarnation with the French Revolution. Instead of "saying that the state is a natural fact like the family, a necessity as a result of sin and human cruelty, a power given directly by God to the Prince, or an organic assembly of corporations, orders and cities, it will be said that it emanates (by a delegation whose modalities can be quite varied) from the originary will of legal subjects, the ultimate repositories of the source of sovereignty."[29] Whereas the monarchical state held an arbitrary relationship to its population, the modern nation-state supposes a principle of organization based on the expression of a particular people through the institutions of the state. Only in this context does laying a claim to representing the will of this people matter.

The idea of the modern representative state and its effects on social practices are thus crucial to my analysis. In deploying this concept, I disagree with those who claim that we cannot understand the functioning of power unless we train our eyes away from this idea and cut off the sovereign's head. This position may today most readily be associated with Michel Foucault's studies on power and governmentality, though many argue along those lines. The anthropologist A. R. Radcliffe-Brown, for example, writes that "there is a good deal of discussion about the nature and origin of the State, which is usually represented as being an entity over and above the human individuals who make up a society, having as one of its attributes something called 'sovereignty' and sometimes spoken of as having a will . . . or as issuing commands. *The State in this sense does not exist in the phenomenal world; it is a fiction of the philosophers.*"[30] What does exist, he says, in words not unlike Foucault's, "is an organization, i.e., a collection of individual human beings connected to a complex set of relations . . . ; there are only, in reality, powers of individuals—kings, prime ministers, magistrates, policemen, party bosses and voters."[31] Not only does the state not exist, the sociologist Phillip Abrams argued thirty years later, but "it is itself the mask which prevents our seeing political practice as it is . . . ; it starts its life as an implicit construct; it is then reified—as the *res publica*, the public reification, no less—and acquires an overt symbolic identity progressively divorced from practice as an illusory account of practice."[32] Yet such a position does not take into account the material effects of a reified notion of the state. Abrams's critique assumes ideology to be a false consciousness of reality that can be dissolved by pointing to things as they "really are." But, as Slavoj Žižek writes, such a concept of ideology is prey to a basic, constitutive naïveté: "the main point is to see how the reality itself cannot reproduce itself without this so-called ideological mystification. The mask is not simply hiding the real state of things; the ideological distortion is written into its very essence."[33] Žižek here follows Althusser's lead in critiquing a notion of ideology as existing in a simplified notion of ideas; he insists that ideology is instead materialized in our effective social activity. A certain regulative idea of the state (reproduced in state institutions) is thus crucial for forming subjects as citizens who, as Lloyd and Thomas write, "by definition and for all practical purposes accept the forms and precepts of the state at least to the extent that alternatives become literally and figuratively the state's 'unthinkable.'"[34] Thus, for instance, Žižek takes the important point to be that we act as if we believe the president incarnates the will of the people, as if the state were a unitary body. Perhaps the state "exists nowhere in reality," but, Žižek argues, it "is none the less implied by 'reality' itself as a point of reference conferring on it its symbolic consistency."[35]

But Žižek is speaking of the late twentieth century and of parts of the world where the hegemony of such an idea of the state was successfully established. My concern, however, lies in the threshold of different and competing notions of sovereignty. This regulative idea of the state was certainly the symbolic reference point for da Cunha and others who looked to Europe for the latest models to emulate, but Canudos revealed that it did not apply in the same way for the entire population of the territory called Brazil. Indeed, we should keep in view the multiplicity of political cultures at this juncture in Brazil. What is visible and sayable about the state? What passes for self-evident and what is still contestable within the economy of images and enunciations regarding the state? In what way might the public hysteria over Canudos have played a role in the process by which "specific forms become dominant and established, as opposed to the potentially infinite variety of possible forms that 'might have been'?"[36]

The possibility that we might understand a state and its relationship to a population in more than one way acquired particularly visible form in Brazil throughout the nineteenth century through the competing projects of a monarchical versus republican state. (This does not exclude the possibility that a single label—"republic"—can itself harbor different kinds of projects.) Unlike the rest of Spanish America, Brazil established itself as a monarchy when it declared its independence in 1822 as the Empire of Brazil, which lasted until 1889. During this period, Brazil had two emperors—Pedro I (1822–1831) and Pedro II (1840–1889). Three appointed regents ruled from 1831, when Pedro I voluntarily abdicated in favor of his five-year-old son, until 1840, when the young emperor was crowned at fourteen years of age. Nonetheless, the nation adopted a constitutional monarchy, claiming adherence to principles of representational government. Brazilian republicans, therefore, did not have a monopoly on the idea that the state's source of authority was popular sovereignty and that it represented the people. This "idea" could be and was defined in different ways.

How was Brazil to participate in a transatlantic discourse founded on appeals to universal principles of liberty, equality, and popular sovereignty? This question preceded the passage from empire to republic; indeed, it was raised early in the nineteenth century, before official independence, with the Portuguese king João VI's pledge of allegiance to a new constitution in 1820. The

king had made Rio de Janeiro his residence and the seat of the Portuguese empire following Napoléon's invasion of Portugal in 1807. The displacement of
the royal court was not well received in Portugal, where it raised the specter
that Portugal had now become the colony of a colony. In 1820 "a diverse group
of property owners, merchants, low ranking military officers, magistrates,
clergy and some members of the nobility in Porto, Portugal called on the king
to return to Lisbon and proclaimed the 'regeneration' of the Portuguese nation
by convoking the Cortes, a formerly consultative institution representative of
the kingdom as manifest in the reunion of the three estates (clergy, nobility and
the people), for the deliberative task of writing a new constitution."[37]

According to the historian Kirsten Schultz, who analyzes the years of
Dom João's court in Brazil in *Tropical Versailles*, the proclamations of this group
("Long Live our Good Father" and "Long Live the Cortes, and with them the
Constitution") made clear "both the movement's loyalty to the monarchy and
the fact that this loyalty depended on the king's own allegiance of the Cortes
and a new constitution that, in turn, would circumscribe royal power and restrict it to the role of the executor" (235). In other words, she writes, the nation
rather than the crown would be sovereign. In February of the following year
constitutionalists in Rio de Janeiro staged a rebellion asking that the king accept the constitution being written in Lisbon and that its norms apply equally
in Portugal and Brazil.[38]

Although expectations and understandings of this new system's implications ranged widely, they all turned on the recognition that constitutionalism
entailed the creation of new political bonds and a new political language. One
remarkably consistent shift in political language—one that is of particular
significance to any understanding of the way the state was imagined in Brazil—was the proclamation of a new source of sovereignty (also portrayed as
the restoration of a sovereignty that had been trampled with the consolidation
of absolutism): the people. Schultz points out, "Whereas royal officials in the
1790s and 1810s had sought to ensure the resident's allegiance to His Majesty,
'Our Lord' and 'Common Father,' constitutionalists celebrated the triumph
of contractual government over paternal rule; they praised the new political
agency of 'the people'; they hailed the rise of 'the public' as the defeat of narrow,
private interests associated with absolutism" (256). According to one pasquinade, the adoption of a constitution implied an act of political "union" between
king and the people (250). According to another pasquinade:

> From the people to the king, power is given,
> Thus the people can legislate,
> If upon this notice the king does yield
> To arms his inert power will be ceded. (257)

The verbal proclamation of this new form of political community was also registered in the language residents used during the royal audience. Schultz quotes the memoirs of the royal counselor Silvestre Pinheiro Ferreira, who reported that after the constitutionalist rebellion in Rio de Janeiro, residents began to appear before Dom João not to request the grace of royal patronage but rather to make demands "in the name of the people" (251).[39] Accompanying such a change was the increased use of the term *citizen* over the previously used *vassal.* Whereas the term *citizen* had previously designated "well-regarded members of an urban community who fulfilled their duties to God and sovereign," it began to acquire the meaning of a national political identity, and unlike those whom the term *vassal* designated (understood as dependent on the crown), this newly fashioned citizen was cast as an equal member of the sovereign nation. The citizen was also, in contrast to vassals, deemed to have the privilege of deliberating on the future of the political body (257). Public opinion had previously been understood as simply "truthful collective judgment," but a concerted effort now sought to place it "at the center of the exercise of national sovereignty" (260). Public opinion, declared one pamphleteer whom Schultz quotes, "expressed the vote of the people" (260). Another pamphlet declared that in constitutional politics "'words' and 'printed discourses' were 'thrown out,' so to speak, into a vast stadium, where each citizen is allowed to enter and fight, having the whole nation as an arbiter who can freely pass judgment" (261).

But who counted as a citizen and a member of the public? While the abstract principle of popular sovereignty was enshrined, there was a struggle to define who exactly constituted "the people" that had been called into being as sovereign by the constitution. Schultz reports that even as constitutionalists celebrated equality before the law and popular participation in politics, even as they claimed that "the entire nation" could cast judgment in this vast stadium, many "also claimed that the majority of the people were not 'capable of profound deliberation'" (264). In his study of the Rio de Janeiro press during the 1820s, Marcos Morel points out a bifurcation between two essentially different conceptions and uses of public opinion (although the separation was not neat and absolute, and both could be invoked in succession on the same page). The first of these was the Rousseauian (or Jacobin) idea of the general will or popular sovereignty; the second comprised opinions voiced in the "republic of letters" by literate or enlightened individuals. In general, writes Morel, the latter understanding was preferred, in deliberate opposition to the example of the French Revolution, where anarchy and excess were seen to have prevailed.[40]

Both versions had circulated in France, too. Whereas Morel's research suggests that the term *public opinion* indistinctly referred to both possibilities (general will vs. the republic of letters), Keith Michael Baker argues that in France it referred to a particular ideological construct that took form briefly in prerevolutionary France (its hegemony, he says, lasted barely twenty-five years) and that was central to the transition from the ancien régime to the French Revolution. It was also, unlike its later uses in Brazil, specifically a liminal concept set between absolute authority and revolutionary will.[41] Even as the construction of this abstract category helped transform political culture, with ultimate authority transferred from the public person of the sovereign to the sovereign person of the public, even as it was deployed to signify a tribunal, a barrier against the monarch's arbitrary will and the abuse of power, public opinion was also understood as a source of peaceful, rational, universal, and objective judgment. It constitutes, says Baker, an image of "a politics of rational consensus" rather than a "politics of contestation."[42] It is also tied specifically to the invention of the printing press and the growth of literacy.[43] An example of this connection occurs in the French statesman and minister Chrétien Guillaume de Malesherbes's proclamation that "the art of printing has thus given writing the same publicity that the spoken word possessed in the midst of the assemblies of the nation during the first age. But it has taken many centuries for the discovery of this art to have its full effect upon men. It has required that the entire nation gain the taste and habit of informing itself by reading. And it has required that enough men become skilled in the art of writing to lend their ministry to the entire public."[44]

Malesherbes suggests that the entire public or nation can access this new art through reading but also that a specific group of people—those skilled in the art of writing—occupy a privileged place within the larger body of the nation and must lend their ministry to it. This privileged position was specifically articulated by Jacques Peuchet, a theorist and writer who Baker says elaborated in "relatively systematic terms the meaning of the notion of public opinion as a central feature in the theory and practice of politics on the eve of the French Revolution."[45] In an essay in the *Encyclopédie méthodique* (1789) he argued that "true legislative authority had already passed from the monarch to the enlightened elite, whose public function it was to lead the nation toward greater knowledge and rationality."[46] Peuchet wrote that "public opinion has its source in the opinion of the enlightened. . . . Writers have become the true legislators of peoples."[47]

Such arguments were possible for a Brazilian context, however, only after the arrival of the court in 1808, since the printing press had been banned until then. In Brazil, as in the rest of Latin America, the technology of writing had largely served to mark the exclusive nature of a specialized social group that Angel Rama calls "the lettered city." It had functioned, therefore, as a marker separating barbarism from civilization, and not until the twentieth century did it begin to function as the means for a more inclusive social and political project. Throughout the 1810s the Portuguese crown alternately policed oppositional pamphlets and newspapers and sponsored its own organs to meet criticism with praise. It was only in 1820, with the constitutionalist movement, that the crown finally suspended its censorship of the press, leading the number of newspapers in Rio de Janeiro to jump from one to eleven.[48] Both Schultz and Morel argue that this constitutes a transition from a public space marked by the ancien régime's forms of communication (gazettes, the cries of street hawkers, posters both printed or written, flyers on the streets, collective readings, and proclamations) to a public space where the debates were consolidated in the press and where private and individual readings acquired ever more importance. Schultz emphasizes the displacement of an iconic and spectacular public life by a textualized symbolic order, however, whereas Morel proposes instead that older forms of communication did not disappear but subsisted alongside newer practices, producing a hybridity in the public spaces in Rio. As a regular, consistent press emerged, he argues, Rio de Janeiro saw a proliferation of other types of printed materials: *folletos*, manifestos, proclamations, denunciations. Still, even if reading had a wider impact on the society of Rio de Janeiro than its restriction to a small elite suggests, reading—and the values of education, reason, and mediation—clearly served to evoke a threshold that demarcated those who could truly participate in this new public.[49]

Brazil's postindependence constitution of 1824 reflects continued ambivalence surrounding the capacities of the population at large and the concept of representation and popular sovereignty. The constitution included many classic components of European liberalism: the division of power into executive, legislative, and judicial branches; relatively broad-based suffrage; the reduction or elimination of trade restrictions; freedom of the press; public education; and formal equality before law. Yet, as the historian Judy Bieber puts it, "the leaders of the new nation were more concerned with the consolidation of a strong, unified state and the economic and political integration of the center-south than in promoting representative institutions."[50] Individualism, competition, pursuit of profit, order, and progress received particular weight, though the slave regime was left intact. And although the constitution guaranteed representative government, it invested the emperor with a moderating power that allowed him, for example, to arbitrarily dissolve the parliament and to nominate senators, thereby limiting the autonomy of elected representatives.

The two-tiered electoral system also seemed to address the ambivalence concerning the inclusiveness of the people. The system was direct at the municipal level but indirect at higher ones. Voters were divided into two categories, *votantes* and *eleitores*. The former category had minimal property restrictions (most artisans and small landholders could meet the criteria) and was limited by neither race nor literacy. The minimum age was twenty-five years except for married men, military officers, university graduates, or priests, who could vote at age twenty-one. *Votantes* could vote in primary elections that selected justices of peace and municipal councilors, and they elected the members of electoral colleges from an eligible pool of *eleitores*. The requirements for the second category were narrower: income requirements were double those of *votantes,* and freed slaves as well as those with criminal records did not qualify. *Eleitores* could run for town council or justice of peace and participate in electoral colleges, which voted for provincial and national representatives. Over 50 percent of the adult free population enjoyed either *votante* or *eleitor* status until the system was changed in 1881.[51]

The question of suffrage raises further issues. How did this larger population relate to the newly installed Brazilian monarchy and the discourse of constitutionalism? To what extent were these new ideas about the political bonds between king and people and among the people themselves taken up, accepted, and naturalized in the rest of the Brazilian territory, particularly in the backlands? Were there other, competing discourses? Schultz herself points out that "certain understandings of monarchy and empire were formed in Rio de Janeiro and then projected beyond the city but were not necessarily shared or incorporated into other local contexts. In 1824 northeastern provinces rebelled against government in Rio proclaiming their own, often republican, understandings of the end of the colonial system" (280). How were such understandings of popular sovereignty—tied to literacy and to notions of education and rationality—articulated with other, more popular understandings of politics?

These and other questions have been raised with particular force in recent historiography on Brazil, marking a departure from past assumptions of a gulf between life at the court and in the rest of Brazil during most of the nineteenth century. In "Postcolonial Brazil," Barbara Weinstein points to deeply ingrained assumptions in Brazilian historiography about Brazil as a nation composed of a tiny ever-powerful, and privileged white elite and a huge disfranchised and multicolored popular mass, the two groups divided by a yawning chasm. These assumptions have influenced historiography concerning nineteenth-century politics in particular, leading to an almost exclusive focus on politics in Rio, at the imperial court, that removes the vast majority of Brazil's population from political life; to an emphasis on the relative cohesion of imperial elites and the weak presence of popular actors; and to the belief that where popular classes were tied in to the political system at all, when they participated in electoral politics, their participation was channeled almost exclusively through the system of patronage, so that ideology had little, if any, bearing. This last position is exemplified by Richard Graham's *Patronage and Politics in Nineteenth-Century Brazil,* which argues that representative government was "an exotic imported ideology" and that elections were held only so that the Brazilian ruling class could define itself as part of a European civilized world. Graham argues that political men were primarily concerned with patronage (instead of representing the interests of an autonomous state). The heart of the system was the large landowner, who expected loyalty from his family, free workers, nearby small farmers, and village merchants, a loyalty demonstrated in many ways but that included voting for the party and candidates of the landowner.

Appointment to official positions helped expand a leader's circle, and this fact impelled him to solicit such appointments from provincial authorities, members of the national parliament, cabinet ministers, and even the prime minister. To demonstrate his worthiness for such appointment, he had to win elections, so that he was leader because he won elections and he won elections because he was a leader. The local patron found himself enmeshed in a system that made him client to someone else who depended on still others in a series of links reaching all the way to the national capital. For their part, cabinets exercised their authority not against local leaders but through them, and these landed bosses in turn sought not to oppose the government but to participate in it.[52]

In this view, ideological differences between liberals and conservatives were irrelevant: "citizens divided politically not because of party loyalties, much less ideological considerations, but because of personal ties, making party labels seriously misleading at both the local and national levels."[53] Indeed, Graham also disputes the notion that the end of the empire was impelled by the rise of a new class with a distinct ideology, arguing that the emphasis on patronage continued throughout the republic. Weinstein, however, notes a concerted effort (slower in Brazilian historiography than in recent Spanish American historiography) to change this paradigm and to construct a narrative of "everyday forms of state formation" (a phrase taken from the title of a watershed volume, *Everyday Forms of State Formation: Revolution and the Negotiation of Rule in Modern Mexico*, which investigates how popular sectors participated in and contributed to the construction of states).

Judy Bieber's work on rural Minas Gerais in the nineteenth century exemplifies the historiography Weinstein describes. Bieber sets out to challenge the existing scholarship's emphasis on the traditionalism of the Brazilian interior, its cultural propensity to violence, and its inability to participate in political life beyond the level of patron-client relationships. Her study makes two main points useful for considering how rural populations may have understood "the state" and their relationship to it during the empire (1822–89) and its transition to the republic.

In her first challenge to those past assumptions, Bieber claims that the elites of the small interior municipalities did slowly internalize new political ideologies and rhetoric. She argues that municipal elites shifted their perspective, moving from a political horizon limited to local spaces at independence to an increasing involvement in national politics and an identification with a wider "imagined community," even if the center never imagined the small rural communities as integral to their national project. Bieber never disputes patronage's centrality to the functioning of politics—indeed, patronage was critical to the way in which the central government linked up with the smaller units— but disagrees with Graham and others in arguing that new political norms and ideologies are eventually integrated, so that this shift in the language of politics was not simply for show. Rural peoples genuinely incorporated new ways of thinking about political relationships, mobilizing concepts of governance, citizenship, order, and progress in dialogue with a larger political community and beyond the level of rhetoric (even when it yielded few immediate material or pragmatic rewards). Not surprisingly, she points to newspapers, which began to appear beyond the confines of the coastal cities in the early to mid-nineteenth century (in the 1830s and 1840s in Minas Gerais) and proliferated in the following few decades (1860–1880s), as crucial to the consolidation of this emerging political culture.[54] Increasingly, local letters, diaries, government documents, and newspapers associated with these small municipalities voiced defenses of values such as moderation, judicial impartiality, electoral fairness, and partisan fidelity, which were used to define a moral economy of appropriate political behavior. Favoritism determined by kinship or party alliances was rejected. Following independence, municipal leaders initially produced documents—letters and such—that presumed the traditional relationship to a monarch, that of a submissive vassal to paternal sovereign, but by midcentury patriarchs were sending their sons to coastal cities to acquire university degrees, and as Bieber says, these young men "became citizens of a modern state, not subjects of a patriarchal emperor" (203–4).

In a sense, Bieber's argument is that ideology—claims about governance, citizenship, and sovereignty—was not used simply to mask the way things really were run (i.e., by patronage) but was slowly inked into material practices of daily life and processes of subject formation, even if it did not work as it did in Europe and even if this process was hybrid and uneven. Indeed, the language of liberalism was often articulated with older senses of honor and older notions of kinship (201). Bieber argues, for example, that the Brazilian state successfully grafted party politics and partisan identifications onto a preexisting system based on kinship ties and personal loyalty so that "partisan politics came to serve as a kind of fictive kinship that superseded localized family loyalties" (153). Such identifications, moreover, were spread unevenly in the backlands: in part, her study shows that those towns that adopted the language of liberalism and communicated frequently with the provincial government thrived, while those that did not stagnated.

Bieber's second important point is that this process of integration into a new political culture during the Brazilian Empire, particularly during the reign of Dom Pedro II, went hand-in-hand with the municipality's decreasing political autonomy and self-determination and that it dramatically increased—rather than decreased—levels of political and electoral violence. The municipal council had functioned as the basic administrative unit of Portugal's empire, reaching the height of its powers in the mid-seventeenth century (largely because of poor communications and limited resources). The imperial government sought to reverse this autonomy early on through the Lei dos Municípios of 1828, which stripped municipalities of many powers (including political and judicial functions) and redefined them as purely administrative units. The Additional Act of 1834 further diminished municipal autonomy by requiring town councils to submit all budgets, ordinances, and projects for public works for the approval of provincial legislative assemblies. As Bieber notes, by the 1850s the municipalities had lost their right either to elect or nominate the personnel responsible for maintaining law and order (magistrates, police delegates, and officers of the National Guard) (47–51). Patronage—based first on kinship and then, after midcentury, increasingly on party ties—was slowly turned into the underlying logic of local administration. Officials used their positions to deliver votes, and the municipal office became a benefit bestowed to loyal clients. This political machine was institutionalized under the reign of Dom Pedro II, under whom the centralized government became increasingly intrusive and top-down pressures to force particular outcomes grew.

One consequence of this process was a marked increase in electoral and political violence. Bieber argues that elections in Minas Gerais had proceeded in a relatively orderly fashion until 1848 (although this era has been considered unstable and formative at the national level). Widespread violence, however, became an endemic feature of electoral contests at midcentury (1850) and thereafter. Such electoral violence was blamed on the backwardness of rural areas and the voters themselves (seen as dupes or puppets of political patrons) and eventually led to the restriction of suffrage through a series of electoral reforms, culminating in the 1881 electoral reform, where direct voting finally became law. With this reform, while all *eleitores* would vote directly for the candidates, the group of *votantes* was essentially eliminated. The income requirement was the same as that for the *eleitores* in 1824 (but it required specific and complex documentation to prove it), and after the initial registration was completed, only literates would qualify thereafter. Bieber notes that under the new law, only 150,000 voters registered nationwide, less than one-sixth of the one million registered in 1870 (105). (The literacy requirement became universal in 1892 under the republic.) While blame was therefore placed on rustic *sertanejos* deemed to be operating beyond the reach of law and order, Bieber argues that the responsibility for chaos surrounding elections lay with the institutional connections binding dependent municipal authorities to the will of the political party in power. The *sertanejos* resorted to a "culturally acceptable response to destabilize electoral rituals that they saw as hollow representations of liberalism by a corrupt, hypocritical, and intrusive government" (106). In this way, she argues, the imperial state "laid the groundwork for the política dos governadores of the First Republic and ensured that abuses inherent to machine politics during the empire would be perpetuated in a republican Brazil" (154).

Bieber's study therefore directly challenges positions such as that expressed in 1841 by Paulino José Soares de Souza, a leader of the Conservative Party and minister of justice, when he wrote, "[Our rural populations do not] participate in the meager benefits of our nascent civilization[;] they are lacking in moral and religious instruction because there exists nobody to provide it. Imbued with dangerous ideas of a poorly understood liberty, ignorant of the law, they laugh at the weakness of the authorities, every time they come up against the whims of the people. It [the *sertão*] thus constitutes a part of society separate from our coast and many of our districts and villages, and is characterized principally by barbaric customs, ferocious acts, and horrible crimes."[55]

As I discuss more fully in chapter 4, Paulino's position was to be echoed and systematized in *Os sertões* as one of the principal causes of the attacks on Canudos. Versions of this position, moreover, have been responsible for the previously described dominant vision in historiography in which the vast majority of the racially diverse poor were deemed to exist outside the narrow circles of political life in nineteenth-century Brazil. Bieber reads against the grain of this dominant narrative and suggests another story, one in which the *sertão* was not so separate from the coast and in which political violence was brought on the *sertão* by the consolidation of an increasingly centralized state apparatus, not by "barbaric customs." In this way Bieber maps how a certain regulative *idea* of the state was spread even as she makes visible the violence and losses that accompanied it and the fact that many of the people subjected to the new forms of governmentality saw its claims as hollow and did not accept its forms and precepts.

Representation and the Work of Culture

The phenomenon whereby "the public" is restricted to the literate and enlightened and a discourse of popular sovereignty gets taken up in Brazil despite subsequent efforts to restrict popular participation in the electoral process is described by Agamben as a curious disjuncture within the notion of "the people." In modern European languages, he writes, the term designates both the "whole of the citizenry as a united body" (the constitutive political subject) and the class that is de facto excluded from politics: the poor, the wretched, *les mi-sérables*.[56] For Agamben, this fracture between the people and the people, the presence of misery and exclusion, becomes an "intolerable scandal" precisely with the French Revolution, "when it [the people] becomes the sole depositary of sovereignty."[57] The French Revolution thus names a transition after which the modern nation-state will desperately try to erase or heal this fracture and make the people coincide with the people. Hence, says Agamben, "the people is what always already is and yet must, nevertheless, be realized."[58]

The principle of representation is brought in to suture this gap and, particularly after the Terror, displaces the ideals of transparency that informed revolutionary sensibility. The revolutionary moment itself was more Rousseauian in inspiration. For Rousseau, representative democracy is a contradiction in terms. Such representation can only alienate the general will and substitute for it, replace it, hence his famed quip: "The English people believes itself to be free; it is gravely mistaken; it is free only during election of members of parliament; as soon as the members are elected, the people is enslaved; it is nothing."[59] What is needed instead is immediacy, the absence of mediation between people and power. Democracy, in this sense, must be modeled after a festival in which all are out on the streets, participating in full daylight, rather than the theater, where the audience, seated separately in the dark, is united only through mediation of the performed spectacle.[60] As Lloyd and Thomas put it, "Where all stand in the same space, in radical equivalence, no one can stand for any other, nor any voice speak for any other."[61] Rousseau's call for immediacy notwithstanding, the notion prevalent after the French Revolution was a version of what Baker identifies as Emmanuel Joseph Sieyès's social theory of representation, which privileged "the rational representation of social interests" over a Rousseauian aggregation of particular wills.[62] Sieyès declared, "The people or the nation can have but one voice, that of the national legislature. . . . In a country that is not a [direct] democracy—and France cannot be one—the people, I repeat, can speak or act only through its representatives."[63] These words were echoed by one constitutionalist newspaper in Rio de Janeiro when it avowed that "what the 'school of revolutions' taught was that popular sovereignty was better expressed through representative institutions than in the 'Jacobin usurpation of power by the people.'"[64] Sovereignty could be exercised only through legal representation.

Jules Michelet, the paradigmatic historian of the French Revolution (and one who exercised great influence on da Cunha), exemplifies with particular clarity an attempt to heal the fracture to which Agamben referred through a representational project. It is clear, in the first place, that if Michelet was to write the history of the French Revolution, it could not be a history of kings and their downfalls; rather, it had to be a history about the actions of a people. In this sense his project exemplifies the centrality of the people to the emerging political project in the transition from the monarchical state to the modern bourgeois state.

In the kind of history Michelet struggled to write, he imagines the historian as the "guardian of the graves," the medium through which the dead speak. "Suppose we were to constitute a guardian of graves, a kind of tutor and protector of the dead," Michelet proposes. "Yes, each dead man leaves a small property, his memory, and asks that it be cared for. . . . This magistracy is History. And the dead are, to speak in the fashion of Roman Law, those miserabiles personae with whom the magistrate must be concerned."[65] The relationship between the historian and his or her subjects thus mimics the political project that Michelet finds manifest in the French Revolution. The subject, first, is "each dead man"—each man not as exceptional but as one integer in a series. But this everyman is also dead, and if a live people may be said, as Deleuze wishes, to speak for itself, the dead clearly cannot, except to "ask" for the custodial mediation without which their memory would languish. The agency that binds the historian to this dead man shifts: this "man" requests representation (asking for his memory to be cared for), but the historian is also described as his "tutor" (speaking to and not only for this man). Moreover, the injunction on the historian to "represent" this man comes from above to the extent that it is described as isomorphic with the custodial relationship of the magistrate to the people as determined by Roman law. Proxy cannot be separated from portrait for Michelet, or better, Michelet transforms the problem of producing a portrait into the problem of acting as a proxy. If Michelet was to produce an image of the political event of the Revolution, he had to represent (speak for) the agents of that event as he understood it. Writing history therefore is about transforming silence into voice: "the silences of history must be made to speak, those terrible pedal points in which history says nothing more, and which are precisely its most tragic accents."[66] At first glance these silences do not seem particularly hard to retrieve. Despite the lacuna achieved by separating the dead people from the live historian—the transformation of voices into silence—the process seems to be easily reversed. Michelet's ideal is a homogeneous, seamless world in which everything in the universe shares the same smooth skin, the same common denominator. Events in history are merely different moments of a single surface extending itself ever onward, like a rug, a sheet, or a film, so that the historian is always able to recognize and verbalize any other point further along the same surface. If death is no barrier to those restless dead seeking a magus to decipher their meaning, it is because there is nothing exterior to the underlying structural unity. "Now they live with us, and we feel we are their relatives, their friends," says Michelet; "thus is constituted a family, a city shared by the living and the dead."[67] Michelet thus demonstrates the narration of a particular form of representation that is also a form of government—since history is also a magistracy—that protects and transmits the "property" of each individual of the people. (The exclusion harbored at the heart of "the people" appears in the equivalence Michelet establishes between "memory" and "property"; however faceless and nameless this man is, his relationship to his own existence is defined as ownership of property. Not all dead men accommodate themselves to the implied series of "each dead man.") Death both installs the difference or division, which is traversed by the historian (and government), and by that same move justifies the place of transmission.

Yet Michelet also finds what he calls the "people's language" mysteriously inaccessible to him. "I was born of the people[;] I have the people in my heart. . . . But the people's language, its language was inaccessible to me. I have not been able to make the people speak."[68] From this painful admission Roland Barthes will extract an image of Michelet gazing like Moses on the Promised Land but unable to step into it. The people's frontier shakes his ideal at its very core. As Barthes says, it is his own speech, his own work, that bears him, lacerated, far from paradise, so that he is "perhaps the first author of modernity able to utter only an impossible language."[69]

Whereas Michelet attempts—and fails—to speak for the people, Lloyd and Thomas identify a temporal logic that arises to resolve the fracture between people and representative (between people as political subject and people as excluded from politics) so that there is a time lag between the state (which embodies the people as political subject) and the people. In other words, the state expresses the people not as they are but as they will or should be realized. Thus, they write that the state "must be understood as representative in the fullest sense: it is at once an institution that derives from the people and one which expresses at a higher level the still developing essence of that people."[70]

This leads me back to education, that marker that circumscribed the boundaries of true "public opinion" for so many at the time. Indeed, Michelet himself touches on this formulation when he speaks of the historian as both representative of and tutor to the dead. Speaking *for* the people turns into speaking *to* the people. Or, as Lloyd and Thomas put it, rephrasing Marx's famous comments on the French peasants who supported Louis Bonaparte, "They may not represent themselves[;] they must learn to be represented" (5).

Lloyd and Thomas develop a rich and powerful argument about culture's role in this project. Culture, they say, becomes the means of producing the people that will be adequate to their representation in the state. The term *culture* means something specific here. While it includes the ensemble of artifacts and aesthetic practices traditionally associated with "the cultured version of culture," it designates primarily the disposition of the individual in relation to those objects and nature, not those objects per se. In other words, Lloyd and Thomas's argument turns around a historical moment in which culture was understood principally in terms of cultivation. What needs to be produced is this disposition.

When Lloyd and Thomas cite Matthew Arnold's comment that "Culture suggests the idea of the State," therefore, they mean two things. First, they point out parallels between the two concepts. In particular, they underscore the way both culture and state are understood as sites of reconciliation for a society that is otherwise riven by conflict and contradiction (1). Hegel, of course, is the inevitable reference point for any concept of the state as subsuming particularities and contradictions. Lloyd and Thomas argue that culture is analogously posed as a sphere in which the human subject could cultivate all its capacities at a time when the division of intellectual and manual labor was increasingly forming specialized or partial individuals (2). This fashioning of a whole self took place above all through an education in aesthetics insofar as, after Kant and German Romanticism, aesthetics and art have been posited as the site where the individual's freedom can be reconciled with the universe's determinism. Exemplary of these arguments, for example, is the following passage that Lloyd and Thomas quote from Friedrich Schiller's *On the Aesthetical Education of Man*: "Every human being, one may say, carries within him, potentially and prescriptively, an ideal man, the archetype of a human being, and it is his life's task to be, through all his changing manifestations, in harmony with the unchanging unity of this ideal. This archetype, which is to be discerned more or less clearly in every individual, is represented by the State, the objective and, as it were, canonical form in which all the diversity of individual subjects strives to unite" (47). Schiller's remark shows a relationship between culture and state that goes beyond simple parallelism and in which aesthetic education is supposed to bring every human being closer in harmony to this ideal individual represented by the state. In other words, as Lloyd and Thomas write, aesthetic and ethical judgment becomes the condition of possibility for the formation of the modern citizen.

This, then, is the second sense in which culture suggests the idea of the state. The education in culture, Lloyd and Thomas say, interpellates "individuals into the disposition to disinterested reflection that makes the state's mediations possible" (14). Through a relationship of substitution or supplementation, they thus argue, culture "comes to mediate between a disenfranchised populace and a state to which they must in time be assimilated" (5).

In pragmatic terms this disposition was to be transmitted to the population through state educational institutions. For intellectuals such as Matthew Arnold, teachers and educators exemplify the "ideal citizens," reversing the chain of representation so that they are the state's representatives to the people. Borrowing a phrase from John Stuart Mill's *Considerations on Representative Government* (1861), Lloyd and Thomas write, "'the instructed minority' becomes a corrective to the unenlightened will of the majority acting at once as tutors in citizenship and representatives of the state at the local level" (5). Their argument that culture becomes a place of mediation between the populace and the state thus concerns both the development of an ideology of culture, centered on the cultivation of aesthetic judgment, and the way such an ideology is materialized in the development of educational institutions in England. This was not "self-evident" at the time, as is shown through their analysis of the challenges articulated within radical working-class circles in nineteenth-century Britain.

Postcolonial Failures and Compensations

Euclides da Cunha could cast education as the means for crossing the gap painted by Paulino Soares de Sousa, for ushering the barbarian hordes into civilization, because such models had been imported to Latin America—especially following independence, when the region faced the pressing need to build new nation-states out of the ashes of the colonial order. Thus the nineteenth-century writer-statesman Andrés Bello could write: "The *belles lettres* were an instrument in the formation of disciplined subjects, subject to law, subordinated to the general order and capable even of administrating it."[71] Bello's wording alerts us to the fact that in Latin America the problem was not the cultivation of wholeness to remedy fissures and divisions internal to civil society (the product of an increasing differentiation of labor in industrializing societies) but rather a colonizing project to discipline and subject that which was still considered outside civil society. Accordingly, Bello's instrument of education was grammar rather than aesthetics. Nonetheless, literature, too, was understood to play a role in constructing a citizenry. As Julio Ramos writes, literature was the space where "one saw projected models of behavior, norms necessary for the invention of citizenship, symbolic frontiers and limits, the very imaginary map of the states being consolidated."[72] The nineteenth-century novels that Doris Sommer identifies as "foundational fictions" provide examples of this attempt to educate readers into the imaginary identifications necessary for nationalism. Sommer argues that the ill-fated romances that drive these novels are meant to persuade readers to identify with the lovers, who are drawn from different classes, parties, and ethnicities, so that they can imagine a new social order in which the hitherto prohibitive differences the lovers represent are subsumed, allowing the relationships to succeed.[73]

Yet such attempts took place in a postcolonial context in which, as Ranajit Guha said, the nation failed to come into its own. Even as late as the First Republic, the politician Alberto Torres could measure out his disenchantment in the following formula: "This State is not a nationality; this country is not a society; this population is not a people. Our men are not citizens."[74] Intellectuals in Latin America faced challenges and contradictions even greater than those Michelet faced, for they were trying to make the people not just speak but speak in the grammar developed by movements on the faraway European continent. Success and failure were measured against that model, and as Torres's words indicate, reality often stubbornly resisted adapting itself to European norms. Michelet at least believed a people existed (though their language was inaccessible to him), but Torres doubted even that. And if there was no nation, no society, and consequently no people to have a language, where did the intellectual who wanted to express that language fit in? Nicolau Sevcenko points out that no one defined this state of affairs better than da Cunha, who argued that the difficulties confronting the government's expeditions against Canudos were due to the fantastic circumstance of waging a war against a completely unknown nature and people.[75]

Because of this position, da Cunha became a model for writers, such as Silvio Romero, José Veríssimo, and Araripe Júnior, who saw the country's main problem as the elite's incapacity to understand the country and its people and who opposed what they perceived as the Europeanizing trends of Machado de

Assis and others like him. Writing in 1897, Silvio Romero described Brazil's situation as an "absurdity": "A tiny intellectual elite separated itself off from the mass of the population, and while the majority remained almost entirely uneducated, this elite, being particularly gifted in the art of learning and copying, threw itself into political and literary imitation of everything it found in the Old World. So now we have an exotic literature and politics, which live and procreate in a hothouse that has no relationship to the outside temperature and environment."[76] As Roberto Schwarz suggests, there is more than one contradiction in this position, where the "sin of copying" is deemed an absurdity in contrast to "the norm of an organic, reasonably homogeneous national culture with popular roots,"[77] a norm imported from abroad. But da Cunha's text was considered a model that avoided such a sin. According to Regina Abreu, while the consecration of *Os sertões* resulted in part from the emergence of a new "modern and scientific criticism," da Cunha's book was also fundamental for "the exercise and affirmation of this new criticism."[78] Da Cunha's initial canonization was thus inextricable from the ascendancy of a new discursive formation that sought to produce intellectuals who, cognizant of their country's difference from Europe, would truly represent the people. Muniz de Albuquerque wrote, "In the following decades [after its publication] critics would attribute to this book the beginning of the search for the authentic country, for the people, having banished the illusion that we were a European nation and revealed instead the importance of being American. With this book, we had begun the search for our origins, for our past, for our people, our customs, our traditions. . . . *Os sertões* is definitely a framework in the sense that it outlines the elements with which the problem of national identity would hitherto be thought. It is a book which furnishes images and enunciations for the different regionalist discourses."[79]

The regionalist discourses to which Durval Muniz de Albuquerque refers here took shape in Brazil after 1920, arising from the ruins of a diffuse and provincial nineteenth-century regionalism. For Albuquerque this shift was possible only after crisis undermined older paradigms, such as naturalism, and older forms of sociability. A new way of looking at space and a new social sensibility emerged from this crisis, "producing the need to think questions of national identity, national race, [and] national character, as well as the need to elaborate a national culture capable of incorporating the different spaces of the country."[80] In this new imaginative geography, the Northeast became the other of São Paulo, a great medieval space ruled by banditry, messianism, and feudal power structures, a place associated with nostalgia for the past or the desire for revolution.

According to Albuquerque, after 1930 Brazil adopted this discursive construction of regionalism under the geopolitical enterprise of integrating its vast interior lands into the nation-state.[81] Like the Peronist state in Argentina a decade later, Getúlio Vargas's Estado Novo (1930–1945) was a populist project defined as the inclusion of a previously excluded people in the sphere of politics. Under the Estado Novo, the state was supposedly capable of integrating national differences into a whole: "The nation was represented fundamentally as territory, as geography, and the State was to articulate regional diversity under the leadership of São Paulo. This representation, which predominated during the Estado Novo, was based on the negation of a model of State and nation that had, according to Cassiano Ricardo, dominated in the previous period, one that was 'contaminated' by European 'isms' and constructed by the 'coastal cities.'"[82]

According to Regina Abreu, da Cunha became a "model writer" for Vargas's regime.[83] One sign of his adoption is the impetus given to the movement of self-proclaimed da Cunha fans and followers during the Estado Novo. Abreu, who traces the government's deliberate policy of consecrating da Cunha, notes as one example the "Semanas Euclidanas," instituted in 1935 in São José do Rio Pardo (the city where he wrote Os sertões). These yearly weeklong celebrations of Euclides da Cunha, which still take place, are organized as intellectual "marathons" for young students; they include a series of classes and a municipal parade and are capped by public talks on da Cunha's work given by important intellectuals. Under Vargas, the cabin where da Cunha wrote Os sertões was turned into national monument, and his biography and work were disseminated by official vehicles such as the Instituto Nacional do Cinema Educativo, which produced a educational film on him in 1944, and the newspaper A Manhã, which devoted two special numbers of their literary supplement to him in 1942. In addition, Abreu argues that the large-scale diffusion of Os sertões was the basis for the inauguration of the genre of "estudos brasileiros," wherein da Cunha's book was read as the "parable of Brazilian history, which demonstrated Brazilian's ignorance with its own territory and history."[84] Abreu cites a study by Heloisa Pontes of the coleções brasilianas, books that, starting in the 1930s, were edited for the purpose of increasing knowledge of Brazil; she concludes that they bear a structure similar to the da Cunha's model for

apprehending reality—land, people, struggle—and that they themselves are
conceived as *"entradas bandeirantes"* (the name given to the inland incursions
of colonists that expanded Portugal's effective control over the inner reaches
of the South American continent).[85] It was also during the Estado Novo that
Os sertões became required reading in the school curriculum. Finally, *Os sertões*
gained the status of national patrimony during this period, a period when the
very idea of "national patrimony" was inaugurated and institutionalized in
Brazil.[86]

To the extent, then, that "what governs the canonicity of culture's texts is
their approximation not so much to reality as to a regulative *idea*,"[87] Euclides da
Cunha has acquired canonical status because he acts out the "regulative idea,"
common in Latin America, that intellectuals are social glue. He is understood
as something akin to Michelet's magistrate: speaker for the dead and tutor to
the people, representing the truth of the people of Canudos to Brazil as well as
offering a model to represent Brazil to its people.

Yet da Cunha's canonization is also symptomatic of a peculiarly Latin
American, or postcolonial, vision of the mediating effects of culture, since—
to cite Roberto Schwarz's argument about the importation of liberal ideals in
nineteenth-century Brazil—the instrumental ideal of culture proved to be "out
of place." Schwarz's analysis turns on a contrast between the way these ideas
functioned in their places of origin and in places where they were adopted.
According to Schwarz, liberal ideology was the expression of the triumphant
bourgeois consciousness in Europe, but this ideology, which postulated the autonomy of the individual, the equality of all citizens, the universality of law, disinterested culture, and a commitment to thrift and labor, was manifestly out of
place in Brazil, where production was based largely on slavery.[88] Nonetheless,
such ideals still constituted the frame of reference. Schwarz calls them "second-
degree ideologies" to describe the peculiar function of ideologies that do not
describe reality—not even falsely—but are still used by the elites for other purposes. In the case of Latin America, therefore, we should attend to what one
could call a "second-degree ideology of culture." Taken strictly, Schwarz's argument can lead to positions such as Richard Graham's (where liberal ideology
is meaningless and acts simply as a cover for the practices of patronage), but
Schwarz suggests that such ideologies instead worked in different, often hybrid
ways in Latin America. For Latin America, then, what emerges is—contrary to
the tradition analyzed by Lloyd and Thomas—an economy in which culture

acquires an additional, secondary function wherein it is deemed to compensate for a precarious state's inability to set into motion the machinery that would produce the kind of citizenry imagined by the likes of Matthew Arnold.

Instead of a context in which education in aesthetics is understood solely as a means to cultivate the qualities needed for a citizenry, the situation is marked by repeated failures to produce a people. By the twentieth century, literature acquired a special demand to be not only the site of resolution for a heterogeneity that extends beyond the internal conflicts of a civil society but also the site of compensation for the lack of any resolution. This compensatory function becomes thematized as such in the self-reflective novels of the "Latin American Boom," almost as a last effort to preserve the power of the literary. In *The Untimely Present* Idelber Avelar remarks the tendency in Boom writers' critical pieces to portray

> literature as disproportionately "advanced" ahead of its time vis-à-vis the continent's economic and social backwardness. . . . What has to be attended to is the rhetoric in which the diagnosis of a *dissymmetry* between the social and the literary came to be equated with the postulate of a *substitutive* operation whereby the latter was said to *compensate* for the former. "No matter how accentuated our technical isolation," we write the best literature in the world. The relationship between culture and economics then took a twisted form: they were so far apart that the development of the former bore no relationship to the backwardness of the latter; yet they were close enough that one could remedy, cure, function as a corrective for the other.[89]

Whereas this substitutive operation is phrased in terms of dissymmetry in modernization (social backwardness vs. literary advancement), I have been emphasizing the question of unity and disunity (perceived as a symptom of this social backwardness), so that the literary is advanced to the extent that it mediates what remains divided and disintegrated in reality.

The compensatory function of culture is what drives Angel Rama's theory of transculturation, a hermeneutic model that has been one of the most important and widely used in Latin American literary and cultural criticism over the past twenty years. The starting point of transculturation is the existence of two or more original worlds that enter into contact and, "as in the genetic coupling of two individuals,"[90] produce a new, third term. As originally conceived by the Cuban anthropologist Fernando Ortiz in his *Contrapunteo cubano del tabaco y el azúcar*, transculturation describes the "transitive process from one culture to another."[91] Culture is thus envisioned as a meeting ground for peoples and societies that do not otherwise meet, as this passage from Ortiz shows:

> If these American Indies were a New World to the European peoples, Europe was a very New World for the American peoples. Two worlds collided and discovered each other. The contact of the two cultures was terrible. One of them perished almost completely, as if quickly struck down by lightning. A failed transculturation for the indigenous peoples and a cruel and radical transculturation for those newly arrived to these lands. The human indigenous sediment of the society was destroyed in Cuba, and it became necessary to uproot and bring over all her new population. . . . What a curious social phenomenon, that of Cuba; all her peoples and cultures have been invaders since the sixteenth century, either bearing force or by force; all her peoples and cultures are exogenous and dislocated, and they harbor the trauma of the original uprooting and the brutal transplantation to a new culture in formation.[92]

Although the indigenous groups perish almost immediately, Ortiz still understands a transculturation (a cruel and radical one) as having taken place between Europeans and indigenous groups. They vanish but leave a trace—if only through an absence that makes a new labor force necessary—that continues to mark the new culture being formed. Ortiz's words show that the point of view from which this history is surveyed is the presumed outcome of the process: "Cuba." Culture (a new Cuban culture) is thus both the outcome and the ground on which a violent clash between worlds turns into the creation of a new one.[93]

Latin American literary and cultural criticism, however, took up not Ortiz's model but rather Angel Rama's version of it, which moves the terrain from culture defined in broad anthropological terms to the sphere of the literary. "In Latin American literary criticism written under the aegis of dependency theory in the 1960s and 1970s, literature was conceived as a vehicle for the cultural syncretism necessary to the formation of an inclusive nation-state. Rama's idea of 'narrative transculturation,' . . . exemplified for him by the novels of the 'boom,' was perhaps the most influential expression of this general idea."[94]

Just as significant is the fact that this change was accompanied by decreased emphasis on violence and an increased emphasis on a positive outcome. In other words, the increased emphasis on the specifically aesthetic, literary place of mediation led to an increased emphasis on the positive outcome of mediation. Rama lauds the term for the agency and creativity implied in the mixing of what he calls the interior-regional (traditional rural cultures) and the external-universal (cosmopolitan modernizing cultures). It is an antidote to considering nonmodern cultures as "merely passive or even inferior," destined to losses without a creative response, what the Peruvian writer José María Arguedas called the idea that "the defeated nation renounces her soul . . . and acquires the soul of the winners."[95] Whereas Ortiz, speaking of Cuba, points out that all Cuban inhabitants—dominant and oppressed—are products of displacements and travel, Rama constructs an opposition between a relatively untouched and static interior region and an outside world that generates change. The interior-regional structurally resembles the psychoanalytic unconscious: "an unknown cultural background that methods of knowledge can only clumsily account for" or "cognitive structures in incessant emergence."[96] In Rama's version of transculturation, the interior-regional is also simultaneously the bearer of the roots of identity, the site of a deep continuity, and that which changes in contact with the exterior. But this transaction between the interior-regional and external-universal culture takes place specifically on the terrain of literature. Writers mix regional traditions with the literary vanguard and produce novels that for Rama expand the original "cosmovision" "so that it is better adjusted. This cosmovision is authentic, artistically solvent. It is even modernized. Yet its identity is not destroyed."[97] The literary form thus becomes the place where two worlds meet. As José María Arguedas, Rama's principal example, put it, "I attempted to transform into written language what I was as an individual: a strong living link, capable of being universalized, between the great, walled-in nation and the generous, humane side of the oppressors."[98]

Two things should be noted, however. First, the process is unidirectional, at least in Rama's version. When literature comes into contact with anthropology, letters, and indigenous myths, it "devours" them, including them within its province, but literature is not undone in the process, not transformed into something unrecognizable. Second, the relationship between the literary and other practices in society is not visible in Rama's theorization. In other words, Rama's theory suggests that cultures meet in the literary realm without asking what happens outside literature. Literary transactions seem to take the place of other kinds of hybridities or meetings or are in any case the most important register of such transculturation to the extent that the literary is the place where the cosmovision of the interior-regional culture is preserved and transmitted. The exclusive focus on the literary suggests that it substitutes and compensates for other realms of society—even though Arguedas expressed his desperation at his inability to overcome the divisions fissuring Peruvian society. He may have forged a hybrid language and a narrative practice, but this could not be universalized to other sites of Peruvian society.

This is the point of Cornejo-Polar's theory of heterogeneity, which takes into account the productive process of literature and the lack of coincidence between the universe represented within literature and the universe in which it functions. A literature such as the *indigenismo* of which Arguedas was a part (a variant of Latin American regionalism) could interpret a referent that was indigenous, agrarian, oral, and Aymara or Quecha speaking, but it did so through a narrative production that included writing, the Spanish language, European artistic conventions, and particular ideologies and social interests (e.g., positivism, Marxism, nationalism) and was destined for reception by middle-class sectors in Lima.[99] The theoretical proposal of heterogeneity is thus primarily historical rather than aesthetic. It is premised fundamentally on the conceptualization of a reality that "is characterized by its abyssal fissuring, by its unsalvageable disharmony."[100] In such a context form cannot be perceived as neutral terrain over which battles can be fought or lost or as a place for their resolution; rather, it must be confronted as an artifact delivered inescapably by one side of the equation.

This second-degree ideology of culture expressed in Rama's theory of transculturation is manifest in the canonization of da Cunha's text, too. In this respect, it is striking to note the slow inscription of *Os sertões* within the canons of the literary. If, as Terry Eagleton says, "some texts are born literary, some achieve literariness and some have literariness thrust upon them,"[101] then da Cunha's text certainly falls in the third category. The text defies conventional generic classifications, moving between an anthropological essay, a testimony, a political document, and a historical account of the events. When it was published, its generic indeterminacy was noticed and yet accepted so that, for example, in 1902 José Veríssimo wrote: "The book of Mr. Euclides da Cunha is at the same time a book of a man of science, a geographer, a geologist, an ethnographer, a man of thought, a philosopher, a sociologist, a historian, and a man of sentiments, a poet, a novelist, an artist."[102]

Da Cunha himself, who was an engineer by profession and had not previously entered the elite literary circles centered on Rio de Janeiro, acknowledged that he didn't properly fit the category of a "literary man." In his acceptance speech following his election to the prestigious Academia Brasileira de Letras, he began, according to Abreu, by "taking on the identity of a 'man of science'

and reflecting on the difficulties of entering into a house of 'men of letters.'"
Even so, argues Abreu, such a reflection and its occasion—the fact that he was
invited to be part of an academy of letters—also signals that "there wasn't a
clear distinction between the frontiers of literature and science and that there
were not yet consecrating institutions in the field of science with the same
prestige as the Brazilian Academy of Letters."[103] Like many other texts in the
nineteenth century, especially Domingo Sarmiento's *Facundo* (perhaps the text
closest to *Os sertões*), da Cunha's book arrived before the full differentiation between literature and rationality in Latin America, a process that Julio Ramos
analyzes in his *Divergent Modernities*.

Later in the twentieth century, however, the multiplicity of *Os sertões* had
to be decided in favor of its literary or scientific qualities. Whereas Antonio
Candido favored its scientific value, claiming that *Os sertões* signaled "the end
of literary imperialism and the beginning of a scientific analysis applied to the
most important aspects of Brazilian society"[104] (thus claiming da Cunha as the
founder of Brazilian sociology), most often and increasingly the literary value of
the text was underscored. On the surface, the valorization of the literary seems
to have been a response to the thorny question of the text's "truth-value" in
relation to what had become da Cunha's outdated science: his theories on the
autochthonous origin of the American individual and his positivist concepts
of race in which stronger races triumph over weaker ones and miscegenation
is largely a force of degeneration. Thus, for instance, the critic Franklin de
Oliveiro assures the reader that "the greatness of Os Sertões . . . is an eminently
literary greatness. The scientific knowledge rusted early: the beauty of science
resides precisely in an incessant revision of postulates and hypotheses."[105] It is
a way of excusing and brushing aside the racism of *Os sertões*, and the model of a
visionary da Cunha now holds: da Cunha was no slave to the now oxidized but
then novel imported European models of thought but strove to remain faithful to the Brazilian reality he witnessed. Da Cunha saw the essence of Brazil,
despite the trappings of this oxidized science.[106] In this way, then, the text's literary dimension is increasingly put forward as the justification for a continued
insistence on the text's sight. González Echeverría's and Costa Lima's readings
are the culmination of inscribing da Cunha's text within a literary register. It is
in this sense that *Os sertões* becomes not only an example of effectively integrating the population of the hinterlands (an example deployed in the schools to
this effect) but also the symbolic instantiation and compensation for what the
government had failed to do.

CHAPTER TWO

A PROSE OF COUNTERINSURGENCY

> There in that corner, he [Antônio Conselheiro] . . . spoke to the people. He was
> a dry and bearded old man and prayed in such a manner that it was wonderful
> to listen to him.
>
> —Antonio Carola, 1955

The various biographical accounts of Antônio Conselheiro—also known as Antônio dos Mares, Santo Antônio Aparecido, Santo Conselheiro, and Bom Jesus—differ as to details of his early life (e.g., date of birth, his relationship with his wife, and the date he left Ceará for Bahia). Most stories concur, however, on the following points.

The Conselheiro was born Antônio Vicente Mendes Maciel in Quixeramobim, Ceará, in 1828 (or 1830, the year of his baptism). His father, Vicente Mendes Maciel, was a smalltime merchant who owned a few houses. His first wife having died, Vicente remarried when Antônio was six. Tradition has it that Antônio's stepmother was mentally unstable and mistreated the boy. His father apparently hoped he would become a priest and sent him to study at a school where he not only acquired literacy in his native language but also learned arithmetic, Latin, and French (which, given the levels of literacy then common in Brazil, placed him among a privileged minority). Antônio soon abandoned his studies and went to work in his father's commercial establishment, taking control of it on his father's death. He was unsuccessful commercially, however, and closed his father's business in 1857, the same year he married his cousin Brasilina Laurentina de Lima.[1] From 1857 until 1871 he tried his hand at several jobs, from primary school teacher to wandering merchant to a legal advocate for the poor. At this time he also separated from his wife, who is said to have cheated on him. According to these stories, Antônio's mother told him about the affair and advised him that he should hide in the bushes and watch to see for himself. To convince her son, she decided to play the part, dressing up as a man and creeping out of his wife's room. In this account, the enraged Antônio shot her only to discover that it was his own mother when he removed the clothes. Antônio was indeed jailed in 1874 in Bahia, charged with his mother's murder, but after he was sent back to Ceará, the accusation was deemed false.[2] (His acquiescence to the arrest is often cited to show his acceptance of governmental authority under the monarchy.) The story has continued to circulate, however. Antônio is supposed to have had two (and according to oral culture, perhaps even three) sons—one by his wife and one by Joana Imaginária, a mystic artist who carved wooden statues of saints. In 1871 he was brought to court for a debt that he paid off by selling all that he had. Soon thereafter, apparently, he turned to a wandering religious life.

The first record of him from this era occurred in November 22, 1874, in a note published in *O Rabudo*, a newspaper from Sergipe, announcing that a certain Antônio dos Mares, with bare feet and long hair and wearing a blue robe, was preaching about morality and customs. He did not accept alms, ate little, and constructed churches and cemeteries. The tone of the piece is nonchalant, but by the end of the Canudos conflict, the Conselheiro would be described as a madman and a fanatic, a throwback to barbarism. Everything about him would connote excess and rupture, reducing and finally eliminating any possibility of understanding the man as an ordinary figure, as did this note in *O Rabudo*.

Within the space between the note in *O Rabudo* and da Cunha's text, published over twenty years later, emerged a prose of counterinsurgency. I borrow this term from Ranajit Guha, who used it to underscore the way accounts of peasant insurgencies found in colonial India's governmental letters and dispatches were not neutral, factual accounts; rather, they were organized explicitly by a code of pacification through which the state sought to put down insurgency in words and actions. To say that government memoranda are interested in combating insurgency may seem obvious enough; Guha's main point, however, is that the governmental optics in these sources is preserved in secondary and tertiary accounts of the events. In other words, even seemingly neutral historical accounts produced years later secretly reproduce many of the assumptions embedded in the first level of immediate accounts (which constitute the bulk of the primary sources available, for the peasants enjoyed far less access to the technology of writing). Since the discourse on peasant insurgency "made its debut . . . as a discourse of power," its central problematic is the security of the state.[3] As it is written into the historical record, therefore, peasant insurgency is also assimilated into "an element in the career of colonialism. In other words, the peasant was denied recognition as a subject of history in his own right even for a project that was all his own."[4]

Guha's project in *Elementary Aspects of Peasant Insurgency in Colonial India* was to recover the distorted consciousness of peasant insurgents through a reading of their praxis of rebellion, but his scrupulous attention to the consequences of assimilating such peasants into another history cleared space for other historians and critics in the Subaltern Studies Group to elaborate the concept of subalternity as a discursive effect. Guha notes, for example, how peasant consciousness and praxis are misread in the historical archive according to the terms and categories of the discourse of power. If, for example, an uprising lacked a clear program and objective that the government could recognize as political (i.e., that operated according to a Western, modernized bourgeois notion of the political), it was considered nonpolitical. The peasants are thus excommunicated from the category of the political as well as the categories of reason and agency (so fundamental to a post-Enlightenment notion of the human) and assimilated to other, nonhuman categories. The "natural" rhetoric that organizes many representations of peasant insurgency noted by Guha (peasant rebellions "heaved like earthquakes" and "spread like wildfire") indicates how the subaltern becomes unrecognizable in human terms. In other words, since the act of insurgency shows that these peasants have not fully been subjected, their actions cannot therefore be understood through the category of the subject. When Dipesh Chakrabarty, Gyan Prakash, Gayatri Spivak, and others developed the concept of subalternity on the heels of Guha's analysis, they underscored the extent to which we can have access to the subaltern only through the discourse of power. To put it differently, we do not have access to the subaltern as an autonomous agent external to a discourse of power; we have access only to the way subaltern rebellions were committed to paper, rendered unintelligible, turned into the equivalence of nonsense or noise. The subaltern "emerges between the folds of discourse, in silence and blindness and overdetermined pronouncements."[5] Subalternity designates not the peasant per se but the excommunicated peasant, the peasant as assimilated into another's history.

The Priests

One of the markers Guha isolates to demonstrate the misreading of the peasant rebel's "consciousness" in even radical and seemingly sympathetic historiography is the inability to confront religion. Religion presents no less an obstacle in the case of Canudos, but we can understand the vexed relationship between religion and the narratives of the conflict in more than one way. First, we can follow Guha and locate religion squarely on the side of the Conselheiro and his followers; we can, that is, echo Chakrabarty by saying that "gods, spirits, and the so-called supernatural" had "a certain 'reality'"[6] for the Conselheiristas that they lacked both for the Brazilian government at the time and for subsequent historical discourse. Religion, in this sense, would be an index of an exteriority that cannot be grasped within elite discourse.[7]

Rui Facó's account of Canudos in *Cangaceiros e fanáticos* (1965) is a textbook example of the problems that Guha ascribes to Marxist analyses of peasant insurgency. Facó analyzes a series of crises—economic, ideological, and sociopolitical—that are characteristic of the fifty years spanning the turn of the twentieth century and are expressed in peasant rebellions in Brazil's vast backlands. Facó argues that the recurring Brazilian banditry and fanaticism, labeled by some as "extra-historic phenomena," were not themselves backward phenomena but rather fruits of Brazil's own economic backwardness and the decadence of its socioeconomic system (the "latifundio pre-capitalista"). According to Facó's analysis, the religious beliefs of people such as the Conselheiro's followers constituted an ideology, but one that functioned as an instrument of social liberation for the *sertanejos*. The spread of "fanaticism" revealed the drastic separation between the ideology of dominant classes and that of poorer sectors in the *sertão*. But Facó defines religion as the primary conscience people have of themselves when they lack control over their own persons and are weak and impotent. For Facó, then, mysticism in the *sertão* becomes an essentially passive element (in contrast with the more active "*cangaço*," or banditry) that nonetheless enters into conflict with the surrounding society. The elites react by attributing fanaticism and aggressive intentions to the groups. For Facó, the next phase of conflict in the case of Canudos, in which the "fanatics" became active, coincided with what he calls the slow ascension of power of João Abade, the military leader of Canudos, and with the eclipse of the Conselheiro himself. Facó insists that Abade "decided in practice on the destiny of that collectivity, while the Conselheiro remained simply as the spiritual chief, an almost symbolic feature. His importance was minimal for the unfolding armed struggle. . . . He fades into the background at the moment of struggle."[8] This counterpoint between a passive religious response and the more active response of banditry in the Brazilian *sertão* would be repeated in one of the most important movies of Brazilian Cinema Novo, Glauber Rocha's *Black God, White Devil* (1964).[9]

While Facó is obviously sympathetic to the community, his dismissal of religion and his assumption that the Conselheiro had to have vanished as an active agent during the violence reveal the extent to which Canudos has acquired the status of an allegory behind which one must read and identify the true meaning of the community and its fate. In other words, Canudos is incorporated as a datum within a history of capitalism's expansion in which the revolutionary proletariat becomes the main subject. In this view of the history of insurgency, says Guha, all moments of consciousness are assimilated to the highest moment of the series—an ideal and secular consciousness. Religion is written out of the story.[10]

Yet religion is also central to many narratives about Canudos, which suggests that instead of marking a self-exceeding otherness, it becomes a strand in the construction of a self-constituting otherness (to use Gyan Prakash's formulation of subalternity). Understood in this fashion, religion becomes not simply a reality that cannot be grasped by secular, modernizing forms of thought and narrative but rather one of the principal story-telling devices by which the difference of the peasants is processed. As an example of this, we can take Mario Vargas Llosa's rewriting of da Cunha's text in *The War of the End of the World*. In this novel, the Conselheiristas are described as fighting a kind of war essentially different from the one the government thought it was fighting. The former viewed the republic as the Antichrist, and the logic under which they fought "was only apparently that of the outside world, that of men in uniform against men in rags, that of the seacoast against the interior, that of the new Brazil against traditional Brazil. All the jagunços were aware that they were merely puppets of a profound, timeless, eternal war, that of good and evil, which had been going on since the beginning of time."[11]

In an essay on the Quebra-Quilos riots in Brazil, Vargas Llosa offers an argument against materialist rewritings of popular revolts (such as Facó's) that can be understood as justifying his choice to foreground a religious logic in his representation of the Conselheiristas. There he expresses his disagreement with

> this attitude of explaining everything that the poor do through a classifying table in which the people always appear to be rebelling in defense of their material rights, understood in terms of modern ideology. There is a secret paternalism, and even condescension, in understanding those rebels as "irrational" minors who do not know what they do and which the contemporary historian, master of ideology, clarifies by turning those poor people retrospectively into adults, recruiting them into a history understood as an ineluctable progression towards the triumph of good and justice. To treat those people who wagered their life attempting to destroy the indestructible like this is to pile on one more injustice: it is to steal the little they have after all that was stolen from them in life: their originality.[12]

This statement resembles Guha's analysis in several ways, yet Vargas Llosa nevertheless does not effectively restore "originality" to the rebels in his literary account of Canudos. In *The War of the End of the World*, Vargas Llosa uses his literary arsenal to conjure a multiplicity of perspectives that crisscross and clash without comprehending one another. This includes the previously mentioned construction of the Conselheiristas as obeying a logic entirely different from that of the Brazilian government. But this effort at multiplicity does not provide what Chakrabarty, for example, argues that we need: "history that will attempt the impossible: look toward its own death by tracing that which resists and escapes the best human effort at translation across cultural and other semiotic systems, so that the world may once again be imagined as radically heterogeneous."[13] Rather than look "toward its own death," the novel reserves for itself the vantage point from which it surveys the totality of perspectives, condemning the violence as an example of the destruction wrought by ideologies, whether religious or developmental. In this way Vargas Llosa's novel shows that, despite its pretensions to a nineteenth-century realism, it shares a number of features with the Boom novels of the late 1960s and 1970s, including the belief in the transculturating ability of literature to suture gaps in the social, political, and cultural histories of Latin America. Religion enters the novel under a form of a magical realism. It is admitted, in other words, as a sign of literature's ability to include all that colonizing narratives have excluded from reason and reality. Returning religion to the rebels therefore becomes simply another form of inscription within a history not their own.

In analyses of the stories on Canudos, religion has been subject to both processes (it is both misunderstood but also used as a device of understanding). Rather than attempt to determine what religion is "really like," however, it seems more fruitful to track the logic by which religion becomes part of the fabric of a prose of counterinsurgency. One of the ways Guha lays out the irreducibility between the code of insurgency and a code of counterinsurgency is as an opposition between two columns entitled "fine" and "terrible." Thus "peasants" (fine) are set against "insurgents" (terrible), "Islamic puritan" is set against "fanatic," "resistance to oppression" is set against "daring and wanton atrocities on the Inhabitants," and so on.[14] Another way to describe this difference is to say that what appears ordinary or acceptable in the first column becomes extraordinary and excessive in the second. Comparing early representations of Canudos with those that prevailed by the end of the conflict allows one to outline how perceptions of the Conselheiro's religiosity moved from its being a rather ordinary phenomenon to being an extraordinary one. We can track, therefore, how it becomes one of the terms through which a prose of counterinsurgency is expressed.

One of the earliest and most extensive descriptions of the Conselheiro and his activities before he settled in Belo Monte comes from a certain Durval Vieira de Aguiar, a member of the Bahian police, in his *Descrições práticas da Província da Bahia*, originally published in 1888:

> When we passed by the village there was a famous Counselor. He was short and dark-skinned, with a long beard and hair, and dressed in a blue robe. He lived alone in an unfurnished house, where pious women amassed, showering him with gifts of food. This guy is more of an ignorant fanatic than a hermit, and his occupation consists in preaching a patchwork of messages, teaching prayers, making banal predictions, and praying rosaries and litanies with the people. He uses local churches for these activities. Passing by, the civilized traveler is treated to a ludicrous spectacle, especially when he recites in Latin and none of his listeners can understand him. The people tend to gather around any religious act performed by the Counselor, whose indications they blindly obey. They will even resist laws. For this reason the vicars allow him to pass himself off as a saint, especially because he does not seek to gain from the situation. On the contrary, he is an extraordinary promoter of baptisms,

marriages, . . . festivals, novenas, and other activities from which the Church reaps its profits. On this occasion the Counselor had finished building an elegant church in Mucambo, and he was building another excellent one in Cumbe, where he maintained admirable peace despite the multitude of people.[15]

These and other writings on the Conselheiro and his followers prior to the Canudos conflict offer us our few accounts untouched by da Cuhna's text. This report also provides a representation of the Conselheiro before he was deemed a serious threat to the new republic and before the government sought to contain him physically and discursively. The Conselheiro was not yet insurgent. It is thus a curiously mixed text, containing both the seeds of later accusations against him (an ignorant fanatic whose blinded followers could even resist the law) and rather off-handed appreciative comments (about the elegant or excellent church, admirable peace, and his lack of avarice). Above all it is a rather paternalistic description. Constructed from the viewpoint of a "civilized traveler" who disavows the cultural and religious traditions of the people being surveyed and pokes fun at the Conselheiro's random use of Latin and banal sermons, it is in a sense exoticizing. Nonetheless, it also suggests that the Conselheiro might be an ordinary fixture in his context.

Indeed, when the Conselheiro began his nomadic phase, there were any number of "holy men" wandering the Brazilian backlands. This phenomenon was an accepted part of popular Catholicism. As the historian José Calasans suggests, a system of categorization existed to indicate types of holy men, who did not necessarily have to be priests. The scarcity of ordained priests in rural areas contributed to the lay character of popular Catholicism in Brazil; in 1887, for example, 124 of Bahia's 190 parishes lacked a full-time or permanent priest.[16] According to Calasans, the title *beato* signaled "good man" and denoted someone who prayed, sang hymns, and begged for alms for church construction, while *conselheiro* is supposed to have signaled someone who was better educated in religious matters and could give counsel and sermons.[17] (Other categories indictating religious functions included *festeiro*, or one who organizes religious feasts, and *capelão*, someone well versed in prayers.)[18]

While his activities suggest that he moved within an accepted and ordinary framework of popular Catholicism, this did not mean that all local priests nonchalantly allowed the Conselheiro to pass himself off as a saint, as Aguiar intimates. Indeed, his first systematic group of enemies came from the Catholic

[handwritten marginal note: So what Conselheiro was doing was normal?]

Church, since his activities threatened it just when it was redefining and reasserting its authority. The episcopal reform Pope Pius IX initiated in the 1860s is critical to explaining both the Conselheiro's immense attraction and the Church's fervent reaction to him. Pius IX sought, among other goals, to reaffirm the bishops' control over their jurisdictions and eliminate any heterodoxy within the Catholic community. The pope's measures ended up drawing the Church away from people such as those of the Brazilian interior, classifying their popular expressions of faith as fanaticism and superstition. This effort to exterminate such Catholicism and replace it with a purer one intensified the confrontation between traditional lay Catholicism and the Church.[19]

A series of letters from priests and secular authorities to the archbishop of Bahia beginning in the 1880s constitutes the first written evidence that the Conselheiro emerged within a field of already extant tensions. Letters in the largest cluster concern accusations and counteraccusations among three men in the parish of the Divino Espírito Santo do Inhambupe: a Capuchin missionary named Júlio Fiorentini (Capuchin missionaries from Italy had played a large part in the settlement of the northeastern interior);[20] Antônio Porfirio Ramos, vicar of the parish; and Caldas Brito, the district's chief of police. These letters attest, first, to a series of tensions and accusations that exceed the matter of the Conselheiro's presence. In 1887, for instance, Caldas Brito accused Fiorentini of despotism, citing actions such as insisting that three people who lived with unmarried women and died without confession be buried by the river's edge and stopping a wedding because the bride was not a virgin. Porfirio Ramos accused Fiorentini of meddling in politics and sowing dissent: "After destroying our main church, into which a great sum of money was uselessly poured, part of the construction came down and the remaining part began to crack and show faults. Father Julio Fiorentini started to spread dissent among my good parishioners; he took an active part in all political plots and finally turned the pulpit and confessional into weapons of war."[21]

In his letter to the archbishop, Father Fiorentini—who had come to the diocese only recently, in 1881—replied with the rigidity of which he was accused, affirming that both other men were guilty of a rupture with authority. For example, he accused Ramos of violating doctrine through syncretism: "Two years ago he gave the holiest of sacraments, that is, a consecrated host, to a certain Salustiano so that he wouldn't be afraid of witchcraft and could dig up money";[22] "when someone is sick and visits him he tells them to perform

a candomblé ceremony."[23] He further accused Ramos of being in league with
Caldas Brito and protecting the Conselheiro. In addition, he charged Caldas
Brito with being both a Mason and the first "Conselheirista" of the town.[24]
Such, then, were the tensions into which the Conselheiro was inserted, local
contests over power that included accusations of excessively rigid or lax interpretations of religion. A year earlier (1886), Fiorentini had complained directly
about the Conselheiro, and his reproaches were structured around the same set
of issues with which he accused Caldas Brito and Ramos.

Perhaps because this first "counter-Conselheirista" discourse took place
within a mutual belief in religion (albeit not a common *sertanejo* culture, for
Fiorentini was a foreigner and seems to have been rather horrified by the daily
life of priests in the Bahian *sertão*),[25] it did not characterize the Conselheiro's
beliefs as sick, irrational, excessive, barbaric, or fanatic, as a fully fledged prose
of counterinsurgency later would.[26] It is not that the Conselheiro was never accused of heresy at this early date; at one point Fiorentini did accuse him of heresy in words that seem to anticipate some of da Cunha's: "It seems as if we were
in the midst of the thirteenth century, when the Albigensian heresy devastated
Old Europe, especially Catholic France. We lack only the martyrs, who won't
take long to appear; everything else is there. And all this in the nineteenth century!"[27] Nonetheless, statements such as these were countered by others from
priests who felt comfortable asserting the Conselheiro's orthodoxy. Ramos,
who protected the Conselheiro, defended his position by assuring the archbishop that the Conselheiro presented no threat to the religion: "I can guarantee Your Excellency that I have sought to listen to him to know the doctrine he
announces and I found nothing offensive to religion. In fact, to the contrary,
his explanations are but the true law of God, and his life true penitence."[28]

The historian of religion Alexandre Otten's analysis of the Conselheiro's
sermons makes Ramos's defense seem entirely reasonable. These sermons
form part of a manuscript attributed to Antônio Conselheiro that was found by
the soldier João de Souza Pondé after Canudos was defeated and later delivered
to Euclides da Cunha.[29] Otten, who has undertaken one of the most extensive
analyses of these texts, displays revisionist historiography's tendency to depict
the Conselheiro as not just nonheretical but indeed ultraconservative by the
standards of traditional lay Catholicism. Otten argues that the Conselheiro's
sermons are completely orthodox, combining an insistence on the marvels of
God's love and the value of imitating the evangelical Jesus with "a belief in the
imminent end of the world, which produces an eschatological devaluation of

life and a characterization of the church as elitist."[30] Still, Otten discards the notion of Canudos as an essentially messianic and apocalyptic movement, emphasizing the Conselheiro's desire to be viewed not as the Messiah but as a prophet—and an optimistic one, at that—counseling an exodus and return to a primitive Christian community. Otten further dismisses the characterization of the Conselheiro's discourse as a simple holdover from a primitive past (i.e., the resurrection of an archaic form of religion) and emphasizes instead its connections to the external conditions of the time, including a general decline in faith in the *sertão* due to socioeconomic crises that closed off many traditional models of religiosity there and favored such prophetic discourse.

Indeed, despite a few comments such as Ramos's, the letters of the Bahian priests tend to register a preoccupation not with the question of the Conselheiro's heresy or orthodoxy but with the preservation of clerical and hierarchical authority at a time when these difficult socioeconomic conditions and the scarcity of priests made institutional religion less attractive even as the episcopal reform pushed priests to comply more fervently with spreading the word.[31] The fact that the Conselheiro himself was accomplishing the tasks established by the episcopal reform—since he not only prayed and built churches but also preached—and often doing it more successfully put him at cross-purposes with the Church's drive to reassert its authority. What the letters display above all is thus a jockeying for power within a shared domain. In 1882, for example, the archbishop of Salvador circulated a letter to all Bahian parishes prohibiting them from allowing the Conselheiro to speak in their parishes. This letter clearly frames its argument against him in terms of legitimate authority instead of orthodoxy versus heterodoxy. While it grants that the Conselheiro may have been virtuous, it insists that he lacked the authority to preach and that this lack was the crux of the issue: "The people of the parish should know that I absolutely prohibit them to gather and hear him preach. According to the Catholic Church only the ministers of Religion to the Saintly Mission can indoctrinate the people; the secular person, whoever he is, even if virtuous, does not have the authority to preach."[32]

Such a position can be contrasted with the decision of another Bahian archbishop nearly two hundred years earlier when he received word of another holy man, a certain Francisco Mendonça Mar—bearded, dressed in a rustic tunic, and living in a cave at the edges of the São Francisco River—who, like the Conselheiro, attracted large crowds with his fame for oratory and healing. The Archbishop Sebastião Monteiro da Vide (1702–1722) called Mar to Salvador and ordained him, whereupon he returned to serve as the chaplain of the region where he had been living.[33] The police captain of Inhambupe, José Geraldo de Aragão, proffered a similar solution regarding the Conselheiro in a report to the head of police in Salvador on November 8, 1886. In this report he attributed the threat of public disorder to the lack of "authorization on the part of ecclesiastic authority and attention on the part of civil authority," adding, "It would be best if either the large group that accompanies him be dispersed or that he be placed under clerical authority and employed in the kind of life that he has chosen for himself. If neither of these options are taken, it will lead to anarchy and confusion."[34] With its hierarchy undergoing reform, however, the Church did not consider acceptance an option.

A protest by Fiorintini in 1888 also reveals the worldly nature of this battle for authority. Those who supported the Conselheiro received both money and influence; those who opposed him recei̇   ̇her: "The two previously mentioned pastors support him, allo̊̇   in their parishes, and protect him because those who a⌐   ̇f money, and these pastors also perform all th⌐ ̇   gs, of the followers of the Conselheiro   ̇   ven more scandalous is that they even ̇   ̇ptized by a priest that protests the Co̊   ̇iorentini had dwelt more explicitly on   ̇ty over the people: "While the pastors were su̇   ̇ı assembly, he, Antônio Conselheiro, called to order ̇   ̇ch had been left without pastors. There he taught the people ẘ   ̇ear of being rebuked because the flock lacked its shepherd; when the shepherds returned, the wolf had already devoured the flock, they were already used to the enemy and no longer believed in the pastor, [and] they turned against any priest who had the audacity to reprimand the actions of the above mentioned Cons."[36]

Despite Fiorentini's animalistic rhetoric, the battle here is perceived as being fought over a common terrain, within a common, accepted understanding unmarked by heterogeneity, the issue that prevailed later on. One could argue, against Fiorentini, that the definitional battle over Catholicism resulted from a postcolonial situation with social, historical, and cultural fractures (a European institution and its representatives vs. the syncretic beliefs of a colonized people), a position closer to that of da Cunha, for whom the Conselheiristas' beliefs were, above all, a symptom of the inferiority and backwardness of his race: "All the naïve beliefs, from a barbarous fetishism to the aberrations of Catholicism, all the impulsive tendencies of lower races given free outlet in the un-disciplined life of the backlands, were condensed in his fierce and extravagant mysticism."[37]

For Fiorentini, however, people are not divided into superior and inferior races. They are fundamentally homogeneous; they are all sheep, for example, and can be either ruled by their shepherd or devoured by the wolf. They do not necessarily naturally tend in one direction or another; in other words, no principle of identity links the flock of sheep to one particular form of rule or another. What make the difference are contingent circumstances—for example, the mere absence of the shepherd. In this respect, Fiorentini's rhetoric foreshadows later accounts of the Conselheiro's popularity among *sertanejo* populations in its ascription of blindness, ignorance, and lack of agency on the part of the people. They are simply tossed here or there depending on external circumstances. What fractures exist are defined with reference to previous moments of schism within Church history (i.e., to stress the point again, they are internal to Church history rather than potentially external to and incommensurable with it).

Otten and many other contemporary historians echo some subaltern studies historians' attempts to return agency to peasant rebels against assumptions such as Fiorentini's by, in the case of Canudos, highlighting the revolutionary and democratizing potential of Christianity, especially at its origins, as an explanation for its powerful attraction. Otten cites the following popular verse, which emphasizes Jesus' poverty and a concomitant call for justice:

> Jesus said, I am God
> Son of the true God
> Who will come save the Christians
> Without need of money
> I came poor into this world
> So that I could mete out justice.

> [Jesus disse, Deus sou eu
> Filho de Deus verdadeiro
> Que vem salvar os cristãos
> Sem precisar de dinheiro
> Vim as mundo pobre
> Para poder ser justiciero.][38]

This verse, Otten concludes, articulates the substratum underpinning religious movements of social protest. The religious person, whether a messiah or
prophet, is a "charismatic person who knows how to reappropriate the stolen
image of god and give the poor a new identity. The exclusion they suffer as the
dispossessed and exploited transfigures itself into election, . . . the disinherited
see themselves as sons of god, a chosen people summoned to a new life."[39] The
semantic rearticulation afforded by such versions of Christianity—of an identity of dispossession as one of election—turns the *sertanejos*' receptivity to the
Conselheiro into an entirely rational choice instead of a blindly ignorant one.
In effect, according to this perspective, the Conselheiro articulated a counter-
hegemonic discourse that granted them a measure of relief from their state of
exploitation and a ground from which to resist it.

In 1887 the archbishop of Bahia was no longer content to consider the
Conselheiro a problem simply for religious authority and wrote the president
of the province asking him to do something about the individual known as Antônio Vicente Mendes Maciel, who, he said, preached "subversive doctrines,"
thus doing "great harm to religion and the State, distracting the people from
their responsibilities and dragging them after him, trying to convince them
that he is the Holy Ghost and rebelling against constituted authority, which
he does not obey and orders all to disobey."[40] Perhaps the archbishop used
this more alarming rhetoric and coupled disregard for authority with a charge
of heterodoxy because he was addressing the state. In any event, this is the
first time the Conselheiro is characterized as an insurgent (*insurgindo-se contra
as autoridades constituídas*), the first time he is described as a threat not only to
religion and local authorities but to the state. The response to this request is a
marvelous combination of, on the one hand, the emerging modernizing discourse that would establish an incommensurability between itself and that of
the Conselheiro and, on the other, a residual, more laissez-faire approach to
governance. The president of Bahia requested that the Conselheiro be shipped
off to a mental hospital, but he was informed that there were no spaces left.
And that, says da Cunha, was "the beginning and end of the legal measures
that were taken under the Empire."[41] Despite the opposition of the Church and
the disdain of "civilized" travelers, this response shows that the Conselheiro
might well have continued wandering the *sertão* for another twenty years. Yet
six years later everything had changed.

The Local Landowners

The settlement of Canudos/Belo Monte in 1893 marked a sea change from more than one perspective, as is registered in a letter by one local landowner to another in January 1897. Antônio Conselheiro, he wrote, "is not the man that many judged as a harmless maniac. . . . Many good people were taken in by him but now try to annihilate him because his politics are completely different, being an intractable monarchist."[42] Landowners around Canudos figured critically in the development of the conflict (although they do not play a prominent role in *Os sertões*), and at least one historian, Consuelo Novais Sampaio, argues that the confrontation resulted from infighting and manipulation within the local Bahian oligarchy. Sampaio attributes too much power to the local elite, however, when she writes that "the phenomenon of Canudos can be understood only through the actions and behavior of the upper classes,"[43] as if the actions and behaviors of the Conselheiristas were irrelevant to the process, but her work does help to lay out the local construction of a prose of counterinsurgency that in key respects differed from the early anti-Conselheirista discourse proffered by local clergy. The previously quoted letter shows how these local landowners actively helped construct an impression of threat that had been first verbalized by the Catholic Church and was later spread nationally by the press.

One of the Conselheiro's early and principal enemies, a man who, according to reports, played a role in organizing the first police-force expedition,[44] was Cícero Dantas Martins, the baron of Geremoabo (or Jeremoabo) and the real-life prototype for Mario Vargas Llosa's Baron de Cañabrava in *The War of the End of the World*. The baron owned sixty-one farms in the *sertões* (including two in neighboring Sergipe), ranking him among the largest landowners there.[45] He was also politically conservative, a founder of the opposition party in Bahia loyal to José Gonçalves da Silva (of the Partido Republicano Constitucional). On February 24, 1897, he wrote a letter to the Bahian *Jornal de Notícias* defending himself against accusations that he supported the Conselheiro. Such accusations were commonly traded back and forth between area landowners, as attested by a collection of letters that friends and dependents wrote to the baron in 1894–1897; Sampaio organized and published these letters as *Canudos: Cartas para o barão*.

Conselheiro becomes economic figure

The most interesting aspect of the baron's letter (quoted anonymously by da Cunha in *Os sertões*) is the emergence of the Conselheiro within a discursive arena organized by economic rather than religious interests. Religion as such is irrelevant to this grid of intelligibility; the Conselheiro matters only insofar as he relates to economic considerations. In the following fragments, the baron expresses dismay (*causava dó*) at the movement of people who sold all their belongings, leaving their regular lives behind, to serve the Conselheiro. He comments in some detail on the apparently strange and unbelievable sight of livestock, objects, land, and houses being sold for almost nothing (*por preços de nonada*).[46] Even more scandalous perhaps is the burning of goods considered "luxury": "In plain daylight, in the houses, streets and highways, there would be piles of shawls, dresses, skirts, hats, shoes and any object that contained wool and silk. These were delivered over to the voracity of flames, because luxury was contrary to the doctrine preached by the stubborn missionary."[47] Such behavior is antieconomic; the baron expresses concern because such acts violate a semiotic code of value (both exchange- and use-value) that he deems natural and that, by refusing to participate in it, the Conselheiristas destabilize.

The baron's letter also expresses how the Conselheiro was written into a general landscape of economic deterioration as Brazil's coffee-producing Southeast overtook its sugar-producing Northeast in economic importance.[48] The monarchy's greatest support base had been the long-standing oligarchy of landowners based mostly in the Northeast and tied to the production of sugar and to slave labor. These sugar barons had managed to maintain their monopoly on political representation until the republic was ushered in, but their economic power had been gradually waning throughout the nineteenth century.[49]

economic depression

Unable to compete with new techniques in the world market or to withstand a drop in prices, the sugar industry went into a slow decline, pulling the Northeast into economic depression. This decapitalization caused a labor shortage that disrupted the region's power structure; well before abolition, many slaves had been sold off to the coffee plantations in the South. Any remaining capital was invested in increasing the amount of land dedicated to planting sugarcane and centralizing labor, which thus limited the cultivation of subsistence crops and caused food shortages and high prices.[50] A cycle of droughts that marked much of the future Third World at the end of the nineteenth century (including northeastern Brazil) wreaked further havoc on the sugar economy and the inhabitants in the *sertão*.[51]

The baron's letter registers the threat Canudos posed to the surrounding region by draining away labor: "With the abolition of slaves, the effects of the propaganda were felt even more for the lack of free hands for work. The population lived in delirium or ecstasy . . . [;] thus agricultural labor became scarcer and scarcer, and now it is with great difficulty that any property can function, and without the necessary regularity."[52] The baron was not the only one to display such concern. Indeed, when the archbishop had finally written to the province's president in 1887, he had already anticipated this problem by declaring that the Conselheiro "distracted" people from their responsibilities. Many letters written to the baron show the same fear. The mayor of Tucano, for example, complained that the labor shortage forced him to pay workers double to build a wall in his city: "Because of the plague of Conselheiro there are no workers."[53] Such letters may at least partially explain why the Conselheiro was able to wander the *sertão* largely unimpeded for twenty years; he incurred disfavor from religious and civil authorities, but in general they left him alone. With the founding of a community, however, the Conselheiro set himself up, unknowingly or not, as a rival "patron"—and one who drained away labor and possibly even votes from neighboring landowners. Within the patronage system through which Brazilian politics functioned, this capacity was tantamount, as Ralph Della Cava puts it, to "political power."[54]

The Conselheiro's settlement in the region also produced fears that his followers would not only withdraw from the economic relationships undergirding the region's power structures but also violate private property by invading and stealing from neighboring farms. Ironically, a number of lawsuits against the government after the conflict reveal that farms were indeed destroyed and livestock pillaged during the attacks—but by the soldiers, not the Conselheiristas. "I ask for indemnification," wrote one man, "not for the cattle that the jagunços ate, because you well know that the conselheiristas did not use the 'goods of the republic,' since they could count on the great resources furnished by their fanatics, but for the cattle that were eaten by the government's forces, when in those faraway lands they found themselves without resources and haunted by the horrors of hunger."[55]

Yet even if the inhabitants of Canudos did not literally attack private property, the antagonism between the Conselheiro and his followers and the local landowners became inscribed as a conflict with private property. Indeed, the baron ends his letter by exclaiming that the Conselheiro's doctrine is communism, with an exclamation point indexing his horror. One can see this gene-

Canudos as drain on labor forces

alogy and interpretation in the present-day Movimento Sem Terra's claim of
Canudos as one of their precursors (and in the fact that one settlement in the
state of São Paulo is called Nova Canudos).[56]

The baron's letter has two faces. It not only disparages the Conselheiristas but also criticizes the governor of Bahia, blaming him for having escalated
the problem: "The Bahian government's criminal and culpable tolerance . . .
allowed the followers to multiply astonishingly. . . . That was the nefarious administration of Sr. Dr. Rodrigues Lima. Let public condemnation fall upon his
head."[57] This aspect of the baron's letter introduces another dynamic in the process by which a prose of counterinsurgency was constituted: to the extent that
the actions of the Conselheiro were slowly written into another story, they become available as a surface of inscription for tensions and problems that exceed
the Conselheiro himself. In letters such as the baron's, Canudos was rendered
equivalent to a series of disruptions and disorders for which the governor was
held responsible. Canudos thus became one in a series of elements marking a
conflict between two factions in the Bahian oligarchy. This use of Canudos as
a pawn on the landowners' political chessboard leads Sampaio to argue that
local infighting constituted the real impetus for military action. This does not
mean that there was no antagonism between Canudos and members of the
local Bahian oligarchy; rather, the antagonism becomes overdetermined. Nor
does it mean that the chess game played out as the various oligarchic factions
intended (thus ascribing to them—in an inverse of subalternization—an intentionality and effective agency greater than they enjoyed). Nonetheless, there
was both a process of accretion by which external antagonisms were projected
onto a representation of the Conselheiro and a certain element of contingency
in the way it unfolded. Much of the discourse that ended up dominating by the
conflict's end took a particular form: it sought to counter a threat that Canudos
was perceived to pose to a version of a political community. A prose of counterinsurgency emerged, but it need not have. A recourse to arms was not the only
outcome possible. Things could have been otherwise. The conjuncture that
produced the conflict thus included not only the slowly spiraling and extending
groups—local priests and landowners, the Bahian oligarchy, and members of
the fledgling republican government—that felt threatened by the Conselheiro
but also all that was aleatory in their combination.

At the end of the century there were essentially two power factions in Bahia, one headed by José Gonçalves (Geremoabo was a leading figure in this faction) and the other by Luís Viana. The differences were not quite political, for

both men had been conservatives under the monarchy and adhered at the last minute to the republic. They had even been friends. Their contest for power instead began when the two men split after the first president of the new republic, Marechal Deodoro da Fonseca, dissolved the National Congress. Gonçalves had been the governor of Bahia until Doedoro's failed bid for more power but was forced to renounce after having supported it. The Vianistas came into power first with Rodrigues Lima (1892–1896) and then with Viana himself. Novais Sampaio argues that the Gonçalvista faction saw Canudos as a way to invite federal intervention and invert the power balance. It was not an uncommon ploy; in fact, before the First Republic ended there would be three more federal interventions in Bahia: in 1912, 1920 (with the *revolução sertaneja*), and 1923. The opposition was able to come to power only with the last of these, when the governor lost federal support.

In Bahia the 1890s were years of continuous violence and banditry, so that Viana's primary interest lay not in the Conselheiro but in the more pressing conflagrations elsewhere. These included, among other events, bonfires in which residents burned tax decrees, which took place in 1893 and 1894 in several towns; an attack by bandits on the city of Lençóes; ruffians threatening the Lavras Diamantinas; a mob siege of the village of Mendes Brito; and a series of violent crimes in the town of Jequié.[58] In fact, referring to the Conselheiristas' opposition to the republic in an 1897 interview, Viana declared, "Their ignorance is such that I can't actually believe that they bother themselves with the issue of the form of government."[59] The opposition, however, which included the baron, used Canudos (among other incidents) to accuse Viana of incompetence. In an interview in the *Jornal de Notícias*, José Gonçalves claimed, "The action of the governor of Bahia, which is despotic in all other respects, is as we see dubious, indecisive and incomprehensible in the case of Canudos."[60] Even further, according to speeches opposition members made in the Bahian senate in 1897, Viana, like Rodrigues Lima before him, was deemed to have a plan to "provoke the bandits of Antônio Conselheiro . . . in his hole in Canudos, to alarm the surrounding populations so as to impede the electors of the fifth district (under control of the opposition party) from appearing at the urns. In this way the governor would be able to falsify the electoral results so that only his three candidates would appear to have received votes."[61] One senator even identified the governor with the holy man: "We need to finish off the Conselheiro Luís Viana in order to then liquidate Canudos."[62]

The National Stage

According to the official story, the war was sparked by a misunderstanding between residents of Canudos and a lumber merchant in Juazeiro in 1896. The residents, so the story goes, had requested and paid for lumber that would be used to build the church. The lumber was not delivered, however, and when the townspeople declared (either threateningly or nonthreateningly) that they would pick up the lumber themselves, city officials at Juazeiro claimed they were being threatened and requested protection from Viana.

Viana responded by sending 100 armed men in October 1896. When the police force arrived in Uauá to spend the night, most of the city's inhabitants fled, many of them going to Canudos to warn its residents. On October 21 a procession of either 300, 500, or 1,000 (the versions differ) left Canudos to meet the attackers, singing, carrying standards, and bearing muskets, knives, and icons. The police battalion was beaten and forced to retreat.

The Bahian press inflamed public opinion, and the government organized a second expedition, this one comprising 543 men from both the army and the police. This expedition included federal forces led by General Solon (commander of the district and, curiously enough, da Cunha's father-in-law), but Viana insisted on Bahia's autonomy and dismissed the need for federal intervention. Solon was demoted, and the expedition was sent to Canudos under Febrônio de Brito in January 1897. Soon after leaving camp in Frei Appolônio de Todi, the expedition was encircled by *jagunços* and forced to withdraw (the term *jagunço*, which literally means "thug," came to designate those who fought for the Conselheiro).

According to several historians, the defeat of Febrônio's expedition marked the turn whereupon Canudos ceased to be a "chess piece in the game of the local Bahian oligarchies" and became visible on the national stage.[63] From this point on, the press was to play a large part in the construction and spread of an increasingly alarming Canudos.

In *Humor e sátira na guerra de Canudos* Lizir Arcanjo Alves charts the changes in journalistic coverage of the Conselheiro from his settlement in Canudos until the end of the conflict, focusing principally on the use of humor and satire. She demonstrates that when Canudos was first settled in 1893, the Bahian newspapers employed two opposing representations of the Conselheiro (the South did not hear of him until the second expedition): the good man versus the religious maniac. One example of the former appears in a letter written to the

Jornal de Notícias in 1893; the writer declares that, drawn by curiosity, he visited the Conselheiro and found his conversation to have been "pleasant," although his house was filthy and had only one place to sit. In his practices, the visitor wrote, "he counsels only the good of the people; if they follow him around, it is because they want to. . . . How is this citizen offensive? Whom does he harm? . . . He counsels the people not to abandon their homes for his sake; the people disobey him because of their fanaticism and follow him around. He is an honorable man; if he wanted to, he could become rich overnight, but he accepts only food and nothing else."[64] The more negative references generally poked fun at the Conselheiro, much as did the previously cited passage from Durval Vieira de Aguiar, and advised the government to combat ignorance and fanaticism, but because he was not yet perceived as a threat, they did not demonstrate much concern. The following verse published in a Bahian newspaper in 1894 exemplifies the often jocular, nonchalant tone used when referring to the Conselheiro:

> All who want to eat, drink
> Have money, without working
> Should enlist in the troops
> Of Antônio Conselheiro
>
> [Quem quiser, sem trabalhar
> Comer, beber, ter dinheiro
> Va na tropa se alistar
> Do Antônio Conselheiro][65]

Alves shows a progressive change as the rising necessity to combat an insurgent population produced ever more extraordinary visions of the Conselheiro. The defeat of the first two expeditions led to an increased urgency in the effort to oppugn the image of the good, inoffensive holy man and portray him instead as a criminal and dirty *jagunço* who needed to be destroyed. What others described as "fine" needed to be turned into "terrible." In January 1897 the *Diário da Bahia* editorialized in this vein:

> It is necessary to extirpate [this evil] . . . in the interests of the implementation of order and the development of the State. . . . It is painful to see the soldier's bullets fell poor and ignorant men misled by fanaticism and emboldened by the indifference of our governors to constitute a State within a State.
> By now this malady will be extirpated only by a hot iron, and as painful as

medical language
the "objective"
truth"

the *operation* may be . . . , we have only one wish: that the *doctor* in charge of the operation be successful and that it last for all time.[66]

Here we already see a fully fledged prose of counterinsurgency at work. At this juncture I want to underscore three points. First, such medical rhetoric bears an implicit polarization leaving no room for neutrality: the "objective" truth is that the Conselheiristas have fallen prey to a sickness that must be uprooted, however painful the operation may be. Sickness is incommensurable with a healthy body. Second, there is no room for the intentionality of the Conselheiristas, just as the diseased lack agency over the symptoms of their disease. They are poor, ignorant people sick with fanaticism. In other words, they know not what they do and must be cured. Third, the aim of preventing the construction of a state within a state reveals a code already operating under the perceived interests of an abstract state. While questions of order, authority, and governance marked previous representations of the Conselheiro, the grid through which he was rendered intelligible was increasingly marked by an ideology of the state even when it was not proffered by state functionaries.

Arcanjo Alves argues that sympathetic treatments were generally limited to Bahia, where one could confront such representations by claiming personal contact with and knowledge of the Conselheiro, as in the previously quoted letter from the *Jornal de Notícias*. This was not possible in the South, however, where the Conselheiro was exponentially more distant and unknown, so that newspapers there generally followed the lead of the most rabid newspapers in Bahia.

Nonetheless, the South was not bereft of more conciliatory views. The monarchist party had been founded in 1895, and the following year had witnessed the growth of monarchist newspapers that were especially prominent in offering some of the most consistent early critiques of the government's actions. The *Gazeta da Tarde*, for instance, lambasted the government: "What does the government intend with the tremendous and horrible hecatomb of those populations, whose only crime is the faith of their pure hearts, the ardent and fantastic vision of a feverish and dreamy imagination?"[67] The motor of such critiques was perhaps less a sympathy for the people of Canudos than a distrust of everything being claimed under the name of the campaign against Canudos. The monarchists, in other words, did not share in the lines being drawn between Canudos, monarchy, and barbarism, on the one hand, and science, humanity, civilization, and the republic, on the other. Indeed, they attempted to reverse such equivalences, as the following passage from an editorial attests: "Yes, it's true. We forgot that no one in these times of so much science, of so much spirit, of so much Compteism, wants to venture to defend the ignorant who die for the fanaticism of their beliefs and their honor. Let these people die like dogs thrown in the fields, at the edges of roads, as an example of the scruples of consciousness and a rotten Catholicism which still remembers to make faith the enchanting light of salvation. It is written—this republic can not live without blood and more blood!"[68] As the war went on, however, the consequences of seeming to support the *jagunços* became increasingly severe, and the voices raised in their defense became fewer and fainter.

The third expedition—when the events had already acquired meaning as a conflict between Canudos and the Brazilian state—was the most dramatic and most dominant in historical memory. Canudos became a source of public obsession during the last year of the conflict and dominated the press, which was thriving by that time; twenty-nine newspapers were founded in Rio de Janeiro in 1897 alone.[69] Whereas some newspapers had received dispatches from the front during the War of the Triple Alliance (1864–1870), against Paraguay, the third Canudos campaign marked the first time that eight of Brazil's main newspapers sent journalists to the front: from Rio, *O País, Jornal do Comércio* (which sent Manoel Benício), *Jornal do Brasil, A Gazeta de Notícias,* and *A Notícia*; from São Paulo, *O Estado de São Paulo* (which sent Euclides da Cunha); and from Bahia, the *Jornal de Notícias* and *Diário da Bahia*. New telegraph lines linking the North and South (telegraphs and roads were extended toward Canudos to facilitate the movement of the army and its attendants) helped the quick transmission of whatever news made it through army censors. As a consequence of this attention, the incidents of Canudos "invaded" (to borrow a term from the Brazilian critic Walnice Nogueira Galvão) all aspects of the newspapers, finding their way, like a virus, into editorials, *crônicas*, reports, humor, and advertising. The following ad for shoes reveals the ductility of Canudos: "People who have recently arrived from Canudos tell us the following: in the last attack a valiant group of soldiers, after having exhausted their munitions, decided to run after the Conselheiristas and kick them, so confident were they in the durability of the shoes they had bought in the popular store *O Monomento*. What a great idea!"[70]

The use of Canudos to sell goods—the fact that it seeped through different genres within the spaces of the newspaper—raises the question of its larger popularity. What claims can one make about the relationship between the ubiquity of Canudos in the newspapers and more widespread public opinion? Newspapers had by this point existed in Brazil for eighty years and were, at least in the big cities, on the cusp of a transition from the artisanal, solitary endeavors of the nineteenth century to the industrial institutions they were to become in the twentieth century,[71] but their circulation was relatively small, and literacy was still limited (estimated at 15 percent in 1890).[72] To what extent were the opinions being expressed—on both sides—simply those of the lettered elite? (And to what extent were they merely expressions of bias, since, even within these restricted circles, newspapers were often extensions of various political parties and groups, tools for manipulation of political affects and fears?) At the same time, recent research suggests that the press had an impact on urban centers that went much further than the restricted circle of readers, combining with older forms of communication to produce a hybridity in the public spaces. In a short newspaper piece from February 1897, Machado de Assis addresses how Canudos seeped from one medium to another—from the written word to visual iconography and then to oral history. Assis writes of a woman who goes to a newspaper seller and says she wants "the paper with the picture of the man that fights out there." "Which man?" asks the vendor, and she replies, "I forgot his name."[73] The man, of course, is the Conselheiro. Even if she can't remember his name, however, she has heard enough of the events to want to buy a newspaper with his portrait. Assis comments, "The name of Antônio Conselheiro will end up entering in the memory of this anonymous woman and it won't ever leave. . . . One day she'll tell the story to her daughter and then later to her granddaughter."[74] There are many indications that news and opinions of the Canudos War did cross a variety of frontiers and circulate through other forms of transmission and communication, such as flyers, collective readings, and rumors—for example, costumes of the Conselheiro and his men were popular choices for Carnival in Rio de Janeiro during 1897.

Canudos shows up as well in so-called *cordel* literature, a popular form of transmission that even today provides news, entertainment, and instruction to illiterate or semiliterate individuals in Brazil's city streets and country markets (the name comes from the Portuguese word for "string" and refers to the way these pamphlets were displayed for sale). *Literatura de cordel* draws on the centuries-old Iberian *romanceiro*, or ballad tradition, as well as chapbooks, biblical stories, exempla, folktales, and a variety of African and indigenous elements.[75] The influence of the poet-improvisers known as *cantadores* (similar to the Argentine *payador* tradition), however, means that *cordel* literature almost exclusively takes poetic form.[76] At the same time, although their contents are thus close to the *corridos* found in other parts of Latin America, these pamphlets are collections of stories designed specifically to be read (they are printed on newspaper-weight paper usually measuring four by six and one-half inches and generally containing eight, sixteen, or thirty-two pages), whereas *corridos* are generally sung to melodies. Also, *cordel* draws on a narrative corpus foreign to *corridos*. While "there are *cordel* versions of news events, the exploits of famous bandits and religious topics . . . , there are no *corridos* about Romeo and Juliet or Sleeping Beauty."[77]

José Calasans's anthology entitled *Canudos na literatura de cordel* includes two pieces, one written by an inhabitant of Rio de Janeiro and the second by a soldier who participated in the conflict, both notable for the way they echo the prose of counterinsurgency visible in public writing and its justification for the military campaigns, including the subordination of the events at Canudos to concerns of the state's security. The first of these, "A Guerra de Canudos do fanático Conselheiro," addresses the army's final moment of triumph over Canudos and articulates the conflict through a sense of nationhood. Here, a wide panoramic shot shows us the Brazilian nation rising spontaneously to defend the republic, which has been threatened by a fanatic and his band of ruffians. This poem is fundamentally a lesson in a geography of affects:

> In the states of Brazil
> The youth arose
> And organized battalions
> In every town
> To defend the Republic
> Which was threatened
> By the fanatic Conselheiro
> And his horde of jagunços.

> [Nos estados do Brazil
> Levantou-se a mocidade,
> Organisando batalhões
> Em toda a localidade.
> Para defender a republica

Que se achava ameaçada,
Pelo fanático Conselheiro
E mais a sua jagunçada.][78]

The poem foregrounds the idea of a nation that is unified and that defends itself. The supporters of the Conselheiro are condemned according to the same modernizing code we see in many of the newspapers: they are outside the law (bandits) and irrational (fanatics):

This horde of bandits
fanatics, traitors
Were finally beaten
By Brazilian soldiers

[Esta horda de bandidos
Fanáticos e traiçoeiros,
Afinal foram batidos
Pelos soldados brazileiros].[79]

They are also characterized as simultaneously inside and outside the nation-state, a paradox with which da Cunha will grapple. To describe them as "traitors" is to assume that they have turned their backs on their own nation. But since they fight against the "Brazilian" soldiers, they are excluded from the category of citizen. And Bahia itself is characterized as being far from the "patria," as not quite inside the nation:

Glory to those who died
With Republican faith
Defending their motherland
Far away, in the land of Bahia

[Glória àquelles que morrerão
Com a fé republican
Defendendo sua patria
Longe, na terra bahiana].[80]

In addition, this and other *cordel* poems are interesting because they participate in an emergent discourse on the army as the embodiment of the nation. Until the (failed) attempt to institute an equitable draft with the 1874 Recruitment Law, most soldiers were impressed. Those who had wives, honorable jobs, or powerful patrons were largely protected from impressment, but the idle poor (under- and unemployed unskilled laborers) were not. Indeed, the historian Peter Beattie argues that the army was an important—perhaps the most important—tool of state social control of the free poor in Brazil, one that functioned more as a semicoercive labor system than as an instrument of fighting. As became obvious in the campaign against Canudos, soldiers were often only minimally trained in warfare; instead, they were assigned tasks such as guard duty, paperwork, helping on public works such as railroads and telegraph lines, tending fields or herds, and running orphanages or else worked as musicians, masons, plumbers, carpenters, gunsmiths, metalworkers, tanners, and tailors.[81] When they were called to arms, it was usually for internal social control, such as quelling slave rebellions and other kinds of police work, not war against an external enemy (with the exception of the War of the Triple Alliance). Beattie argues that although scholars seldom consider soldiers under the rubric of labor and in the context of other forms of coercive labor, such as slavery, indentured servitude, serfdom, and debt peonage, Brazilians in the 1800s often did. The military was also, Beattie argues, a protopenal institution (a preventative rather than punitive institution of social reform) since impressment was often the punishment for nonviolent offenders.[82] Hence the association of soldiers with slavery, low wages, dishonor, emasculating punishment, and criminality.

These associations began to change by the end of the nineteenth century, and much of the rhetoric on the Canudos conflict, both in *cordel* poems and in da Cunha's text (though the latter reflects a continued ambivalence regarding soldiers and the army), registers an emerging discourse of a quasi-mystical union associating soldiers with the nation and its defense. In this respect, the public reception of soldiers after the Canudos War contrasts tellingly with their treatment after the War of the Triple Alliance. Whereas Canudos veterans were received with "unusual patriotic fanfare,"[83] according to French- and English-language newspapers, the people of Rio manifested their opinion of the unpopular War of the Triple Alliance by abstaining from the army's homecoming parade, so that the emperor ended up having to order guards "who held back the city's uninvited 'rabble' to enter the 'utter solitude' of the stands bringing a 'simulacrum of popular life' to them."[84]

It is difficult to assess the extent to which common soldiers identified as a whole with the new role being carved out for the army, but the second poem in Calasans's anthology, "A Guerra de Canudos," was written by a soldier who participated in the conflict. It is similar to the previously quoted poem, but the rhetoric is even stronger. Where that poem strives to glorify the patriotic defense of the national imagined community, this one lingers on a denunciation of the tyranny of the Conselheiro and a detailed narrative of the battle. The Conselheiro is nothing but an outlaw leader ("chefe cangaceiro") and a cruel bandit who murdered his mother and deluded a "great people" with false doctrine and miracles. His followers are demonized even further than in the previous poem:

> The most perverse of men
> With instincts for bedlam
> Deserters, horse-thieves
> Criminals and witches
> Came to join the troops
> Of the fanatic Conselheiro
>
> [Os homens mais perversos
> De instinto desordeiro
> Desertor, ladrão de cavalo,
> Criminoso e feiticeiro,
> Vieram engrossar as tropas
> Do fanático Conselheiro.][85]

The defensive war is justified not so much through a matrix of nationhood as in terms of danger to the (republican) state. In other words, the conflict is voiced in terms more related to problems of governmentality. The coordinates for this matrix are given by details of the Conselheiro's setting up his own churches, city, and government; attacking neighboring farms; and declaring state taxes null in his own territory:

> He raised two Churches
> And built a city
> Making himself governor
> With much ferocity.
> He conquered the twenty leagues that surrounded the city
> With cattle-ranches
> Killing the ranchers
> Destroying buildings
> And many, in order to escape,
> Joined him.
> Believing in banditry

And in his crimes
He did away with taxes
In the center of Bahia
Saying that later on
He would restore the monarchy.

[Levantou duas Igrejas
E construiu uma cidade
Se fêz governo dela
Com muita ferocidade.
Tomou vinte léguas em roda
Com as fazendas de gado
Matando os fazendeiros
Deixando prédios arrasados
E muitos para escaper
Foram os seus recrutados.
Confiados no cangaço
E nos crimes que fazia
Acabou com os impostos
Pelo centro da Bahia
Dizendo que mais tarde
Restaurava a monarquia.][86]

These two examples of *cordel* literature speak to the possibility, therefore, that the discourse visible on the pages of the newspapers should not be understood as restricted to a small literate elite. The newspapers intersected with other conduits of information, rumors, and beliefs in the hybrid public spaces of Brazil, and the prose of counterinsurgency that sprang up there leaked into other forms of transmission.

As with the early notes and caricatures of the Conselheiro in Bahian newspapers that Alves analyzes, the humor displayed in the advertisements and carnival costumes was possible only at the outset of the third expedition, in February, when it was generally assumed that this expedition of 1,300 men, led by Colonel Moreira César (the first expedition to involve federal soldiers from the South), would easily prevail over the poor, dirty fanatics at Canudos. Moreira César was well known as the "corta cabeças" (throat slitter) for having brutally put down the Federalist Revolt in Santa Catarina, and no one doubted that he would whip Canudos into shape,[87] making his defeat all the more shocking. As da Cunha would later argue, this defeat and the others before can be explained by an almost complete ignorance of the terrain and the enemy and the drastic underestimation and misreading of both, as well as by the poorly trained, un-equipped, and probably unenthusiastic soldiers fighting for the government. One example is telling. The third expedition brought well-drilling equipment improper for the *sertanejo* terrain, leaving the soldiers plagued by a lack of water. The army fought according to books and theories, while the Conselheiristas responded with guerrilla tactics. Despite suffering an epileptic fit on the way, the supremely confident and thus incautious Moreira César moved the expedi-tion in a forced march to Canudos; once there, he ordered a bayonet attack. Wounded, he died that same night.[88] Pedro Nunes Tamarindo took over and ordered a retreat under fire, one that proved a blessing to the Conselheiristas, since the army left behind copious amounts of munitions.

The shock over the defeat birthed a series of spectacular, sensationalist, and vindictive representations, stemming principally from incredulity that a hinterlands prophet and his ragged group of followers could defeat a military expedition. Events were chaotic elsewhere, too, as both the government and mobs of up to three thousand people perpetrated increasingly violent and op-pressive attacks on monarchists, destroying the facilities of Rio's three leading monarchist newspapers and, in March 1897, assassinating Gentil de Castro, the director and owner of the *Gazeta da Tarde*.[89] As the arson attacks on news-papers that displayed less rabid views indicate, the code of counterinsurgency was not entrenched equally throughout the nation, but it ended up dominating the press and public opinion in the urban centers of the South. The following excerpt from *O País* on July 18 provides an example of the rhetoric used during this period: "The monster, far away, in the depths of the mysterious backlands, opens its insatiable gills, asking for more people, more fodder of Republican hearts, an opulent snack of heroes, and the beast will continue filling itself and devouring until, in fit of rage, feeling the lack of provisions, this meal of bodies, it shakes its mane and with one step of its monstrous paw wants to crush the motherland, draped in mourning for the death of her most beloved sons, for the massacre of her glorious army!"[90]

The metaphor used here to represent the enemy is not sickness but a monster, indeed, not a sickness about to be extirpated but—after the defeat of Moreira César—a monster so monstrous that it could crush the nation with one stomp of its angry feet. An inversion underpins this switch in metaphor. The verbs employed give the monster the intentionality that sickness lacked, but it is a baneful, pernicious intentionality: it asks for people to eat; it wishes to crush the nation. This intentionality comes at the expense of the Consel-heiristas' humanity. We no longer have poor, ignorant individuals tricked by fanaticism in this scenario. The only people here are those being eaten: the republicans. The monster's motivations, however—hunger and anger—are largely irrational. What does this monster really want?

We have perhaps the most spectacular example of denied agency in the flourishing theories regarding a vast conspiracy, complete with international support for the Conselheiro, to restore the monarchy; according to these theories, modern arms were being smuggled into Canudos, and Italian fighters were leading the attacks on the Brazilian army. The monarchist theories became so popular, Galvão argues, that some newspapers began inventing their own conspiracies, following the murky steps of a fictitious Canudos supporter to increase their readership. On March 10 *A República* carried an editorial asserting the presence of such forces:

> Really, no one believes that the brutish and taciturn jagunço, cloaked with sordid rags, sandals on his feet, his locks long and filthy, disoriented by religious megalomania, is the leader of this sinister movement, which has already robbed the motherland of so many precious lives. Antônio Conselheiro is a vile instrument, less than an instrument. He is only the pretext that has served to bring together all the elements contrary to the Republic, grouped in ignorance, banditry, and crime. Behind this sinister figure are the real authors of this tremendous hecatomb wrought by the expedition to Canudos.[91]

The monarchists, of course, contested these theories, sometimes with indignation and offended pride. On February 22, 1897, for example, *O Liberdade* announced, "One must have obliterated all moral sense to suppose and propagate the idea that the illustrious men of the Imperial regime would be so inept and incapable as to entrust the great cause of the liberation of the motherland to instruments of such poor quality."[92]

Several points about these rather extraordinary conspiracy theories bear consideration. First, they deny agency to the Conselheiro and his followers, who are portrayed as instruments of the real but hidden agents. Such theories emerged for perhaps a fairly obvious reason. So far, the Conselheiristas had beaten back all military attempts to control them. Since the prevalent discourse had already denied them any possibility of political agency, the only way to explain how these poor, dirty, irrational fanatics could successfully challenge the modern nation-state was to posit other, more modern, and minimally rational agents behind them, even if those agents, too, were archaic for being monarchist, even if they still represented ignorance, banditry, and crime.[93]

Second, this is yet another example of the way Canudos became a surface of inscription for a series of antagonisms. This is not to say that the Conselheiro was not a monarchist, a point I'll discuss in more detail in the following chapter, but the clearly fantastic dimension to these conspiracy theories suggests the degree to which his opposition to the republic was translated into a different kind of story. When it reached the "national" stage, therefore, Canudos began to function as an element in two different kinds of struggles. It became a screen onto which to project the conflict between monarchists and republicans and a pawn in the internal power struggle between the two allies who had pushed for the new republic, the military and the São Paulo landowners.

The military and the São Paulo landowners disagreed about what the change of regime should mean. The army was in a process of great change, and though it had been largely denigrated and considered marginal throughout most of the imperial period, such attitudes had begun to change with its triumph in the War of the Triple Alliance (1864–1870).[94] Several postwar reforms were passed to modernize the army and improve the recruitment and training of competent soldiers. Such measures included the abrogation of corporal punishment (which many felt had furthered the equivalence between slaves and soldiers); reductions to or elimination of the privileges held by men of higher social status; the improvement of salaries; and the Recruitment Law of 1874, which instituted supposedly "universal" male conscription. In addition to serving as an impetus for the construction of a larger, more "modern" army, the War of the Triple Alliance had also emboldened its members. Officers "increasingly strove to emulate the organization, ideology, and esprit de corps of Europe's model armies: Germany and France"—efforts that included an emphasis on the army's role in "galvanizing national unity."[95] Influenced by positivism, many youths felt the army had a "saving mission" to correct mistakes in Brazil and that this could be done only by ousting the ruler or even overthrowing the empire.[96] Their republican vision, then, took the shape of a military dictatorship that was both modernizing and moralizing.[97] The coffee bourgeoisie, however, wanted a state that could help integrate Brazil into the capitalist system through agriculture and landed estates. During the first years of the new regime, the military faction had held the upper hand (hence the nickname "Republic of the Sword"), but by the time of Canudos, the president was a civilian (in part as a result of Deodoro's ill-fated attempt at a coup). Many historians have argued that the conspiracy theories were thus intended to incite the more "Jacobin" republicans associated with the military, fueling their violence against both the monarchists and the president. Although the publicity campaigns did deal a deathblow to the monarchists, it ultimately backfired on the "Jacobins," since the São Paulo coffee bourgeoisie emerged decisively as the victor in the crisis of hegemony during the Prudente de Morais government. Despite the final victory over Canudos, the army's disastrous failures during the campaign proved to be the death knell for the political hopes of many military officers who had aspired to regain control of the government by using the Canudos campaign to harness popular support for a military coup.[98]

The fourth expedition was rapidly organized and took place in June 1897. The minister of war, Marshal Carlos Machado Bittencourt, was himself responsible for troop logistics. The expedition of about 11,000 soldiers was divided into two columns and placed under the command of Artur Oscar. Artur Oscar opted for a war of attrition, one whose end was perhaps decided by factors such as the presence or absence of food, water, and munitions. The Conselheiro, it is said, died around September 22 of disease or exhaustion. The confrontation ended in October.

According to da Cunha, no one gave up. Local oral history, however, tells of many survivors. One such individual, Manuel Ciríaco, described the denouement in a personal deposition:

> It was frightening. The rot stank from leagues away. We would see the animals running around the bodies and the buzzards formed a great cloud. All was abandoned. No one was buried. That was when Angelo dos Rios, out of charity, brought some men and buried the dead jagunços there. All of these hills that you see there are filled with bones of jagunços. Canudos was over for about ten years; people only passed by here on their way to somewhere else. There were no houses until 1909. And those that survived lived on the farms.[99]

A second Canudos formed slowly after 1909, made up of both former Canudos inhabitants and newcomers. It was destroyed again in 1968 when the region was flooded by the Cocorobó Dam. The population moved to a nearby locale now called the third Canudos (formerly Cocorobó). The ruins of the Conselheiro's church are visible now only in times of drought.[100]

CHAPTER THREE

THE EVENT AND THE EVERYDAY

> Canudos was, appropriately enough, surrounded by mountains. It was a
> parenthesis, a hiatus, a vacuum. It did not exist. Once that fence of mountains
> was crossed, no one could sin.
>
> —Euclides da Cunha, *Rebellion in the Backlands*

The myth of Canudos had the city founded out of nothing, a Troy arising from thin air in the middle of nowhere: the very materialization of rupture.
Envisioned and portrayed as the refuge of criminal elements such as *jagunços*,
fanatics, *sertanejos*, communists, and monarchists, the community was defined
in terms of lacks. Its houses were squalid, disoriented, and disordered, like so
many bits of wood and mud thrown together, as if they had been "built rapidly,
feverishly, in a single night by a multitude of madmen!"[1] Euclides da Cunha
gave us the most well-known portrait, but others, too, defined the community
in such terms, depicting a city that was not really a city, with roads that were
not roads ("There aren't really roads, because that is not a word that one can
use for the paths that cross each other tortuously in an inextricable labyrinth")
and public plazas that were not really plazas ("the only two plazas that exist,
excepting those in front of the churches, are the inverse of the ones that we
know, since the houses face away from them so that they form something like
a common backyard").[2] The logic of this representation permits no space for
mundane preoccupations. One could say of its inhabitants what Raimundo

Nina Rodrigues, the Bahian medical criminologist, said of the Conselheiro: they did not sleep, and they did not eat (or only barely did so). Their lives were one continuous prayer in the ubiquitous presence of God.[3]

At the same time, Canudos has taken on the face of a utopian community, the inverse of a monstrous city. This characterization generally emerges in later rewritings of Canudos, particularly after the 1960s, but an early version of this other vision of Canudos appears in a marvelous little piece by Machado de Assis entitled "Canção de piratas" from July 22, 1894 (in *A Semana*):

> Newspapers and telegrams tell us that the followers of Conselheiro are criminal; this is the only word that could emerge from brains that toe the line, that are registered, qualified, voting, contributing brains. For those of us who are artists it is a renaissance, a ray of sun which pierces the monotonous, light rain to lighten our windows and soul. It is the poetry that lifts us up among the hard prose of this end of century. . . .
>
> Yes, my friends. The Conselheiro's two thousand men are the pirates of the poets of 1830. . . .
>
> Believe me, this Conselheiro in Canudos with his two thousand men is not what the telegrams and public papers tell us. Imagine a legion of gallant, audacious adventurers, without profession or reward, who detest the calendar, the clocks, taxes, social graces, everything that regiments life, forcing it in line. They are men who are sick of this dull social life, the same days, the same faces, the same events, the same crimes, the same virtues. They cannot believe that the world is a secretary of the State, with his appointment book, the fixed start and end of his workday, his pay docked for days missed. Even love is regulated by law; marriages are celebrated by law in the house of blacks, and by a ritual in the house of God, all with etiquette of carriages and coats, symbolic words, conventional gestures. Not even death escapes regulation. The deceased has to have candles and prayers, a closed coffin and a carriage that takes him to a numbered grave like the house in which he lived. . . . No, by Satan! The followers of Conselheiro remembered the romantic pirates, shook their sandals at the gates of civilization, and left in search of free life.[4]

Machado de Assis turns to Victor Hugo for models—though he references "Chanson de pirates" and not, like da Cunha, *Quatre-vingt-treize*, where Hugo narrates the Vendée peasant revolt against the postrevolutionary French republic—and produces a Canudos that assumes the hues of renaissance and romance rather than monstrosity. In both representations, however, Canudos takes on the face of a negativity, of a rupture, a "No!" to civilization.

Others have come after Assis. One could cite, for example, the Hungarian novelist Sándor Márai's *Veredicto em Canudos* (1969). Márai, who knew of Canudos only from Samuel Putnam's English-language translation of *Os sertões*, uses it as a metonym for a utopian, anarchic dream processed through his experience of May 1968. The heart of his novel is the story of an English-speaking aristocratic couple who abandon their comfortable, bourgeois lives to find "reality" in Canudos.[5] Later historiography, particularly by Marxists, similarly rewrote it in utopian terms as an egalitarian, communist community.[6] More recently Slavoj Žižek reflected this utopian representation by using Canudos to exemplify "sites of eternity that interrupted the flow of temporal progress":

> Canudos, an outlaw community deep in the Brazilian backlands . . . , was a home to prostitutes, freaks, beggars, bandits, and the most wretched of the poor. Canudos, led by an apocalyptic prophet, was a utopian space without money, property, taxes, and marriage. . . . The Canudos liberated territory in Bahia will remain forever the model of a liberated space, of an alternative community which thoroughly negates the existing state space. Everything is to be endorsed here, up to the religious "fanaticism." It is as if, in such communities, *the Benjaminian other side of the historical Progress, the defeated ones, acquires a space of their own.* Utopia EXISTED here for a brief period of time— this is the only way to account for the "irrational," excessive violence of the destruction of these communities (in Brazil of 1897).[7]

In reaction to both these versions, much historiography on Canudos after the 1960s or thereabouts has tried to downplay the radicality of differences, to get away from these dramatic versions and draw out instead Canudos's continuities with other *sertanejo* cities in terms of ethnic composition, hierarchical structures, economic activity, and popular culture. Such a shift forms part of the attempt to think of the Canudos community in terms of its everydayness rather than solely as an event, an attempt to cut it back down to more recognizable and human proportions. Alexandre Otten's rewriting of the Conselheiro's religiosity as ordinary exemplifies this shift. Dain Borges measures out these changes in an ironic formula: "In the light of revisionism, Canudos itself now seems almost ordinary; the reaction of the state and federal governments seems mysteriously vicious."[8] This same formula, however, also reveals that even when ordinary, Canudos (as an event) remains enigmatic, with the mystery now shifted onto the "irrational, excessive violence" (as Žižek put it) of the government's reaction. It is not so easy, in other words, to render Canudos ordinary following its subalternization, since one of the effects of such subalternization was the erasure of its everydayness as a meaningful category. The everyday vanished, rendered invisible.

Everydayness

According to some theorists—Maurice Blanchot, for example—the everyday is always invisible. Blanchot makes this claim because he understands it as a level where structures of order dissolve, much like statues crumbling suddenly into salt. Thus, for example, he denies the possibility of the subject at the level of the everyday. Subjection has not yet happened, since nothing happens in the everyday: "When I live the everyday, it is anyone, anyone whatsoever, who does so, and this any-one is, properly speaking, neither me, nor . . . the other."[9]

Henri Lefebvre, however (to whom all contemporary theorizations of everydayness, including Blanchot's, are greatly indebted), conceives of the everyday as the level at which structures of order are constructed as well. He describes it as a point of mediation between the controlled and uncontrolled: "Its apparent solidity bursts asunder to reveal it as the point where nature and culture come together."[10] Not only do subjects vanish at the threshold of the everyday, then, but they are constituted there as well. The everyday may escape or may even act as a black hole, pulling structures apart or condensing them into invisibility, but it is also the site of emergence, the "condition stipulated for the legibility of forms."[11]

If the everyday is to do this, the part must imply the whole, much as, according to a passage from Lenin, occurs in commodity exchange (Lefebvre quotes this remark on the first page of his *Critique of Everyday Life*): "In his *Capital*, Marx first analyses the simplest, most ordinary and fundamental, most common and *everyday relation* of bourgeois (commodity) society, a relation encountered billions of times, viz. the exchange of commodities. In this very simple phenomenon . . . analysis reveals *all* the contradictions (or the germs of *all* the contradictions) of modern society."[12] The concept of everydayness presented here designates not only the most common of activities or states, those that are therefore trivial or ordinary, but also activities and states that are repeated a billion times. The everyday is thus a place of continuity. To the extent that, as Lenin says, such repeated activities or relations reveal all the contradictions of modern society, we can understand them as the lowest common denominator of that society. Everydayness thus implies a Cartesian totality that, faced with infinity, mathematizes the universe, reducing it to a few numbers and axioms so that the whole universe can be reconstructed, projected, and extended on the basis of these building blocks.

The totality at stake in Lefebvre's book is modern, bourgeois society inasmuch as this model of everydayness is premised on the deep homogeneity required of the citizenry of a modern nation-state, the commensurability required for market exchanges. This perspective shares much with Machado de Assis's critique of a life regimented by calendars, watches, and taxes, a life that produces the same days, the same faces, the same events, the same crimes, and the same virtues—a life against which Canudos becomes a line of flight.[13] In other words, for Lefebvre (and for Machado de Assis), daily life's current tendency toward uniformity, iterability, and sameness results specifically from modernity. In the past, housing, modes of dress, eating, and drinking presented "a prodigious diversity. Not subordinate to any one system, living varied according to region and country, levels and classes of population, available natural resources, season, climate, profession, age and sex."[14] The modern everyday, however, designates "a denominator common to existing systems including judicial, contractual, pedagogical, fiscal, and police systems;" it is "the platform upon which the bureaucratic society of controlled consumerism is erected."[15] Lefebvre operates therefore with a historically specific concept of the everyday. Although he does no more than gesture at forms of everydayness in premodern society, his model leaves open the suggestion of a fundamental transformation of everydayness in which continuities and regularities are turned into iterability or seriality. Switching to spatial metaphors, we can describe this push toward legibility and normalization as equivalent to the transformation of *land* into *territory*.

Michel de Certeau's study *The Practice of Everyday Life* turns Lefebvre's microlevel on its head, pointing instead to the small, minuscule, quotidian ways people manipulate the mechanisms of order and discipline, seeming to conform yet evading precisely by using tactics small enough to escape notice. His everydayness is the domain of numbers rather than names, the space of anonymity (as for Blanchot) and therefore democracy. De Certeau understands such escape, however, not as an ontological property of everydayness but as a result of a multiplicity of orders that overlap at the everyday. In other words, the everyday still evokes larger orders in his model, but each individual and each day constitutes the locus for the interactions of an incoherent and contradictory plurality of determinations. There is no single totality implied by each unit. To the contrary; if there is a whole, it is "made up of pieces that are not contemporary and still linked to totalities that have fallen into ruins."[16] De Certeau's everyday is crammed with cellars and garrets, layered spaces, hollow places in which a past sleeps, encompassing accumulated times that can be unfolded but are silent and blank on the surface. Each place, "like a deteriorating page of a book, refers to a different mode of territorial unity, of socioeconomic distribution, of political conflicts and of identifying symbolism."[17] The legible order overlying such stratification "is everywhere punched and torn open by ellipses, drifts and leaks of meaning: it is a sieve-order."[18]

If we juxtapose the two models, the concept of everydayness becomes a liminal one. It refers to a microlevel that is either the fundamental platform on which a reigning order is erected or the minuscule point showing that any existing order can be eluded. Using different terminology, we can say that this everyday is the level on which hegemony seeks (but may fail) to reproduce itself. It is the threshold at which hegemony seeks to become invisible as such, its violence buried deep, so that it is lived as consent rather than domination.

Such a statement perhaps requires a fuller explanation. Hegemony names a historically specific project of rule irreducible to the mere exertion of power or domination. It is often described in shorthand as operating through consent rather than domination or through persuasion rather than coercion. Antonio Gramsci elaborated the classic formulation of hegemony in his endeavor to formulate the conditions under which the proletariat could become the ruling class in Italy. For Gramsci, the proletariat could do this only if it overcame economic self-interest and won the support of poor peasants and southern intellectuals. This cultural, moral, and ideological leadership of one social group over allied or subordinate groups (as opposed to the subjugation or extinction of antagonistic groups) constitutes hegemony. It was not, therefore, simply the domination of subordinate groups but a process through which the dominant group's ideology acquires legitimacy not just as a tool to further that group's interests or aims but as the solution to more universal problems: their ideology manages "to propagate itself over the whole social area—bringing about not only a unison of economic and political aims, but also intellectual and moral unity, posing all the questions around which the struggle rages not on a corporate but on a 'universal' plane."[19] The development of that particular social group is presented and accepted as "the motor force of a universal expansion, of a development of all the 'national' energies."[20]

Despite a number of problems with the term *consent,* it serves at least two important functions in Gramsci's model. First, although it indicates a rule that operates on the level of ideology and culture, one should not equate hegemony with mystification or false consciousness; it is not simply a question of beliefs or ideas, not even for Gramsci. Indeed, hegemony becomes a much less useful model when understood that way. Derek Sayer, for example, opposes the theorization of hegemony (which he distrusts) to another model of rule in which "the exercise of power pure and simple . . . itself authorizes and legitimates, and it does this less by the manipulation of *beliefs,* than by defining the boundaries of the possible."[21] Power, he says, works materially by forcing subjects to comply with certain rituals, such as carrying a driver's license or passport, sitting in a classroom, standing in line to pass customs at an airport or, we could add, acquiring a marriage license, affixing a number to one's house, and measuring a pound of wheat. This coercive organization of time and space at the most everyday of levels thus produces and reproduces "*material* forms of sociality."[22] Although Sayer contrasts this material operation of power to hegemony, I argue that this operation is exactly how hegemony works. It is about the very naturalization of procedures such as carrying a passport, going to school or—as we will see in the case of Canudos—complying with certain rituals of marriage or taxation.

Since Sayer holds on to a distinction between material practices and beliefs, he appeals to the concept of cynicism to close the gap between them: people accommodate to their social reality regardless of their beliefs. They can comply cynically. But as Žižek puts it, where is the place of ideological illusion in the Marxian formula "they do not know it, but they are doing it"—in the knowing or in the doing? In the doing, Žižek answers, much as did Althusser, who called on Pascal's oft-repeated dictum to illustrate his concept of ideology (kneel down, move your lips in prayer, and you will believe).[23] We know that money is not a magic, immutable substance, but we act as if it were, drawing no distinction between a new coin and one that is old and worn. Žižek (like Althusser before him) dismisses the notion of the private inner realm of ideas posited by the ideology of ideology in which individuals act as a function of their beliefs (and if they don't, they are either inconsistent, cynical, or perverse), since ideology acts precisely by constituting concrete individuals as subjects.[24] Since "ideas" become inscribed in practices, any "idea" not thus inscribed is irrelevant. The term *consent* should be understood, therefore, as pointing to a form of rule that operates at the level of ideology but is irreducible to a question of beliefs. Hegemony, too, is in the doing.

The second important function the term *consent* performs for Gramsci is to indicate the participation of subordinate groups, whether actively or passively. Participation here should not be understood simply as actions of autonomous, rational subjects—as a choice in which coercion or force plays no part. Gramsci's notes suggest a range of possibilities for participation. First, it accompanies Gramsci's idea that hegemony "presupposes that account be taken of the interests and tendencies of the groups over which hegemony is to be exercised."[25] The leading groups must make some sacrifices, although not in regard to their essential—that is, economic—interests. Second, while Gramsci sometimes describes consent as given spontaneously, it can also be inculcated via education or "forcibly extracted" from the subordinate groups.[26] Gramsci describes the ethical state—one that works by hegemony rather than outright coercion—as both requesting and teaching consent. In other words, the ethical state exerts "educative pressure" to produce the "new type of humanity" that will "freely" consent to its rule.[27] Writing of the "educative and formative role of the state," Gramsci identifies its aim as "always that of creating new and higher types of civilization; of adapting the 'civilization' and the morality of the broadest popular masses to the necessities of the continuous development of the economic apparatus of production; hence of evolving even physically new types of humanity. But how will each single individual succeed in incorporating himself into the collective man, and how will educative pressure be applied to single individuals so as to obtain their consent and their collaboration, turning necessity and coercion into 'freedom'?"[28]

The fully functioning ethical state—where the coercive element has withered away as it becomes ever more irrelevant and unnecessary—is the utopia of a perfect and seamless hegemony. This is the end point toward which hegemony tends. More often than not, however, it is more useful to follow Gramsci's elaboration of hegemony as designating a *project* of leadership rather than a seamless achievement (and perhaps a project that comes into being only when the possibility of complete hegemony has already dissipated). Despite hegemony's desire for completeness, for garnering the unqualified commitment of the masses, it can for Gramsci be superficial, incomplete, or unstable. Consent is a more useful term when used negatively. In other words, it designates not so much free, rational choices of subordinate populations as the fragility or instability of hegemony, the possibility for struggle or contention. It designates the possibility of an outside that we should understand not in terms of beliefs or ideas (as does Sayer) but as residues of a residual or emergent alternative order.

The subaltern, writes Alberto Moreiras, is what lies outside the hegemonic relationship. If its everydayness escapes, as happens in the case of Canudos, this happens not simply because the everyday is so banal and familiar as to be unperceived, as Blanchot maintains, but because it has become too unfamiliar to be perceived. This everyday cannot be seen because the "forms" of a society are no longer legible there.

Quebra-Quilos

The Quebra-Quilos (Smash the Kilos) riots, which broke out in northeastern Brazil in 1874–1875, offer an illuminating counterpart to Canudos insofar as they present a moment of insurgency in which everydayness was not written out of the narrative. As the name suggests, the riots often involved the destruction of the scales used to weigh goods in the marketplaces, a resistance to the imperial government's introduction of the metric system over ten years earlier, in 1862. Yet the name masks a variety of unrelated demands. Evidence suggests that the protests were spurred by a series of factors that additionally included new taxes and fears of army conscription following the passage of the Recruitment Law of 1874. Besides destroying scales, rioters also burned official records, including tax records and land titles. Many authorities attempted to blame the riots on religious, especially Jesuit, leadership, but there is no historical record of unified leadership.[29] Priests and clerics were involved in some cases, but Armando Souto Maior, the only historian to dedicate a book-length study to these events, argues that the riots had no connection to any systematic, organized political movement and instead comprised a series of disarticulated but metonymically related incidents that began in the state of Paraíba and then spread to Pernambuco, Alagoas, and Rio Grande do Norte.[30] In Goiânia, for example, the riots resulted from small producers' and merchants' reactions against the monopoly of foreign merchants, especially the Portuguese, so that they often took on a xenophobic or even anticolonial tint.[31] In two cities the Quebra-Quilos riots included the deliberate destruction of house numbers; in some cities where slaves participated, the revolts included a demand for emancipation; and in other cities, Freemasonry was denounced (here the local leadership was religious). According to Roderick Barman, echoing Guha's study of the transmission of peasant revolts, "the means of dissemination appear to have been kinship links between the different villages, the peasant practice of attending markets in several localities, the gossip of itinerant peddlers and other travelers, and newspaper reports communicated by the literate. The rising tended to occur first in satellite markets and then to move, on the following market day, into the distribution market town for the area."[32] The revolts seem to have subsided largely on their even though troops and police officers were often sent to put them down.

If the riots were not exclusively organized by a resistance to changes in the metric system, why did they become intelligible as such? Ernesto Laclau's model of the creation of the hegemonic relation is useful here. Gramsci understood a class or group to be hegemonic when it succeeds in presenting itself as realizing the broader aims of either emancipating or ensuring order for wider masses of the population; for Laclau, this process takes place through the production of an empty signifier. For an example, he supposes a regime opposed by a number of different particular struggles. These struggles differ among themselves even as they all oppose the system. If a hegemonic relation is to be constructed among these various points of opposition, a relation of equivalence must prevail over the differentials, a transitive chain equating a to b, b to c, and so on. The longer the chain, the more abstract the equivalence and the less these separate struggles will share "something equally present" in all. At the limit, their common denominator will be a pure communitarian being independent of any concrete manifestation: the utopia that all believe will come into being as soon as the regime that is blocking its existence is destroyed. Laclau argues that this imagined community cannot have a representation (signifier) of its own, since if it did, it would be simply one more difference in the series of differentials. The imaginary common denominator therefore borrows a signifier from somewhere in the chain of equivalences and empties it of its particular signified. The result is an "empty" signifier that also becomes the signifier of a lack, of an absent totality.[33]

Understood through Laclau's model, then, opposition to the metric system becomes the empty signifier in the Quebra-Quilos riots. It becomes the surface onto which are inscribed all other demands (demands for, e.g., the emancipation of slaves, religious freedom, fewer taxes, or a ban on conscription). In contrast to Canudos, this surface of inscription is marked by the temporality and level of the everyday. The act of smashing scales both identifies and defies changes at the everyday level, which is what makes for the slightly incongruous nature of the riots evident in the words of one commentator who said, "One expects that people will calm down and that the peace won't be disturbed in this municipality for such a frivolous reason."[34] Such an uproar should not happen, he seems to be saying, for something so ordinary and frivolous as a system of weights.

This was not an arbitrary surface of inscription, however, despite the variety of demands articulated in these riots. What this commentator misses is that the structures of society do not change without a change at the level of the everyday, as Lefebvre wrote and as the Brazilian government surely believed. The riots constituted a struggle over *which* and *whose* everyday. They manifested a resistance to the homogenization and unification of the everyday as described by Lefebvre's model and decreed by the Brazilian state in its attempt to increase its extractive and regulative power. Martin Lienhard rightfully grasps the impact and scope of this expansionist movement in nineteenth-century Latin America when he terms it the "second conquest." Lienhard specifically refers to the oligarchy's drive to consolidate its power through the expansion of the *latifundia* system into areas that had remained largely untouched under Spanish and Portuguese colonial rule. Where a large indigenous population still existed, landowners invaded common lands, thus destroying the economic and cultural base of indigenous groups that had managed to survive thus far despite the destruction of their political autonomy with the first colonial conquest.[35] This economic conquest was often matched by genocidal campaigns to eliminate all that smelled of barbarianism, any form of autonomy that threatened the spreading neocolonial order. Lienhard considers the Argentine and Chilean "campaigns of the desert," the Yucatan Caste War, the War of the Triple Alliance, and the Canudos campaign to be variants of this phenomenon. This process thus includes both a horizontal and a vertical component: it involved expanding outward and invading lands that had been outside the direct grasp of the Latin American oligarchs, but it also involved a transforming and intensifying governance, moving from the kind of loose, porous rule that Benedict Anderson associates with medieval sovereignty to a new principle in which the power of the nation-state is assumed to be "fully, flatly and evenly operative over each square centimetre of a legally demarcated territory."[36]

This intensification of rule happened in a number of ways. For example, Judy Bieber argues that throughout the nineteenth century, and in particular after 1850, municipalities across the empire lost autonomy and control at the hands of an increasingly intrusive and regulated political machine functioning through patronage. The Quebra-Quilos riots, however, coincided with what

Jeffrey Needell describes as one of state's three major attempts to construct and impose a national cultural identity before the success of Getúlio Vargas's Estado Novo. Unlike the Estado Novo, though, these first three attempts (which occurred in 1822–1840, 1871–1875, and 1902–1906) pursued an overtly European identity as a kind of "civilizing mission."[37] The second of these took place after the War of the Triple Alliance when the emperor attempted to outflank critiques of the Liberal Party by carrying out moderate reforms with a cabinet led by Viscount do Rio Branco (chief of the dominant Conservative Party). Such reforms included the introduction of the metric system; legislation to gradually abolish slavery; educational reforms; the first national census; continued and new railroad subsidation; the authorization of a submarine telegraph cable between Brazil and Europe; a series of postal agreements with various other nations; reforms of the commercial and criminal codes; a project for a civil code; the opening of the Amazon basin to foreign trade and regulation of the area; private acquisition of public lands; the promotion of foreign emigration from England, Germany, and Italy; and the Parisian-style reform of the port capital Rio de Janeiro. "In a phrase, the nation was to be reshaped in European form through the dramatic imposition of liberal legislation, Eurocentric education, increased European contact, the importation of European 'racial' stock, and striking material amenities closely associated with the metropole."[38] The minister of justice, writing his official report to the legislature for 1874, described the reforms as a "social revolution which, involving the most influential interests, nonetheless was aided and supported by almost all Brazilians."[39] The Quebra-Quilos riots belied the minister's confidence, however, showing that this "magnificent crusade for moral and material development" (in the words of the president of the province of Pernambuco in 1874) was not very popular with Brazilians, and indeed, it met little success.[40]

One of the particularly contentious attempts at reform was the 1874 Recruitment Law, which outlawed impressment and introduced limited conscription: men between eighteen and thirty years of age would be registered in their local parishes, but a draft lottery was to take place only when too few men voluteered. As I mentioned previously, the law was intended to produce a leveling effect, to undo the disproportionate burden that army service had placed on the poor. In practice, however, many of the exemptions that had protected men—especially those in the upper social strata—from impressment would also protect them from conscription under the new law (which exempted those with more than fifty head of cattle, as well as students, lawyers, and physi-

cians), whereas some grounds for exemptions (e.g., marriage) that had hitherto
protected the poor from impressment would not save them from conscription
under the new law.[41]

Several historians, including Peter Beattie and Joan Mezner, have argued
that resistance to this law was the main cause behind the Quebra-Quilos revolts. Beattie, who argues that previous accounts have not sufficiently rec-
ognized the army's importance as a mechanism for social control in Brazil,
maintains that while those who held power could have chosen to emphasize
modernizing other institutions, the primacy of national defense and the political influence of army officers and their allies ultimately made military reform
a higher priority for the central government. Because the army was central to
Brazil's police, prison, orphanage, and judicial systems, "no other set of reforms, save those abolishing slavery, could compare to the scale of its impact
on institutions of social discipline and the lives of the poor."[42] According to
Beattie, "some participants in the Quebra Quilos Revolt dubbed the Recruitment Law 'the law of captivity,' claiming that it 'turned citizens into slaves.'"
He concedes that it is difficult to tell whether protestors believed they would
be literally "enslaved" or whether they simply borrowed from the polemics of
Liberal Party leaders (who preferred an all-volunteer army to a draft lottery),
but in any case, he writes, "vulnerability to impersonal public authority was
equated with a status uncomfortably close to slavery."[43] As Meznar points out,
many poor farmers had been previously able to dodge impressments through
honorable work, family status, or patronage but would now be at the mercy
of an impersonal lottery.[44] It didn't help that the first national census, held in
September 1872, had coincided with a national registration of slaves (and also
with the decree that ordered the adoption of the metric system throughout the
whole country).[45]

Nonetheless, the riots took shape under the name "Quebra-Quilos," under a surface of inscription that singled out the problem of measurement. Benedict Anderson identifies maps and censuses as manifestations of the modern
nation-state's principle of homogeneity. Both are organized around a totalizing
classificatory grid that can be applied flexibly to anything under state control:
peoples, regions, religions, languages, products, monuments, and so on, all
of which are in principle bounded, determinate, and countable—things that
can be serialized, reproduced, and governed once they have been made legible.
One could argue that, like the map and census, the introduction of the metric
system illuminated a threshold for new forms of governmentality and control.

Taxes and slavery had existed before, but a change in the system of measurement signaled a new homogeneity. It implied a standardization not just of commodity exchange but of a series of daily practices. What the standardization of weights—and in a different way, the notion of the draft lottery—made manifest, then, was the principle of homogeneity Anderson identifies, the way everyday life is turned into a space of habits, practices, and regularities to be conquered, transformed, and rendered commensurable. The riots can thus be read as reactions to changes in structures of governmentality—specifically, to an illegitimate expansion into areas that a centralized apparatus of government had previously ignored or been unable to affect, into as-yet uncolonized spheres of an everyday or private life. The popular jokes and songs concerning the Quebra-Quilos riots suggest as much. Discussing the origins of a particular riot, one judge mentioned the rumor of a five-thousand-reis tax to be paid by any woman who combed her hair and alluded to other rumors of taxes on sexual activities that he, out of decency, refrained from verbalizing.[46] The humoristic vein signals the apparent absurdity of such government intromission into arenas of everyday life such as personal hygiene and sex. The jokes and rumors also suggest that the new system of measures and weights was associated metonymically with this illegitimate expansion of government.

Souto Maior misses the point when, in good subalternizing fashion, he reads the variety and disarticulation of the riots as showing them to have been prepolitical and the rioters to have been provocateurs rather than agents, since (he says) they did not really grasp the causes or consequences of their actions.[47] According to Souto Maior, the workings of the state were all but unfathomable to the protestors: "The riots resulted from the historical evolution of the empire's economy, and its most visible agents did not always have a precise notion of what the State was, along with its machinery of soldiers and policemen, tax collectors, class differences, concentration of land, commerce, etc."[48] The historian Robert Levine disputes such an ascription of naïveté to the rioters with an analysis of tax trends that seems to confirm their foresight: "Backland participants in these riots, of course, were portrayed as primitives terrified of modern scientific innovations; yet one could also praise them for figuring out that uniform scales and measures would inevitably lead to a higher tax burden. Examination of the tax records in the affected *muncípios*, in fact, reveals that between 1870 and 1875 new taxes were created or raised in two out of every three *municípios* after standardized weights were introduced."[49] Still, even if the rioters had been wrong about the tax burden, and even if the logic behind the rebellions could not be identified as political actions under certain modern definitions of the political, we could still say, along with Ranajit Guha, that "peasants don't launch into rebellions in fits of absent-mindedness."[50]

Nevertheless, Souto Maior's interpretation, however blinkered, denotes a significant gap between these populations and the state in formation. Several historians have argued that the riots indicate a fragility in the power of both the landowners and the imperial state. The riots thus can be read as an attempt—a particularly successful one—to remain outside the purview of an encroaching state: a draft lottery became reality only after 1908 in a republican Brazil; no new census was taken in 1880, as the new law required; and attempts to enforce the metric system were given up.[51] In a study much indebted to Souto Maior's work, Magnus Mörner argues that the riots show the weaknesses behind the empire's façade in its premature attempt to impose a new modernizing system, to move from patrimonial to bureaucratic domination. They reveal that the provincial presidents and elites of northeastern Brazil exercised no effective control over the hinterlands and had to depend on dominance: "The military intervention and the ensuing repression came too late to be considered 'rational.' It was rather, through its arbitrary brutality, a display of traditional, despotic power."[52] This new everyday—an everyday where citizens were counted and exhorted to defend the nation, their forms of measuring made uniform, their territory brought ever closer to other nations by telegraph and railroads—was not hegemonic. Or not yet.

From Monarchy to Republic

Near the end of his book, Souto Maior suggests that Canudos and the Quebra-Quilos riots shared the same "etiology" and produced similar reactions among elites:

> Antonio Freire is right when he says that the Quebra-Quilos riots lacked an Euclides da Cunha. The tragedy of the Quebra-Quilos remained shrouded in the darkness of episodes that have received little attention and the complexity of its social mechanics, which impeded definitive works on the subject. Often the Quebra-Quilos rioters were social types very similar to the jagunços of Antonio Conselheiro and their motivations almost identical. The optics with which both the jagunços and the rioters of 1874 view social institutions has the same etiology. This explains the repeated comments that the principal cause of the Quebra-Quilos revolts was the ignorant reaction of the people

to military recruitment, which they perceived as unjust, to taxes and the introduction of a system of weights and measurements, based on the French decimal system.[53]

In fact, however, Canudos persists in public memory while the Quebra-Quilos riots have fallen into obscurity not simply because the latter lacked a chronicler such as Euclides da Cunha but because of the way the institutionalization of the new republic provided a surface of inscription for a variety of changes spreading over Brazil. This happened not only in the case of an emerging prose of counterinsurgency but possibly also in the discourse of the Conselheiro himself.

By all accounts the Conselheiro's first physical clash with authorities sounds like a late echo or ripple of the Quebra-Quilos riots. The connection is not so strange since the Conselheiro had been wandering around Pernambuco during the years of the riots. Manoel Benício, a *Jornal do Commercio* correspondent at Canudos and the author of *O rei dos jagunços*, explicitly situates the Conselheiro's beliefs within the terrain of the Quebra-Quilos riots by pointing out that the religious leader "opposed the introduction of the metric system in commerce."[54] In Benício's account this first clash took place when the Conselheiro denounced certain municipal taxes as excessive:

> A poor old woman arrived at the fair . . . to sell bamboo. The tax collector demanded 100 reis for the piece of land on which the poor old woman had settled to sell her goods. The woman, who estimated the value of her goods at 80 reis, complained loudly to those around her, crying and lamenting. A group of people gathered, and they all agreed with her, for how could one pay a tax that was more than the worth of the goods to be sold? . . . In his sermon that night the Conselheiro referred to the old woman, declaring: this is what the Republic is, captivity, working only for the government. It is the slavery announced by maps which now begins. Didn't you see that Aunt Benta [the old woman] is religious and white? Thus this slavery does not respect anyone.[55]

Benício's text situates the Conselheiro within a genealogy of the Quebra-Quilos riots, thus suggesting that everydayness is one level on which explanations for the Canudos conflict should be cast, but it also indicates how that conflict began to diverge from the Quebra-Quilos riots. Many of the themes that showed up in the discourse around the Quebra-Quilos riots show up here, too: resistance to new market taxes and the fear of a new kind of slavery that would not distinguish between the honorable and dishonorable poor. At the same time, Benício's scene shows the Conselheiro associating a new system of domination and slavery with the republic.

To an extent, then, the passage from empire to republic simply gave a name and face to some of the changes that had already been taking place throughout the nineteenth century and others that were attempted during the last decades of the empire. The institutionalization of the republic confirmed, for example, the change from a slave economy to a new capitalist-industrial bourgeois society and the consequent changes in power configurations. It legally instituted the basis for a bourgeois democratic state. This did not lead to real democratization, however, since it also preserved the political and social power of the great landowners and reproduced the political and social marginalization of vast portions of Brazilian society. The institutionalization of literacy as a requirement for voting under the republic, for example, meant that suffrage was actually more limited than it had been in the early days of the empire. Moreover, the new republic advanced the intensification of rule associated with Dom Pedro II, particularly some of the measures that had been attempted—but failed—under the Rio Branco cabinet. Indeed, the baron of Rio Branco—the son and namesake of Viscount do Rio Branco—was the minister of foreign affairs in the administration of Francisco de Paula Rodrigues Alves, an administration that Jeffrey Needell calls the "culmination of the Europhile trends of the previous century," adding, "In this way, we must understand it as a legacy redeemed."[56] Under the First Republic, for example, Rio de Janeiro was remade in the image of Paris (many of its crannies and layers wiped out in favor of wide boulevards, rational street organization, and sanitary modernization); new railroad lines were built to unify the capital with the northern, southern, and western parts of the nation; and an expedition was charged with mapping and linking the hinterlands to the country's administrative center through telegraphs.[57] The new republic, in other words, provided a name and face for new processes of governmentalization.

But is Benício right? What do we know of the Conselheiro's political beliefs? The only written testament left behind is his sermon on the republic. Almost all his arguments against the new republic revolve around his concern that it emptied government and the social order of all religious content. Any source of authority other than God is deemed illegitimate. All authority emanates from God, the Conselheiro writes, and he granted the right to govern

Brazil only to the emperor.[58] Moreover, as the sermon makes clear, the Conselheiro viewed the new republic's separation of church and state as a withering of
religion's power in all spheres of life. The new republic is "a great evil for Brazil"[59] because it undermines religion: "it is launched as the quickest and most
efficient way to exterminate religion."[60] The Conselheiro expressed no doubt
that the republic would fall for having turned away from God: "Convince your-
selves, republicans, that you will not triumph because your cause is born of lack
of faith."[61]

The Conselheiro found this secularization to be particularly egregious
with respect to marriage (foreshadowing current attitudes in the United
States). Give to God what is God's and to Caesar what is Caesar's, he quoted,
arguing that the president of the republic violated this dictum by giving it the
right to marry people. The particular concern over marriage shows up as well
in popular verses da Cunha quotes as examples of "the stammerings of the
people": "A mockery they make of marriage / they'd have all true marriages
cease / And have us all get married / by a justice of the peace!"[62] In fact, the first
penal code passed after the proclamation of the republic criminalized having
a religious wedding before a civil one, making it a crime punishable by a fine
or six months in jail, which certainly did not help matters.[63] The Conselheiro
insisted that civil marriage was unlawful and null since real marriage consists
in the union of souls, and only the Church had the power to unite them. He
encouraged parents to forgo civil marriage, for it constituted a grave offense in
religious matters: it "occasions the sin of scandal."[64]

The only moment the sermon deviates from this preoccupation with legitimate authority is when the Conselheiro explains the overthrow of the monarchy as republican retaliation for the "beautiful event" that was the abolition
of slavery. This interpretation of the empire's fall, attributing it to conservative
dissatisfaction with the end of slavery, was not unique to the Conselheiro but a
common theme in monarchist discourse of the time.[65] "The "origin of the hatred" that republicans had for the royal family, says the Conselheiro, was Dona
Isabel's emancipation of the slaves. This event is inscribed within a salvational
view of history: in doing so, he writes, she was acting on the will of God ("she
did no more than follow an order from the heavens") since "the time had come
which had been marked by God for the liberation of the people from such a
state, the most degrading a human being can be reduced to."[66] The Conselheiro's embrace of abolition is indeed one of his most "liberal" positions, and

in this point, at least, Benício accurately assesses his beliefs. According to the Conselheiro, "the men"—that is, republicans—were astonished with such a beautiful event because "they had become aware of the arms behind the labor that produced their wealth, and they responded to the work of these people with indifference and ingratitude."[67] In the implied opposition between "the men"—he means white men, free men, richer men, slaveholding men—and the "people" (*o povo*), he clearly sides with the latter. The outlines of this other antagonism remain faint, however, and beyond it he mentions only the conflict between religious and secular authority, which dominates the rest of the sermon.

Whereas Benício describes the Conselheiro's political views as rooted in a certain rule and way of life ("enraisado nos velhos hábitos da administração de então") whose rhythms were increasingly subject to a different pattern, the concern with religion articulated in this sermon led da Cunha to characterize Antônio Conselheiro as the site for the violent irruption of barbarism. For Benício, in other words, the Conselheiro and his followers were forced from a place that was properly theirs, whereas for da Cunha, they were already out of time and place, a view that will lead da Cunha to declare the Conselheiro incapable of understanding the abstraction of the new republican state form. If one inserts the Conselheiro within the genealogy of the Quebra-Quilos riots, however, his sermon can be read in terms of a continued struggle with the evacuation of sources of authority and meaning.

The incident of the old woman taxed beyond the value of her goods would have taken on a different face twenty years earlier, but the change in the name of the government provided a new surface of inscription. In *Sangue de irmãos*, José Aras writes that his parents were among the crowd listening to the Conselheiro speak the night of the first clash, which followed the incident with the old woman. According to their memories, the Conselheiro explained the clash at Massaté as evidence that "the Antichrist [had] arrived" and that a new era had opened:

> Satan brought the republic, but the king Don Sebastian will come to our aid. Next will come the good Jesus to separate the wheat from the chaff, the goats from the sheep. And woe to those who don't repent before, because their remorse will be useless later. Fast because we are at the end of times. Belo Monte will be Jesus' pasture, the face of Jehovah. The republicans must not be

spared because they are all for the Antichrist. From now on it will be an eye for an eye and a tooth for a tooth.[68]

Laclau uses this moment to illustrate his concept of articulation in *Contingency, Hegemony, Universality*: "One day Conselheiro arrived in a village where people were rioting against the tax collectors, and pronounced the words which were to become the key equivalence of his prophetic discourse 'The Republic is the Antichrist.' From that point onwards his discourse provided a surface of inscription for all forms of rural discontent, and became the starting point of a mass rebellion."[69] Anger over new taxation is articulated with frustration at unceasing droughts; alienation, with changes in Church structure and the perceived illegitimacy of the new basis of authority. After this incident the Conselheiro and his followers were pursued by a police force of thirty men, with whom they clashed in Masseté. Robert Levine remarks that this clash was not a singular occurrence; troops had been sent to aid Viana's supporters against local landowners elsewhere in the state, and they, too, had met defeat. In public memory, however, this clash was lifted from the stream of ordinary occurrences and took on the weight of an event.[70] Only after beating the police force did the Conselheiro and his followers give up wandering and set down roots in Canudos.[71]

The passage from monarchy to republic should be seen, therefore, less as an empirical, necessary cause of the Canudos War (as the Quebra-Quilos riots show, changes in structures in governance prior to the regime change had set off a number of rebellions, riots, and protests) than as a surface of inscription on which other tensions and changes were articulated. Or better: the "republic" was a name that generated a series of different, competing surfaces of inscription. In one, the signifier denoted a civilization threatened by barbarism; in another, a tyrannical Behemoth enslaving the people. If the change in regime was a determining factor in the conflict, therefore, it was so only insofar as the conflict became understood through it. This does not mean that inscription is simply a question of superstructural appearance; it made all the difference between the Quebra-Quilos riots and the Canudos War. In the case of Canudos, the change in regime came to name a breach that erased continuities between the new regime and the old and concealed the everyday stakes in the conflict. It produced the extraordinary Canudos we know today, the one crucial to the self—constitution of the modern Brazilian state. As Roberto Ventura writes, to the extent that the republican form found its mold in the presidency of Prudente de Morais, Canudos was central to this process "through the conversion of the military campaign into the revolutionary crusade for the consolidation of the regime."[72]

Canudos versus Belo Monte

In *Os sertões* da Cunha writes that in 1890, three years before the Conselheiro arrived, Canudos was "a backwoods hamlet of around fifty mud-thatched wooden shanties."[73] The historian José Calasans, however, argues that Antônio Conselheiro did not settle in the abandoned Canudos farm owned by Mariana Carvalho, a niece of the baron of Geremoabo, or in the Cocorobó farm (owned by Elvira Fiel Dantas de Carvalho Fontes, another niece of Geremoabo), both on the right bank of the Vaza-Barris (or Vasa-Barris) River, as has generally been believed. Instead, he installed himself in a relatively privileged and prosperous settlement on the left bank of the Vaza-Barris.[74] Calasans relies heavily on oral history that attests to an original Canudos somewhat more substantial than da Cunha portrays it as having been. Manuel Ciríaco, a Canudos survivor interviewed in 1947 by the journalist Odorico Tavares, claimed that there was already a plaza and sheltered stand, a small chapel, and some houses in better condition, one of which was inhabited by Antônio da Mota, a relatively well-off leather merchant.[75] The Conselheiro's Belo Monte later boasted two churches, warehouses, a barracks, cemeteries, munitions houses, roads, five "neighborhoods," and a school for boys and girls that cost 2,000 reis a month.[76] Although far from the biggest urban centers, it stood at the intersection of several major roads and provided an almost obligatory rest stop for travelers.

How many inhabitants did Belo Monte/Canudos have at its height? The original estimate was around twenty-five thousand people, based on the army's count of 5,200 houses in Canudos and the assumption of an average of five people per *sertanejo* household. Recently some historians have contested that figure, suggesting that the population could not have exceeded five or six thousand. For Calasans the original calculations suggest a city that was bigger than any other in the state aside from Salvador. "The calculations are evidently unrealistic," he contends.[77]

Who were these inhabitants, however numerous? Calasans suggests four stages of population: the original inhabitants, those who followed Conselheiro on his pilgrimages, those who came in the first years of community, and those who came to defend the town during the conflict.[78] Surviving testimonies register several categories: religious people and apostles; teachers; merchants; *cangaceiros,* or bandits (including famous ones, such as Pajeú and João Abade, and others who would make up the so-called Guarda Católica, or "Companhia do Bom Jesus"); poorer people; people of some means who sold cattle and land to go to Canudos; indigenous peoples (living perhaps on the Rua dos Caboclos);[79] and ex-slaves, predominating probably on the Rua dos Negros. Although da Cunha remains silent on the issue, many testimonies mention a large population of blacks liberated by abolition (the "May 13 blacks"). In one such account, a letter from Antero de Cerqueira Galo to the baron of Geremoabo, the former man highlights the contingent of ex-slaves, who he believed formed a majority: "There the masses that are generating a revolt are the very same Conselheiro and his followers, including soldiers and deserters from various States and the people of May 13, which is the largest part; indeed there are few whites there."[80] Testimonies such as these led Calasans to suggest that Canudos was the last *quilombo* (runaway slave community) in Brazil.

No doubt a variety of factors drew people to Canudos during the last two stages: the menace of the *coronelista* system, ties of kinship, the Church's persecution of heterodox practices, religious faith, a belief in the Conselheiro as a miracle worker and healer, and the desire to escape economic hardship (according to revisionist historians, rivers and plentiful underground water made Canudos relatively fertile).[81] Goats were the principal economic resource, and a considerable amount of leather was sold to nearby Cumbe and Monte Santo. Cattle were raised in neighboring big farms as well. Accounts mention not only subsistence agriculture but also sugarcane planted on the river's edge. Selling labor to neighboring farms was another mainstay of the city's economy. This last point suggests a significant amount of contact and travel between Canudos and the surrounding regions; such traffic included not only the residents, who would leave to trade or offer labor, but also a large, fluctuating number of people who would have come for a day to trade or to hear the Conselheiro speak. Commerce with the neighboring region seems to have ceased only at the end of the conflict (September 1897), when Canudos was enclosed on all sides by the army.

Some critics take the town's stable, self-sufficient economy and its investment in a school as evidence that the community was not awaiting the end of the world, unlike, for example, the Contestado movement, in which the community did cease economic activity, turning to raids of neighboring communities for day-to-day survival.[82] Levine also suggests that people moved to Canudos not as a retreat to a primitive utopia but as an escape from hard conditions. Thus, he writes, "the formation of Canudos as a settlement should be seen as a precursor to the great migratory waves that occurred decades later, and not as a retrogressive withdrawal from coastal-inspired progress."[83] In terms of Laclau's theory of the articulation of equivalences, the point is therefore that Canudos could have functioned as an empty signifier that measured the distance between a present of deprivation (whether it be poverty, lack of religion, disease, or police persecution) and a future of fullness without any of the individual demands operating as markers of a single identity or demand. Laclau's model thus keeps open a heterogeneity that is impossible within da Cunha's vision of Canudos as a "uniform and homogeneous community, an unconscious brute mass . . . without organs and without specialized functions . . . in the manner of a human polyp."[84]

The testimony of Honório Vilanova, one of the now-legendary figures associated with Canudos, belies this ascription of uniformity. The Vilanova brothers, Honório and Antônio, were merchants in charge of the town's commercial life and the distribution of goods. In his interview with the journalist Nerton Macedo in 1962, Honório, then ninety-seven years old, described everyday life at Canudos, characterizing the site not as millenarian and messianic but as peaceful, well ordered, and relatively prosperous (by *sertão* standards): "I liked the order there so much that I decided to stay. Canudos was a lucky place. It didn't even need rain. It had everything. Even cane sugar from Caririri." In addition, he said, "There was no need to steal in Canudos because everything existed in abundance. . . . There was no scarcity of provisions."[85] The town offered everything but liquor or fighting. "It was an anthill of people, zealous and orderly in their good habits, where there wasn't even a single prostitute. From the balcony I saw around me the peace and quiet of the passing days. The Pilgrim reigned. His word was the law."[86] According to Honório, however, the Conselheiro's demand for order and peace did not include a requirement that residents publicly and constantly demonstrate their faith. Honório himself rarely went to church, he says ("I went to church only every now and again. I don't like prayer much"), and many other men did not either, it being more a "woman's thing": "The men, I repeat, didn't go to the religious services. The women, yes, almost all of them went to the sanctuary, where they prayed and listened to sermons."[87] Honório's testimony leaves the impression of a communal yet open organization where all the inhabitants could do as they pleased: "Great was the Canudos of my time. Those who had orchards cared for the orchards on the banks of the river. Those who had cattle cared for their cattle. Those who had women and children cared for their women and children. Those who liked to pray prayed. Everything was taken care of because none of it belonged to anyone in particular. All of it belonged to everyone, small and great, in the rule taught by the Pilgrim."[88] Honório's Canudos combines the freedom to do what one wills (for men, at least) with a common law, common grounds, and common property, the delicate point at which individual space folds over into communal space. Honório articulates not an ordinary Canudos per se but the fantasy of an extraordinary ordinary. His Canudos lays bare the ordinary peace and prosperity that is the utopia of a merchant, a utopia sharing perhaps nothing in common with the religious longings of women who went to church or those seeking cures from disease.

Honório's testimony also raises the question of the town's economy. Accounts conflict on several economic issues: How egalitarian was Canudos? To what extent did personal property exist? Was republican money allowed to circulate? In this, eyewitness accounts are no less contradictory than any others. In May 1895 the archbishop of Salvador sent a pastoral delegation to Canudos to bring the Conselheiro and his people under church control. One of the many Italian Capuchin missionaries in the Northeast headed the delegation, which spent approximately a week in Canudos (having failed to exert any influence over the inhabitants, the mission was then suspended). An account of the mission, the only extensive written eyewitness account of the town before the military expeditions, was provided to the archbishop when the delegation returned. In his account, the Capuchin missionary suggests that private property did not exist in Canudos: "Whoever had goods disposed of them and handed over the product to the good Conselheiro, reserving for themselves only twenty percent."[89] Da Cunha's account is similar: "Property with them took on the exaggerated form of the tribal collectivism of the Bedouins. Personal property was limited to movable objects and their individual huts; there was an absolute community of land, pastures, flocks, and herds, and the few cultivated products, the landlords receiving merely their quota, while the rest went to 'society.'"[90] Likewise, Manuel Ciríaco claims that land was given freely to the newly arrived and that the Conselheiro permitted newcomers to build houses as long as there were no doubts about their Catholic and monarchist convictions. But not all was freely given. Basing his claims on information from officials, Lélis Piedade, a Bahian journalist at the time of Canudos, observed that the great majority of papers found in Canudos referred to the sale and buying of houses.[91] According to Honório, too, the Conselheiro did not ban private property, commerce, or money, even though he himself did not touch republican or monarchist money and, later in the conflict, demanded that all money stolen from soldiers be burned. In fact, Vilanova and his brother made good profit as merchants in Canudos.[92] The presence of people such as the Vilanovas undermines the vision of Canudos as a radically egalitarian society, with no differences in wealth, suggesting some stratification even if it was perhaps not as severe as in other parts of Brazil. A minuscule difference, then, that makes all the difference?

But the terrain of comparison is slippery, especially when it is haunted by the inevitable question: was life better (even by a little) or worse in Canudos? And for whom? As does da Cunha, the Capuchin missionary describes Canudos as a place of deprivation and inhumanity where the houses were "rude huts, made of mud and straw, with no windows" and "filthy" interiors; "almost naked" inhabitants, he says, "attested to the multiple privations they experienced in their squalid and skeletal appearance."[93] Yet this same account reveals the cultural gaps (not unlike those that may have driven Júlio Fiorentini's early condemnations of the Conselheiro) that surely informed the missionary's assessment. Preaching on fasting, the missionary had assured his listeners that the Church was not too strict about fasting, for it didn't want the people deprived of force, and so one could always drink and sometimes eat meat while fasting. To this one of the listeners exclaimed, "That's not fasting; that's feasting!"[94] His own ignorance about living conditions in the *sertão* undoubtedly underpinned his representations of Canudos as a place of extreme misery.

In contrast, as Vilanova's testimony suggests, oral history tends to portray Canudos as far from being a somber place of deprivation, penitence, and eschatological anticipation. For instance, oral histories of indigenous groups who lived and participated in the city indicate that many were drawn by a vision of abundance. One individual recalled, "My mom . . . wanted to go and catch a glimpse of the beauty in Canudos. . . . She thought it was pretty since they said that there in Canudos there was a river of milk and embankments made of cous-cous."[95] Another said, "The food was in the hands of the Conselheiro, the people were astonished—this man is God, to accomplish so much, to give food to so many people!"[96] For Manuel Ciríaco, too, Canudos was a place of plenty: "In the time of Conselheiro, I don't like to talk about it, so that others don't call me a liar, but there was everything around here. Everything grew, even sugarcane that you could peel with your fingernails, it grew beautifully here. Vegetables in abundance, and all the rain you could want. . . . Those times, it seems unbelievable."[97] Another account extended the abundance to include festivities: "According to the account of Marcos Dantas de Menezes, who met the Conselheiro in the village of the Good Jesus, today city of Crisópolis, the celebrations of the Conselheiro never lacked music and fireworks."[98]

Still, oral testimony does not unanimously contradict the written versions of Canudos. Silvino Pereira, a member of the indigenous community of Massacará, had negative memories of the town (in part, perhaps, because a colonel persecuted his community for having fought on the side of Canudos): "I did not like that place. . . . It was the most idiotic place I have ever seen[;] I don't know how those people fought in that place. . . . They all lived exposed like cattle, like a herd of cattle in the fields. . . . How did those people live?"[99]

These accounts, which juxtapose a bountiful Belo Monte to a Canudos of deprivation, trace the limits of the shift toward the city as *almost* ordinary, facing or not facing one another across what is inevitably a gap, even if perhaps no wider than an *almost*. In Italo Calvino's *Invisible Cities*, Marco Polo provides mathematically precise formulas for the relationships that determine each city in his catalog. One city presents two faces; depending on the viewer's angle of approach, it displays either alabaster gates, glass villas, sunlight, and chandeliers or rusting sheet metal, soot, tins cans, and fading signs: "From one part to the other, the city seems to continue, in perspective, multiplying its repertory of images: but instead it has no thickness, it consists only of a face and an obverse, like a sheet of paper, with a figure on either side, which can neither be separated nor look at each other."[100] The gap, perhaps no wider than a sheet of paper, is a signal of a structure of excess that historians are hard-pressed to undo. Dain Borges, recall, affirmed not only that revisionist historiography portrays Canudos as almost ordinary but also that the government's actions toward it seemed mysteriously vicious—as if an ordinary Canudos should not have elicited such a violent reaction.

J. J. Veiga's novel *A casca da serpente* (1989), however, suggests that even an ordinary Canudos would not have escaped eventual destruction. This novel takes us through the process of transforming the Conselheiro from extraordinary to ordinary by making him survive the war and, as the title suggests, shed his old skin. He prays less (giving up religion), shaves his hair and beard, takes a bath, changes clothes so as to seem more "normal," starts telling jokes, and calls for more equality (so that decisions are discussed and shared in a group). He and his followers found a new community, and he dies of old age; a statue memorializes his image. Still, the book ends with the destruction of this second Canudos: "If only ruins remain of that dream and that effort, this does not mean that the dream was absurd. It worked so well that it needed to be demolished by force, much as Canudos was demolished seventy years before. . . . It was dynamited by invaders in 1965 and the pieces [of the statue were] scattered down the mountain . . . , and the land . . . is now a deposit of atomic waste administered by a chemical corporation with fictitious headquarters in Monaco."[101] The transformation of habitable into inhabitable space echoes the flooding of the real second Canudos in 1968 to make way for the Corcorobó Dam.

Veiga's novel slyly textualizes the limits toward making an ordinary Canudos. It suggests that an ordinary Canudos presented no less of an antagonism to the rising nation-state given that things such as the secularization of daily life and measurement systems lay at the heart of the conflict. Canudos's ordinary everyday was perhaps not the common denominator of this new state; it corresponded to a state that no longer existed or that perhaps never had. Theirs was a denominator, if one at all, of a whole, but made up of pieces that are not contemporary, linked to totalities that have fallen into ruins.

CHAPTER FOUR

OS SERTÕES   Nationalism by Elimination

> We assassinated thousands of Brazilians in Canudos . . . [;] all that remained
> was *Rebellion in the Backlands*: deposition, pamphlet, sentence that will punish,
> on the day we realize what we did, the cruelty of our administrators and the
> incompetence of our leaders.
>
> —Afrânio Peixoto, "Euclides da Cunha"

Da Cunha enters the discussion of Canudos after the defeat of the Moreira
César expedition, July 17, 1897, with an article entitled "A nossa vendéia," in
which he prefigures Canudos through Victor Hugo's novel on the Vendée peasant revolt against the postrevolutionary French republic.[1] Because of this article, *O Estado de São Paulo* sent him to cover the last expedition. Public discourse
was by then already organized by a full-fledged prose of counterinsurgency, and
da Cuhna's articles, like much of the coverage by southern newspapers, cast the
fighters of Canudos as strange, alien beings (*taes seres*):

> They live on the brink of starvation. Many soldiers I interviewed affirmed,
> surprised, that once beheaded the jagunço does not spill even a teacup's
> worth of blood. A coarse hyperbole, perhaps, but even so it is singularly
> expressive. They affirm too that the dead fanatic weighs no more than a child.
> A complete inversion of physiological laws is necessary in order to compre-
> hend these beings in which physical force is replaced by the agility of simians,
> sliding through the brush like snakes, quickly sliding, dropping down into

the ravine like specters, dragging a rifle that weighs almost as much as they do—thin, dry, fantastic, their tanned skin glued to their bones—as rough as the skin of mummies.[2]

Da Cunha wrote this on August 10, before he had arrived at Canudos. What he recounts is culled from rumor. The origin of the enunciation is therefore ambiguous. Is this only what the soldiers say? Is he speaking as if he were speaking for the soldiers, bracketing every word in doubt? Or is he revealing his ideas through their mouths? This ventriloquism constitutes one of da Cunha's rhetorical signatures, both in his articles and later in *Os sertões*. While a slight break thus occurs between the place of enunciation and the representations offered, it is difficult to tell whether he is appropriating the words of others, bringing them closer to him, or distancing himself from his words by putting them in the mouths of others. Nonetheless, the suggestion of a distance, however slight, produces a slight accent on the level of the signifier, flagging these representations as representations. The passage just quoted displays one of the main threads in da Cunha's newspaper articles, the attempt to subject an unintelligible reality to a recognizable system of knowledge (physiological laws or the measures of weight), to tame these people, if only through reason and discourse.

[margin note: da Cunha's ventriloquism]

The soldiers, Da Cunha will tell his readers later, affirm that they have never seen the enemy alive, that they don't know the enemy or even how many there are. Six days later he writes, "I understood that many of those who return from those regions understand the situation as little as those who have not gone" (*Diário*, 30). The eyewitness has no privilege in this situation. There is nothing to which one can testify except that lack of information, because it is an upside-down place where regular laws don't apply and the beings that confront them are alien and fantastic. In such an unknown land da Cunha replicates the techniques of description used by the first travelers to America: comparisons. No one comparison is sufficient; a catalog is required, a list including simians, snakes, specters, and mummies. Each comparison singles out a different attribute: they are like animals; they are untimely; they are not really here. These beings can be measured and studied only when dead; then it is possible to affirm—with surprise—that they weigh no more than a child, that they spill no more than a cup of blood when decapitated.

The fantastic rhetoric inked into the previously quoted passage waned when da Cunha reached Canudos and met the Conselheiro's followers face to face (although he may have spent only fifteen or sixteen days in Canudos proper, passing the rest of his time in Monte Santo, the base of military operations).[3] What persists, however, is their intractability to the laws of (da Cunha's) reason, so that this remains their defining characteristic. Da Cunha notes, for instance, their incomprehensible resistance: "There they are indomitable; a thousand or so guns firing at them incessantly and they don't cede. Such heroism is incomprehensible" (*Diário*, 58). He declares that he cannot read the despair he expected to read in their faces: "They do not tremble or lose heart, and they do not deny the beliefs they were taught by the fatal and sinister evangelizer that dragged them into immeasurable disaster" (63). The women seem to have been particularly problematic for him, and when describing them, da Cunha falls back on the hyperbolic vocabulary that he used before meeting the *jagunços*: "Among the women eight are monsters wrapped in repugnant rags, their features are those of a virago, hard, their eyes treacherous or cross-eyed" (69). The women prisoners have "a gaze of strange, almost menacing self-assurance" (63–64). When waylaid with questions, these viragos with treacherous gazes utter answers that incarnate their intractability to reason. Their oblique speech eludes the linear logic that attempts to subjectify them: "And they twist and avoid all questions, victoriously fleeing the most skillful interrogation. And when they feel that the questions assault them too much, inflexibly, when it is no longer possible to prevaricate—there surfaces the tireless, *e eu sei?* ["and I know?" i.e., "I don't know"] bizarre euphemism, one that is more expressive than the simple, positive *no!*" (*Diário*, 65).

Their form of expression itself constitutes a refusal of the rational. When da Cunha describes himself and the army encountering the Conselheiro's followers, he inscribes the interaction as a confrontation between two incompatible rationalities; the interaction just cited, for example, sets the women's oblique form of speech against what da Cunha understands as "simple" and "positive." Da Cunha renders the Conselheiristas' speech intelligible only as sheer resistance to the attempts to penetrate and understand it.

Although the journalist signals a growing and grudging admiration for the Conselheiristas by qualifying "e eu sei?" as more expressive than a simple "no" and by mentioning their heroism and courage, his discourse does not cease to subalternize them. Da Cunha explicitly represents the Conselheiro as sheer negativity in his recourse to a mathematical metaphor when explaining the coexistence of negative and positive attributes, in this case, in the Conselheiro.

> What is striking is the stubbornness of those who want to ennoble him, who want to raise him to the level of simple agitated mediocrity or stupid, almost inoffensive maniac, yanking and pulling him up from the profound depression in which he finds himself as a fatal man, one who has all the attributes that characterize truly great men but diametrically inverted. Everything is relative; to consider him a vulgar fanatic is to ennoble him to some degree. Mathematics offer us a perfect appreciation: Antônio Conselheiro is not null, not a zero, he is even less, he has a negative value that increases according to the absolute value of his formidable madness. That is why, in a previous article, I called him a great man in reverse. (*Diário*, 51)

Da Cunha writes that to be ordinary or inoffensive would be too noble for the Conselheiro. Yet it may be more accurate to say that he *cannot* be ordinary for da Cunha or that da Cunha does not want him ordinary. According to the logic expressed in this passage, understanding the Conselheiro as the lowest within the order of positive integers, as the zero, as vulgar or mediocre, seems to suggest that he pertains to the same symbolic universe. Da Cunha's recourse to negative numbers is a way of representing the Conselheiro's incommensurability to his world. The leader can be represented as great, in other words, and described and admired as a great man, but only in terms of a greatness that takes him ever further from the horizon of da Cunha's world. The mathematical metaphor thus encapsulates the erasure of common ground that da Cunha's prose effects, the way the Conselheiro and, by extension, the inhabitants of Canudos cease to remain ordinary and are forcibly turned into the extraordinary.

Da Cunha characterizes his own locus of enunciation via a Cartesian dictum: "I systematize doubt" (*Diário*, 52). Within the universe of journalism, such a characterization is not far off. Canudos was commonly described as a sphinx by journalists and others in the press, but da Cunha's articles and field notes tend to draw out the mysterious, incomprehensible nature of the conflict:

> We are irresistibly forced to consider the campaign . . . under its primitive, incomprehensible, mysterious face.
> It has been so from the very beginning, from the moment the disasters began, surprising everyone, unexpectedly falling like a lightning bolt, at the very moment that victory and its triumphal ovations were expected. (29)

Da Cunha suggests that this inability to correctly read what was happening lay at the conflict's core. His writings thus reveal the seams by which the pressure that insurgency put on a system of dominance is translated into a pressure on a system of knowledge, into an issue of epistemology.

Sertanejo versus Jagunço

Even as Da Cunha wrote his articles for *O Estado de São Paulo,* he also wrote scattered, haphazard notes in his personal notebook, a text that was published in 1975 as the *Caderneta de campo.* The *Caderneta* does not follow a strict order since notes sometimes begin on one page and then leave off, only to resume some twenty pages later. It contains notes on the history of Bahia that da Cunha copied from a Bahian library while waiting for the expedition to leave Salvador, as well as temperature and pressure readings; lists of miscellaneous *sertanejo* expressions and words that he found fascinating; first drafts of articles he wired to São Paulo; a transcription of a soldier's diary of the campaign events before da Cunha arrived; notes on rumors or facts about the campaign; and transcriptions of a *jagunço's* letter, the Conselheiro's prophecies, and *cordel* literature.

The *Caderneta* is an extremely fragmentary and heterogeneous text, which makes evaluating it as a whole somewhat risky. Nonetheless, it forms a counterpart to da Cunha's dispatches in at least one important sense: whereas as his published articles contain practically nothing on the *sertanejo*, being preoccupied specifically with the conflict and the Conselheiro's followers, the *Caderneta* demonstrates a greater concern with the *sertanejos* da Cunha observed as he advanced toward Canudos. Da Cunha writes on two axes, as it were: the articles deal with the *jagunços,* and the *Caderneta* with the *sertanejos.* At the risk of sounding formulaic, one could say that the articles deal with insurgent subalterns whereas the *Caderneta* represents noninsurgent subalterns. These axes are later linked in *Os sertões,* and this joining will be significant.

Perhaps because the *sertanejos* are not insurgents, the *Caderneta* is not organized strictly according to the logic of a prose of counterinsurgency. There is an anthropological quality to the *Caderneta,* which means that while it is no less ideological than are da Cunha's other writings, it largely forgoes the rhetoric that characterizes writing directed toward an audience. Except for the drafts of articles submitted for publication, for example, it rarely touches on the fantastic: the enemies are referred to simply as *jagunços* or enemies. Although the *sertanejo* does take form as a figure from another world, one that is more primitive, the figure is not unfriendly, not threatening. The *sertanejo* does not rep-

[handwritten margin note: sertanejo not yet a threat]

resent an intractability. Da Cunha's tone is warmly paternalistic: "They know neither bread nor biscuits. Butter is a myth. Coffee and raw brown sugar can be found in one or another store that they call *farm*!"[4] Da Cunha marks the difference between the two worlds by what the other one does not have or know (bread, biscuits); he measures their distance by the mythical aspect of butter. Much like an anthropologist, da Cunha notes the material aspects of their lives, food, work, turns of phrase, vocabulary, and mythology. Summed up in an appreciative list, the *sertanejo* is "good, simple, intelligent, uncultured, suspicious, arrogant, loyal, respectful, parsimonious, not very liberal, devoted or grateful, honest and upright."[5] The *Caderneta* bears witness to da Cunha's discovery of a society that was perhaps not the topsy-turvy wonderland described by the soldiers and first related in his articles but still previously unknown to him.

Da Cunha was hardly the only visitor to look at the region's inhabitants through an anthropological eye. The views of one such visitor, Lélis Piedade, present an instructive contrast. Piedade served as secretary of the Comitê Patriótico da Bahia, a committee originally assembled to clean the honor of Bahia, supposedly sullied by the Canudos War, by proving that good republicans and patriots lived in the state. The committee initially provided services to the soldiers, but by the end of the fighting its task had shifted to providing assistance and homes to women and orphans, including those from Canudos. Piedade took a team into the backlands to set up an outpost for assistance between Bahia and Canudos; he also served as correspondent for the *Jornal de Notícias*. Piedade underwent a transformation similar to da Cunha's in many respects. He initially used prose laden with exalted republican rhetoric, condemning the Conselheiristas as fanatics and traitors, but after he came into contact with children and women from Canudos, he began to express admiration and compassion, referring to the victims from Canudos as brothers and as "filhos da Bahia" worthy of charity. After some weeks in Cansação, he wrote: "How adorable and simple is the sertanejo toilette! If I could distract myself from the purpose that brought me here, I would attempt to write a few pages of study on sertanejo customs."[6]

Despite such similarities, Piedade differed from da Cunha in several significant ways. The chiaroscuros of da Cunha's prose flatten and soften out in the writings of Lélis Piedade, who was from Bahia and for whom the *sertão* was not so distant. Piedade also presents a more romanticized image of the *sertanejo* as one who preserves a purity lost with progress in the cities (a position that da

Cunha, too, would eventually assume). More important, however, he describes the *sertanejo*'s relationship to the land as perfectly adequate:

> And the sertanejos, those men of the countryside, who still conserve the inge-
> nuity and purity of customs and the loyalty of hearts that progress atrophies
> in the capitals, don't complain.
>
>   No, they don't complain. They only want this to end. And they want to
> replant tobacco, beans, corn and see again the green of their fields, the green
> that is the hope of a stable future, the happiness of the hearth to which chil-
> dren and old men return laughing and calm after a day's work.[7]

This passage details a hope for a future return to a previous and more ordinary existence, where beans and corn are planted anew and where grandparents and children, the past and the future, are not so far apart. Change is understood as a recuperation of a past. The envisioned future is a stable rather than revolutionary one.

Da Cunha, however, could not imagine just letting the *sertanejo* be. He continues to read the *sertanejo* as harboring a fatal flaw that is condensed, transformed, and exaggerated in the *jagunço*. Thus, for example, da Cunha describes *sertanejo* mythology as prey to a vision of humans as weak and powerless before the designs of fate or the divinity. This outlook is, he writes, a consequence of their rudimentary forms of life and the persistence of old indigenous and African superstitions. While it is a more elaborated and subtle discourse, this discussion of a mythology of passivity coincides with the lack of agency imputed to the *jagunços* insofar as they are subaltern. In other words, da Cunha again employs a rhetoric of negativity and lack to render the *sertanejos* intelligible, just as he had done earlier, though now in a more anthropological register: "Isolated in the desert, with no social and historical consciousness, helpless before a land that they scarcely dominate with rudimentary industry, their superstitions logically translate the legacy of errors that they have received, the pressure of the unknown, of everything that seems inaccessible to human action, reflecting the whim of God rather than the natural order. (Thus a mythology without heroes, without the audacious acts of men who are transformed by battle so common in religions that elevate men and in which problems serve to prefigure the future heights to which men tend)."[8] For Piedade, then, the *sertanejos* were perfectly capable of farming the *sertão*, whereas for da Cunha, they can scarcely dominate the land. Rather than return to their patterns of life before the invasions (and the promise of a firm, green future), the *sertane-jos* must therefore *change*. The difference marked between *jagunço* and *sertanejo*, between da Cunha's articles and his private notebook, is not so much the difference between public bravado and private doubts and sympathies as it is the difference between da Cunha's open confrontation with an intractability on one level and his attempt to dissolve the intractability on another level through the slow, secret constitution of a terrain over which he unproblematically exerts mastery and authority. The private notebook therefore elaborates a blueprint of the symbolic alchemy he wishes to operate on Canudos.

Os sertões: Deposition, Pamphlet, Sentence

Os sertões was published four years after the Canudos War ended, and many have read this temporal distance as a condition of possibility for the text's vision. In other words, it is read as a text produced after the author's moment of conversion on the way to Canudos. But it is also fundamentally a text written after the moment of insurgency had past, after a space that one could call the space of the museum of Canudos, or Canudos as museum (or national park, for that matter), became possible. Read in this way, *Os sertões* becomes a swan song for the defeated. This aspect of timing should not be underestimated. Although it is still subalternizing, *Os sertões* is not organized by the need to combat insurgency that marked the earlier texts. It has already integrated a project of mastery.

Undoubtedly this explains in part da Cunha's new willingness to harshly criticize the Brazilian government's actions. But what is the nature of this criticism? What distinguished it, for example, from the writings of Afonso Arinos and Manoel Benício, who, like Lélis Piedade, intimated that it would have been better to simply to have left the people of Canudos alone? What distinguished it from the brief story by Lima Barreto entitled "The False Henry V," in which the prophet is not an anachronistic fanatic but an old "mestizo who had some learning" and who proclaims the return of the monarchy? In this story, the holy man's prophecies spread like wildfire, and the cruel and exploitative republic, which has been proclaimed a few years earlier, is overthrown by a popular insurrection that brings to power a so-called prince, Henrique V. As the title suggests, this prince is probably not the old king's son. The irrelevance of lineage, however, means that the insurrection is at heart a popular rather than monarchist one.[9] If Nicolau Sevcenko is right to label this story an "*Os Sertões* in reverse,"[10] then neither of these two cleverly superimposed options (monarchist restoration and popular revolution) is conceivable for da Cunha. What, then, is da Cunha criticizing?

One of da Cunha's primary targets is the interpretation of the conflict as an antagonism between republicanism and monarchism, where all public discussion of the conflict is dominated by the outcry "The Republic was in danger; the Republic must be saved: this was the one cry that arose above the general delirium."[11] As a battlefield correspondent, da Cunha had himself voiced that cry. He too had been prey to the theories of a vast monarchist conspiracy behind the *sertanejo* insurgency. But in hindsight he ascribes this reaction to incomprehension, panic, and irrationality:[12]

> To begin with, there was widespread alarm; and, in the second place, the public indulged in the wildest variety of conjectures in an effort to explain how it was that so numerous and well equipped a force with a commander of such renown should have met with so crushing a defeat. Out of all this mental confusion there came the idea, at first vaguely voiced by a few individuals here and there but gradually growing into a firm conviction, that the riotous backlanders were not alone in their rebellion against the government but that they represented, rather, the vanguard of unknown phalanxes that were likely to spring up suddenly, everywhere at once, and bear down upon the new regime. And inasmuch as there were to be found in the federal and state capitals, some years back, half-a-dozen platonic revolutionaries of a tame and dreamy sort who were engaged in a futile propaganda for the restoration of the monarchy, this circumstance was taken as the point of departure for a most unproductive line of reasoning. (*Rebellion*, 277–78)

According to da Cunha, the government and the public failed to perceive that the confict could not be understood on the terrain of the political: "to attribute the backlands crisis to a political conspiracy of any kind is to reveal a glaring ignorance of the natural conditions surrounding our race" (280).

For da Cunha, the real antagonism at the heart of the conflict showed itself through the blindness of the Conselheiristas. While they understood the conflict as a battle between republic and monarchy, these terms designated an entirely different set of signifieds for them:

> He preached against the Republic; there is no denying that. This antagonism was an inevitable derivative of his mystic exacerbation, a variant of his religious delirium that was forced upon him. Yet he did not display the faintest

trace of a political intuition; for your jagunço is quite as inept at understanding the republican form of government as he is the constitutional monarchy.
Both to him are abstractions, beyond the reach of his intelligence. He is
instinctively opposed to both of them, since he is in that phase of evolution in
which the only rule he can conceive is that of a priestly or a warrior chieftain.
(*Rebellion*, 160–61)

Da Cunha essentially argues that the antagonism took the form of a religious
rather than political conflict for the Conselheiristas. They understood the republic not as one political form among others but as the incarnation of evil. It
could not have been otherwise, he writes, for they were too barbaric to comprehend the abstraction that marked both the republican and the monarchical-
constitutional forms. The Conselheiristas were capable of grasping only more
primitive form of government, such as that of a warrior or priestly chief. That,
in fact, was how they lived their own relationship to the Conselheiro in da
Cunha's estimation: Canudos was a barbarous clan ruled by a leader whose arbitrary decisions were law.[13] In fact, then, despite the monarchy's disinterest in
the Conselheiro, da Cunha maintains that he was *by nature* the adversary of the
monarchy, too. This antagonism had not manifested itself during the monarchy simply because the Portuguese and Brazilian courts were too distant to care
(assuming thus that the monarchy had existed in name alone over great parts
of the Brazilian territory).

The matrix for this perspective—the idea that the Conselheiro and his followers were too barbaric to comprehend the abstraction of the modern state
form—is first elaborated by Raimundo Nina Rodrigues (1862–1906), the
Brazilian psychiatrist and anthropologist and founder of the Escola Bahiana
of criminology. (Nina Rodrigues had already published the essay "A locura
epidêmica de Canudos. Antônio Conselheiro e os jagunços," *Revista Brasileira*
[1897].) Nina Rodrigues was greatly influenced by Cesare Lombroso, who had
associated race and phenotype with innate tendencies to commit crimes. Lombroso's method involved measuring the cranium and other body parts to identify physical characteristics that he claimed indicate evolutionary degeneracy
and hence criminality. Biological notions of evolutionary and often racial determinism were thus used to produce concrete social policies (e.g., laws governing
crime).

Indeed, Nina Rodrigues, who was well respected in Brazil, was given the
honor of studying the Conselheiro's skull after his body had been exhumed

and his severed head displayed on a pike by soldiers on their homecoming victory parade. The result (published in "A locura das multidões") was perhaps disappointing. The skull was normal, or more precisely, it was the skull not of a psychopath but of a mestizo: "The skull of Antônio Conselheiro did not present any anomaly that would reveal traces of degeneration: it is the skull of a mestizo which combines anthropological characters of different races."[14] Nonetheless, these racial origins, supposedly inscribed like stigmata on the skull, reveal his "normality" to have been the normality of another, more barbarous and primitive epoch. The deliriums of the Conselheiro and his followers, Nina Rodrigues wrote, "revive or repeat phenomena, feelings or beliefs that were perfectly normal in distant times or in primitive phases of social evolution."[15] Da Cunha's argument that the Canudenses belonged not to the present Brazil but to another place and time is taken, therefore, directly from Nina Rodrigues.

In fact, da Cunha often seems to copy Nina Rodrigues almost word for word. It was Nina Rodrigues, for example, who first voiced the argument that the Conselheiro and his followers could comprehend only a personal, fetishistic relationship to power—which for Nina Rodrigues (unlike da Cunha) meant that monarchism was more legible to them—because they were stuck in an inferior moment of social evolution. They lacked, he writes, "the precise mental capacity to comprehend and accept the substitution of the concrete representation of power by the abstraction he incarnates."[16] They would, moreover, continue to relate to their leaders as their "kings," just as they saw their priests and religious images as gods, and should not be required to contemplate the concept of the republican federation as the guarantor of "a future political unity of a vast country in which there necessarily coexist a wide variety of people with different customs."[17] They bear, in other words, the characteristics of the irrational mob or crowd—as opposed to a society or a public—as that concept took shape in late nineteenth-century crowd psychology.[18]

Following Nina Rodrigues, da Cunha shifts the argument away from a question of politics. In effect he restricts the term *politics* to conflicts within a terrain constituted by the possibility of different state forms. Both sides' use of the same signifiers (republic vs. monarchy) to describe the conflict thus produced the misleading impression that the battle was being waged on the same terrain, whereas the real problem was the lack of a common terrain on which to fight. Isolated and abandoned for centuries, the *jagunços* could do nothing other than what they did: "The case, as we have already seen, is a good deal more complex and interesting than that. Isolated in space and time, the jagunço, being an ethnic anachronism, could do only what he did do—that is, combat, and combat in a terrible fashion, the nation which, after having cast him off for three centuries almost, suddenly sought to raise him to our own state of enlightenment at the point of the bayonet, revealing to him the brilliancy of our civilization in the blinding flash of cannons" (*Rebellion*, 280).

This will be the core of Da Cunha's interpretation of the conflict: the lack of a common terrain or a common temporality within the "geographic fiction" of Brazil. Whereas railway stations are normally taken as the "mark of modern progress," places where differences are subsumed under a teleological temporalization, in Brazil they become places of confrontation between two societies, "one wholly alien to the other": "The leather-clad vaqueiro will emerge from the caatinga, make his way into the ugly-looking settlement, and halt his nag beside the rails where natives of the seaboard pass, unaware of his existence" (*Rebellion*, 405). This image perfectly exemplifies what the anthropologist Johannes Fabian terms "the denial of coevalness"—that is, the tendency in both colonial and later anthropological discourse to deny that the subject and object of discourse share the same time.[19] Under the logic identified by Fabian, the world appears "as an agglomeration of inequivalent temporalities, where co-existing entities failed to come face to face and to claim the same moment of time in history."[20] Even when the *sertanejos* and coastal urbanites meet at the same location—at a place where paths cross—they are unable to "come face to face" and continue to inhabit parallel universes. Even when they share the same time and place, they do not really share the same time and place. Their everyday realities are absolutely incommensurable.

Needless to say, this was not the only possible interpretation of the conflict. Many of da Cunha's and Nina Rodrigues's contemporaries did not perceive the people of Canudos as existing outside the time and space of the Brazilian nation-state. César Zama, a Bahian partisan of Governor Luís Viana, for example, understood the conflict as a difference of political opinion. He maintained that the Conselheiro and his followers had the right to proclaim themselves monarchists precisely *because* they were citizens of the Brazilian nation-state. The right to hold differing political views was not a threat to a democratic republic but one of its fundamental elements:

> There was nothing particularly extraordinary in the case of Antônio Consel-heiro and those who followed him. We all know the kind of life they lead: they plant, they harvest, they raise animals, build and pray.

Rude, ignorant, fanatically dedicated to their leader, whom they believed a saint, they did not worry about politics.

Antônio Conselheiro, however, admitted to being a monarchist. This was his right, sacred right, that no one can contest in a democratic republican regime. There was no act—either by him or his followers—which allows one to presume that they threatened the government of the Republic.[21]

For Zama, their status as citizens of the Brazilian nation-state meant that any violation the Conselheiristas committed should be viewed as internal to the state, not external to it. Consequently, if they had been judged guilty of a crime, it was a matter for the police and not for the army, which had been "created to maintain the institutions, when attacked, and defend the honor of a nation, when insulted."[22] And if they were not guilty of a crime, then they should have been defended by the state, not persecuted by it: "If the Union had to intervene, it should have done so only to protect the persecuted against the persecutors. The federal constitution does not make distinctions: all Brazilians are guaranteed their natural, civil and political rights. . . . What happened in Bahia was more than abnormal: a city of more than twenty thousand souls defended—unguibus et rostris—their right to life and property against an audacious, high-handed government who had no notion at all of its responsibilities."[23]

One could argue that Zama errs by dissolving the challenge of the Conselheiro and his people into a liberal defense of property and life and refusing therefore to acknowledge that there are other, more radical positions from which to quarrel with the new republican government. Nonetheless, Zama's position highlights by contrast certain elements of da Cunha's argument. Most notably for my purposes, Zama inverts the place of normality and abnormality in da Cunha's interpretation of the situation. For Zama, the Conselheiro and his people were perfectly normal, while the way they were deemed external to the Brazilian nation-state was abnormal. Da Cunha, who shared with Zama the new idea of the army as something other than a large police force, was not insensible to the ironies of asking the army to undertake this kind of mission and stage, as it were, the invasion of a foreign territory. But for da Cunha, the Conselheiristas had to be external to Brazil. This very externality revealed Brazil to be a "geographic fiction."[24]

When da Cunha characterizes the campaign against Canudos as a crime, therefore, he is referring to the government's use of violence to force the *jagunços* into a national reality that was not yet theirs, which ended up destroying them.

The ultimate goal should have been something else—incorporation through propaganda, perhaps, or hegemony rather than domination or elimination. Such a project would have decriminalized the violence of the war, legitimizing what ended up being a stupid and inglorious campaign. But its dependence on violence is impossible to miss in da Cunha's metaphor of conquest since propaganda follows literally on the heels of artillery:

> It was plain that the Canudos Campaign must have a higher objective than the stupid and inglorious one of merely wiping out a backlands settlement. There was a more serious enemy to be combated, in a warfare of a slower and more worthy kind. This entire campaign would be a crime, a futile and a barbarous one, if we were not to take advantage of the paths opened by the artillery, by following up our cannon with a constant, stubborn and persistent campaign of education [literally, "propaganda"], with the object of drawing these rude and backward fellow-countrymen of ours into the current of our times and our own national life. (*Rebellion*, 408)

Da Cunha's wartime articles had already proposed this solution. On August 15 he had advanced what would become the main hypothesis of *Os sertões*:

> Those who govern recognize the grave problems that are the result, first, of our deplorable lack of knowledge about the interior unknown backlands, and second, of the intellectual degradation in which those who inhabit them live.
>
> This last is, above all, the permanent enemy.
>
> When the forces that converge there now return victorious—let us complete the victory.
>
> Let these roads, now opened by the passage of glorious battalions, these roads which will be deserted and silent tomorrow, lead the way, after the fight, to an anonymous hero, without noisy triumphs, but who will be the real winner: Sir School. (*Diário*, 26)

What has changed between these two passages besides the fact that the battalions, though first deemed glorious and victorious, are later seen to have effected nothing more than the stupid and inglorious destruction of a people? In both cases, da Cunha calls for a project of territorializing new lands, a project possible only after the artillery opens roads. In both cases, this project supplements the violence of the war. In the former version, it will complete a victory already won; in the latter, it will merely decriminalize an operation that has already taken place (and is no longer a victory). The first is a civilizing mission narrowly defined as a triumph of education over ignorance; the second has the broader and rather paradoxical aim of incorporating compatriots into an existence and temporality that still is not theirs. The government must constitute the missing common ground. It must teach the people to be represented by itself (through schools or other means of extending an ideological hegemony). For da Cunha, this meant that the *jagunços* had to become republicans, too. They had to share the nation's identity.

We thus should not explain the differences between da Cunha's wartime articles and *Os sertões* in terms of a move away from his earlier liberal-republican ideology, as Roberto Ventura has suggested we do:

> More notable than the passage from journalism to historiographic essay is his denunciation of the campaign as a "crime," which makes him distance himself from the metaphor of Vendée and of the liberal-republican ideology. His live coverage of the final moments of the war mean that, interspersed between the articles from 1897 and the book of 1902, is a contact with the reality of Canudos, not mediated by republican propaganda, which produces an "about-face of opinion" (W. N. Galvão) through the reversal of his previous horizon of expectations and the consequent introduction, in his discourse, of a critical difference with republicanism, both in its democratic-representative version (civilian) as well as in its Jacobin-dictatorial (militarist) current.[25]

Although da Cunha might have criticized the errors of the new republican government and even have distanced himself from particular versions of republicanism then current in Brazil, he both articulates and embodies a modern state project, and this explains why his text became canonical.

Imagining the State

One can read in a number of ways how *Os sertões* is saturated at its most fundamental structures by a modern nation-state project. One might note, for example, the various places that the text assumes what, following Jens Anderman's study, I will call the "optic of the state." Anderman borrows the concept of perspective from Erwin Panofsky's analysis of Renaissance optics ("a way of setting subjects and objects up for one another and of making calculable the terms of their mutual engagement")[26] to describe how the state manifests itself visually in photographs, maps, and museums in nineteenth-century Brazil and Argentina. Like a museum, then, *Os sertões* assumes a vantage point characterized by an organizing principle of the totality of society, over and above the collection of institutions of government, a central eye surveying the whole and organizing information according to its interests. Sevcenko suggests that such a perspective is not unique to da Cunha but characteristic of a type of writing that circulated at the time: "This literature emerged organized as if its dual visual perspective . . . had a starting point in space and as if this point coincided with the nucleus of political power. These intellectuals rethought the country as if their gaze were located in the very center of decisions, calculating its possibilities, measuring its real limits."[27]

In good nineteenth-century style, da Cunha begins his book by staging an imaginary observer's entrance into the *sertão* after providing a panoramic geological view of Brazil under the authority of a Foucauldian "Speaking Gaze": surveying, classifying, *representing*. By venturing into the territories of history, sociology, geography, and poetry, da Cunha's text mimics newly forming nation-states' support for the study of history, philology, anthropology, and archaeology to justify their uniform organization of wide tracts of land inhabited by peoples bearing specific characteristics (e.g., of race, history, tradition, language, religion, or environment).[28] Da Cunha's career as a civil engineer prepared him for this perspective. Part of the text's early authority, then, arises from its sweeping encyclopedic range and its fusion of poorly differentiated discursive systems, both of them efforts to map and incorporate Brazil's land and people.

Many other moments similarly reveal the idea of a unified people represented by a state to be among the book's governing coordinates. Although da Cunha clearly indicates that he does not share the dominant interpretation produced by the government and the populace at large, the passage where he describes the general outcry (The Republic is in danger!) unmistakably shows the materialization of a unity in response to Canudos:

> The governors and congresses of the states and the municipal corporations
> continued to clamor loudly for vengeance. All the official pronouncements,
> couched in the same resounding phrases, were merely variations on a single,
> monotonous theme, whose burden was that the enemies of the Republic,
> armed by the monarchist leaders, must be crushed. Like the inhabitants of
> the federal capital, the people of the other cities held meetings, listened to
> speeches, and adopted resolutions supporting the government in whatever
> measures it might see fit to take by way of avenging the disgrace that had
> been inflicted upon the army and (the conjunction is equal to a hundred

eloquent pages) the fatherland. A period of national mourning was declared, and formal action to this effect was registered in the minutes of the municipal councils of the most remote towns and villages. There were masses for the dead in all the churches. (*Rebellion*, 283)

Despite da Cunha's disagreement with the "monotonous theme" of conquest, this passage strikingly instantiates a harmony and even unity among different levels and institutions of government (the governors of states, congresses, and municipal corporations down to the most remote municipal sessions). The fantasy goes even further, to the extent that such synchronization not only takes place among different organs of government but seeps down to the level of the "people," who "understand" what is at stake and support the government. The government's monotone message represents them, or they accept being represented by that message. Mourning the republican dead cements the identity between government and people, even in the most remote of churches. Additionally, railroads and telegraph lines—the states' veins and arteries—are activated: "Alarmed . . . , the population prepared to flee. Locomotives with their fires going stood in readiness in the railway stations. All the able-bodied inhabitants who were fit for combat duty were pressed into service. Meanwhile, the telegraph lines carried to all parts of the country the news of this prelude to the backlands war" (*Rebellion*, 188). These are not isolated examples, for numerous other passages slip into similar representations of unity, as when, for example, da Cunha describes a "public opinion" being expressed in the press and in the streets or when he describes how the city of Salvador reacted to the sight of the wounded soldiers returning from Canudos. Behind *Os sertões*, under it and organizing it, therefore, one can discern the faintly outlined idea of the unified Brazilian people, a unity that is to a large degree produced by the very battles being fought.

This regulating ideal rules da Cunha's criticism against the existing government insofar as the state fails to live up to its name. Although *Os sertões* offers a fantasy in which the nation-state coalesces at different moments in response to the threat Canudos posed, the problem it articulates is that the republic, which was proclaimed over a decade earlier, existed in name only. *Os sertões* clearly argues that the people of Canudos were not the only ones who needed to be incorporated into the modern nation-state. The people of Canudos were simply the most obvious manifestations of a more widespread problem in Brazil.

failure of the state

This logic of deficiencies and lacks occurs everywhere in the text. Before turning to the question of territory and to Brazil as a "geographic fiction," then, I want to focus on da Cunha's descriptions of the army and of the lack of a proper relationship between people and government in Brazil. The army is a particularly interesting example, for his text portrays an army that failed to live up to its supposed transformation from a holding ground for shiftless and criminal men to a source of national pride and unity, a transformation effected through a new rhetoric that, according to Peter Beattie, gained ground internationally in the late eighteenth century and that "portrayed the ideal male citizen as a soldier who would willingly lay down his life for love of country to defend national honor. It lent new romance and respectability to soldiering." Under the new paradigm, the armed forces attained a "quasi-mystical" status as "an embodiment of the nation or the 'nation in arms.'"[29] In other words, da Cunha (who had studied at the Escola Militar da Praia Vermelha but left the military after 1894) measures the Brazilian army against this new, largely French and German model of the military and its attending rhetoric and finds it wanting. The Brazilian soldier, he says, was "incapable of imitating the Prussian . . . going in and coming out with a pedometer on his boot"; "He is disorderly, tumultuous, rowdy, a terrible but heroic blackguard" (*Rebellion*, 250). In terms of this new ideal, Brazil's army does not exist:

> We did not have an army, in the real sense of the term, which implies not merely so many thousands of men and rifles, but, what is of greater worth, an administrative, technical and tactical command, embracing all branches of the service from the transport of vehicles to the higher strategy of campaigns—in brief, an organization par excellence for the planning of military operations.
>
> As it was, everything was lacking. There was no organized supply service, and, as a consequences, in a provisional base of operations connected by railway line with the seacoast it was impossible to obtain rations. There was no transport service capable of handling nearly a hundred tons of munitions of war. And finally, there were no soldiers; the bearers of arms that detrained here did not come from rifle ranges or drill grounds. The battalions, moreover, were incomplete, numbering less than companies, their equipment was in very bad shape, and the men lacked the most elementary notions of military tactics. It was necessary to fill out the battalions, to equip them, to clothe them, to supply them with munitions, and train and instruct them. (289)

This passage foregrounds the larger organizational and administrative structures—administration, coordinated services, strategy, a network of transportation—necessary for a modern army. Moreover, as the last lines indicates, the lack of these modern structures meant the absence of the men who should have filled the places within them—namely, soldiers, the majority of whom, da Cunha says, were rowdy and disorderly and came "from the same racial stock as the backwoodsman" (269). Indeed, the soldiers mirrored the inhabitants of Canudos in their tendency to become a crowd, mob, or multitude, so that only the "moral strength of a commander" could mold them into the organized killing machines that the modern army needed:

> Any army is, first of all, a multitude, a "mass of heterogeneous elements in which one has but to strike a spark of passion, and there is a sudden metamorphosis, a kind of spontaneous generation, by virtue of which thousands of different individuals become a single animal, a nameless monster of the wilds, going forward to a given objective with an irresistible finality." Only the moral strength of a commander can prevent this deplorable transformation, by clearly and firmly imposing a directive which will bring order out of chaos. The great strategists have instinctively realized that the first victory to be won in war lies in overcoming this violent emotional contagion, this undependable state of feeling on the part of the troops. Which with equal intensity will impel a man to face the gravest of perils or to take refuge in flight. A plan of war as drawn up with a compass on a map calls for passionless souls—killing machines—steadily functioning within lines that are pre-established. Moreira Cesar's soldiers, however, were far from having attained this sinister ideal. (253)

Instead of the leadership necessary for transforming a multitude into an army, then, there was only disorganization and disorder, particularly for the men of the third expedition under the epileptic Moreira César. To a large extent, the earlier derogatory perspectives on the army and its men pointed out by Beattie govern the representations of the soldiers. In one passage, for instance, da Cunha projects the fetishism that Nina Rodrigues identifies as a marker of the *sertanejos'* primitive state onto the soldiers themselves: "These modern Knights Templar . . . fought with the same immovable faith as their prototypes of old. [They] wore above their hearts a medal bearing the likeness of Marshal Floriano Peixoto, whose memory they saluted in death. They were, in brief, displaying the same delirious enthusiasm, the same absolute self-dedication, and the same fanatic aberrations as did the jagunços when they shouted for the merciful and miracle-working Good Jesus as they went to their death in battle" (*Rebellion*, 365–66). The soldiers' fetishistic relationship with the republic (materialized in the medal depicting Marshal Floriano) is such that they will try to force the *jangunços* to say "long live the Republic" before cutting their throats. When the soldiers cover the walls of *sertanejo* houses with graffiti on their return journey, these "rude chroniclers" leave behind "incredible lampoons and pasquinades intermingled with the most revolting pornography and deep cries of despair, but without a sentence or a phrase anywhere that was worthy of a man" (411–12). This was just one of the many ways in which the soldiers were portrayed as mirror images of their *jagunço* brothers, an equivalence present early on that increased throughout the conflict. Drawing out the significance of the graffiti, da Cunha concludes that it reveals the "major scandal" in Brazilian history, one he thinks future historians will try to cover up by portraying the campaign in glowing terms. If these "outrageous and indestructible palimpsests" reveal the true nature of the war, however, it is because they show the state institutions' inability to live up to the name of a republic. Not even its soldiers have been guided into the time and place of a modern Brazilian nation-state.

The army provides but one among the many examples of modern representative government's failures in Brazil; da Cunha often attributes these failures to a lack of formal structures and institutions but just as often blames a "subject material" that falls short of that which the state and its various apparatuses should represent. If the soldiers can't live up to the Prussian ideal of the army, still less can the Brazilian people (who are not yet a people) find themselves represented by the new republic. For example, da Cunha describes Canudos as "the provisional headquarters of the praetorian guard of gangsters, who would set out from there for certain definite points to reinforce by club and trigger the sovereign will of the people as expressed in the triumphant imbecility of the first petty chieftain who came along, by the tearing-up of records and by those periodical brawls appointed by law, under the name of 'elections'— a euphemism which with us is the most striking instance to be found of the daring misuse of language. Our secondhand civilization, as always, was serving to regiment the banditry of the backlands" (*Rebellion*, 153). As this passage registers, da Cunha, like many in central government and the intellectual elite throughout the nineteenth century, attributes electoral violence to the backwardness of the people in the backlands and their "petty chieftains" rather than to an increasingly centralized and intrusive state machine. If the word *elections*, as well as the mechanism of democratic representation it signifies, becomes a borrowed veneer that overlies the same violent practices of domination already endemic to northeastern Brazil, if these borrowed or copied ideals do not work, then the fault lies not with the ideals but with the backlands people.

This logic is particularly explicit in a long passage in which da Cunha scathingly condemns the disorder of the early years of the republic.[30]

> Still suffering from the lamentable consequences of a bloody civil war which had come to a close amid an uninterrupted series of seditions and revolts that had lasted since the first days of the new regime, Brazilian society in 1897 was one highly favorable to the work of revolutionary and disruptive elements. Whoever later shall undertake, in the light of significant documents, to weigh and define the interesting psychology of this era will have to bring out the inadaptability of the people to the higher legislation of the newly inaugurated political regime.... The civil government set up in 1894 did not possess the essential basis of an organized public opinion. It found the nation divided into victors and vanquished; and it remained impotent when it came to correcting a situation which, without being openly revolutionary, was certainly not normal, and in dealing with which a resort to force and a reliance upon the tranquil influence of laws were alike unavailing. It was faced with a society which, proceeding by leaps and bounds from conditions of the utmost sloth to those of the most rigid discipline, from incessant conspiracies to states of siege, reflected the sharp contrast that prevailed between its lack of organization on the intellectual side and its high degree of political organization which the people were not capable of comprehending. And, inasmuch as it was not possible to substitute the slow process of evolution in elevating the intellectual to the level of the political, what inevitably happened was that the higher significance of the democratic principles became debased—turned into sophistries, inverted, annulled. (*Rebellion*, 225)

The division and disorganization in which Brazil found itself went hand in hand with a lack of correspondence between people and state, for the people in question could not comprehend and adapt to a "higher" political organization. In this sense, the republic is borrowed from civilization. It is, like the word *elections*, a form or name that is out of place and does not represent the actually existing people in Brazil. Yet this does not disqualify the nation-state project as a project. Da Cunha recurs to a logic of temporalization and representation to suture the gap between model and reality. As Lloyd and Thomas suggest in *Culture and the State*, the state always "expresses at a higher level the still developing essence of that people."[31] In other words, it represents the people as they will be—or rather, as they should be, since this passage implies that the natural evolutionary process can be interrupted and inverted, as when out-of-place democratic principles degenerate in Brazil instead of exerting a civilizing effect.

Canudos thus occupies an unstable place in *Os sertões*. On the one hand, Canudos is not what "we" (i.e., modern Brazilians) are but rather the *jagunço* who is not seen by the passing train. On the other hand, it is just a more visible manifestation of something "we" need to eliminate, an external projection of internal lacks. Canudos thus begins to function in da Cunha's text as a key signifier of a past that must be eliminated in a larger narrative. It ceases to be simply a city: "They are the remainders of an old, backward society whose capital is the mud-hut city of the jagunços" (*Diário*, 25). It is, as it were, an old skin to be shed in the process of growth. Such teleology is another reason the conflict is not one of differing political projects, for there is no possibility of choice. Da Cunha has little doubt about the future directions: "We are condemned to civilization. Either we shall progress or we shall perish" (*Rebellion*, 76). Nonetheless, though the conflict is not an issue of competing political projects, it results from the emergence of the Republic, understood not as a political project but simply as the necessary future. Canudos is Brazil's past, like a seed from the days of the pharaohs that, long hidden in the pyramids' shadows, has sprouted after having been exposed to light—that is, the republic, "a more brilliant and elevated social situation, defined by a new political form" (*Diário*, 23–24). For da Cunha, the war destroyed not "the sinister village of Canudos" but "our exasperating apathy, our morbid indifference to the future, our undefinable religiosity spread in strange superstitions, our narrow concept of nation, badly outlined in the inconsistency of a population scattered about in a vast and poorly known country" (*Diário*, 25). The conflict is turned into a process of cleansing a narrow, fetishistic notion of nationhood unequal to the vast, unknown country to which it supposedly corresponds.

Elections, democracy, a functioning army, a united territory, a united society: this is what da Cunha wants, and these dreams of modernization are to be actualized through the institution of the republican state. They perhaps do not yet exist in Brazil; such notions are perhaps out of place. But they still function as the regulating ideals. Da Cunha is no anarchist; rather, he desires greater organization, greater unity, greater centralization (a better system of railroads), real elections, and a true identity between people and government, and he believes that the future should lie in that direction. Although da Cunha perhaps does not speak from the "state" as it exists in Brazil at the time of the Canudos War, he may be speaking from what he thinks to be the future Brazilian state. The *sertão* is the linchpin of that future.

The Land

The real turn in da Cunha's writings is signaled by the change of the text's title from the originally planned *A nossa vendéia* (the title da Cunha had used for his first article on the war) to *Os sertões*. It corresponds to the main difference between his first writings and *Os sertões*—namely, a consideration of the land itself expressed in the book's first section, entitled "The Land."[32] *Os sertões* thus begins with a discussion of Brazilian geography and the geography, geology, landscape, and climate of the *sertão*. The second section ("The Man") comprises a historical discussion of race in Brazil and the specific ethnic type of the *sertanejo* (including traditions, religions, and ways of life), as well as an analysis of the Conselheiro (the document of atavism), Canudos, and the origins of the conflict. The book culminates in the third section ("The Struggle") with an account of the armed confrontations. While "The Struggle" and "The Man" draw heavily on his articles, "The Land" is almost entirely new, barely hinted at before in measurements of latitude, precipitation, and climate jotted down in his *Caderneta*. This division is likely drawn from Hippolyte Taine's *Origines de la France contemporaine* and his own tripartite model for interpreting civilization historically: race, milieu, moment (da Cunha puts milieu first, however, and makes the notion of environment literal).[33] With the exception of Costa Lima, though, critics have paid little attention to the first section. The tripartite division is governed, on the most obvious level, by two relations. First, the move from land to man to struggle is structured by a move from the general to the particular. Second, it follows a line of causality, making the conflict partly due, at some level, to geography. In other words, the real problem rendered manifest by the Canudos War was not simply the existence of archaic elements here and there but the very heterogeneity of Brazil, the lack of a single territory and people, and the real task was not to eliminate Canudos but to produce a people and a territory. But what exactly is the relationship between "people" and "territory," and what is the nature of the conjunction binding them?

Geography and its determining effects play two roles in this argument.

First, it is one of the principal causes for Brazil's heterogeneity:

> We do not possess unity of race, and it is possible we shall never possess
> it. We are predestined to form a historic race in the future, providing the
> autonomy of our national life endures long enough to permit it. In this
> respect we are inverting the natural order of events. Our biological evolution
> demands the guaranty of social evolution. . . . This is scarcely suggested . . .
> by the heterogeneity of our ancestral elements, but they are reinforced by
> another element equally ponderable: a physical milieu that is wide and varied
> and, added to this, varied historical situations which in large part flow from
> that milieu. (*Rebellion*, 54)

This wide and varied physical milieu contains within it sizable tracts of land
that remain largely unknown. A vast extension of territory shows up on Brazil's
best maps as an "expressive blank, a hiatus labeled *Terra Ignota*, a mere scrawl
indicating a problematic river or an idealized mountain range" (9).

By calling attention to da Cunha's use of the word *ignota* instead of the
more common *desconhecida*, Costa Lima suggests that da Cunha conceived of
the *sertão* as something not amenable to a previous scientific grid, but without
doubting the possibility of molding new instruments to serve the totalizing
discourse of science:

> The experience of Canudos conjures up for him a land that remains unknow-
> able and is not simply unknown. It would be unknown if it had not yet been
> explored and measured by existing instruments. It is unknowable because it
> needs to mold its own instruments. Without a doubt, this idea of science as
> something which remains to be accomplished does not oppose the connota-
> tion of a superior and totalizing discourse, which characterizes the general-
> ized notion taken up by Euclides with religious fervor. But it did oppose the
> idea that the science that was needed was merely an application to unknown
> objects.[34]

The *sertão* is *terra ignota*, then, not only because has it not been described
through known methods of classification but because it eludes certain universalizing classificatory systems already in place. The *sertão* is "a geographical category that Hegel does not mention" (*Rebellion*, 39).

The *sertão* escapes Hegel's universalizing categories (e.g., desert, valley,
coast/islands) because it is hybrid, or better, because it oscillates violently, un-

stably, between two of those categories, desert and valley, depending on the season. It is thus both "barbarically sterile" and "marvelously exuberant." With the rain (sometimes as torrential and violent as the prolonged sun), the desolation of the martyred desert is transfigured in "fantastic mutations" into a fertile valley: "It is one vast garden without an owner." Then, says da Cunha, "all this comes to an end. The days of torture return; the atmosphere is asphyxiating; the soil is hard as rock, the flora is stripped bare; and on those occasions when summer meets summer without the intermittency of rain—the dreadful spasm of the drought. Nature here rejoices in a play of antithesis (*Rebellion*, 41)." This play of antitheses, this dynamic of violent oscillations that the book first associates with the climate of the backlands, goes on to contaminate the people who live there; just as the Conselheiro oscillates between madness and greatness (anything but the banal zero), so the *sertanejo* is a "translation" of the extremes between which the *sertão* oscillates. He is a Hercules-Quasimodo who cycles between beauty and ugliness, strength and weakness, violent outbursts and passivity, tirelessness and exhaustion, victory and defeat, devotion and cruelty. Indeed, the entire text projects or performs the image of a plural world fraught with conflicts, which has led many critics to describe it as baroque or to call da Cunha a "poet of conflict," one whose own way of writing performs this ideal through a polyphonic approach, which rarely gives way to the "I."[35]

Costa Lima spatializes some of these contrasts or conflicts as taking place on different registers of discourse. What Costa Lima calls the subscene of *Os sertões* makes its appearance through metaphors that interrupt the scientific discourse just as mirages or illusions interrupt the hegemony of sight. Presented in poetic metaphors, as so many "as ifs" to embellish the account, the Speaking Gaze does not waver in its authority, but its sight is in any case no longer merely transparent. Two particularly suggestive mirages or illusions condense Costa Lima's subscene: the *sertão* as primordial newness and the *sertão* as ancient. On the one hand, da Cunha claims the *sertão* to have been the last part of the South American continent to have emerged from ocean waters:

> Beating against it for a long time, while the rest of the country to the south was already above water and had assumed its present form—beating against it, eroding it, pulverizing it, swirling away to the west and carrying off all the products of erosion, the mighty current continued working on this corner of Baía, until, in accordance with the general movement of the lands, the region

had wholly emerged and had become the shapeless heap of mountainous
ruins that it is today.

...We may well believe that the region, in this incipient stage, was still
preparing itself for life; the lichen was still attacking the rock and fertilizing
the earth. (*Rebellion*, 17)

This passage casts the *sertão* as newness itself emerging into the world,
still embryonic, half-formed, preparing itself for life. Other passages, however, show it as traversed by markers of past life, by ruins. Although this tor-
mented landscape is recently emerged from the bottom of the ocean, what is
foregrounded is its relationship to its past, rather than to a coming future:
"However inexpert the observer may be, upon leaving behind him the majestic
perspectives which unfold to the south and exchanging them here for the moving sight of Nature in torment, he cannot but have the persisting impression
of treading the newly upraised bed of a sea long extinct, which still preserves,
stereotyped in its rigid folds, the agitation of the wave and the stormy deeps"
(15). In the next fragment, the image of ruin is complicated as being the ruin of
"civilization" rather than older geological stages: "gneiss hillocks, capriciously
rent into almost geometric planes, which resemble square blocks, and which
may be seen rising at various points, giving one the illusion at times of suddenly finding himself amid the lonely and deserted ruins of a majestic castle"
(*Rebellion*, 14).

The images of the sea floor and ruins create oxymorons that Costa Lima
expresses in formulas such as "ruin which ferments" or "fecund leftover."[36]
They are contradictory and unintelligible according to perceptual categories,
which Costa Lima takes as proof that mimesis functions in the subscene: "The
machine of *mimesis* operates by overcoming the likenesses on which it initially
rested, so that a final image emerges in which what dominates is something incomprehensible according to the point of view of exclusively perceptual categories."[37] Something remains consistent in this inconsistency, however, namely,
the fragmentary nature of either image—the *sertão* is incomplete because it is a
"not-yet" or because it is an "already-over."

Geography's first role in *Os sertões* is thus to produce the heterogeneity of
Brazil; its second role shows up in the thesis that the *sertanejo* is saved by the
isolation that the *sertão* imposes. The ruling positivist and racial theories of the
time sentenced the *mestiço* to degeneracy, as da Cunha rather unwillingly ad-
mits in a section entitled "An irritating parenthesis": "An intermingling of races

highly diverse is, in the majority of cases, prejudicial" (*Rebellion*, 87). Yet, as almost all his commentators have observed, and as the section on the particularity of the *sertão* eluding the universalizing schemas of science already indicates, *Os sertões* showcases a conflict between a scientific machinery and a "reality" that it cannot explain sufficiently. In this case, instead of constituting a weak and degenerate being, the *sertanejo* is above all a member of "a strong race," someone able to survive the harshest of climates.

Geography resolves this discrepancy between theory and reality. Da Cunha argues that the mestizos' degeneracy emerges not only because their evolutionary heritage includes mixed elements but also because the weaker elements leave such composite beings unable to survive in civilization: "In this latter case the strong race does not destroy the weak by force of arms; it crushes it with civilization" (*Rebellion*, 87). With this argument he follows a point made by Nina Rodrigues, who distinguished between the *jagunço* and other mestizos, arguing that the former "was able to adapt the virile qualities of his savage ancestors, whether black or indigenous, to the social conditions of free life and rudimentary civilization of the centers in which he lived."[38] But the mestizo of the coast (a black-white mixture rather than the Indian-white mixture of the *sertão*) was exposed to "alcohol, an urban environment and an intellectual rather than physical struggle, to a civilization which surpasses the exigencies of his physical and mental organization." All these weakened the coastal mestizo, "accentuating the degenerative note that is already the result of the simple interbreeding of anthropologically different races" and creating "useless, weak types."[39] Da Cunha closely echoes Nina Rodrigues, but his account emphasizes the factor of geographic isolation, which is only latent in Nina Rodrigues's account. Precisely because they were abandoned and isolated, the *sertanejos* could live in more savage circumstances that were entirely compatible with those weaker elements: "The abandonment in which they were left by the rest of the country had a beneficent effect. It freed them from a highly painful adaptation to a superior social state and at the same time prevented their slipping backward through the aberrations and vices of a more advanced milieu. The fusion that took place occurred under circumstances more compatible with the inferior elements" (*Rebellion*, 87–88). Like Nina Rodrigues, da Cunha marks a fundamental difference between the *mestiçagem* of the *sertões* and those of the coast, but he underscores the relationship with the land as a factor in producing this difference. "The inhabitant of the backlands has in large degree taken from the savage the latter's intimacy with his physical surroundings, and this, instead of acting as a depressing influence, has enriched his potent organism. As a consequence, he reflects in character and costume only those attributes taken from other formative races which are most adaptable to his incipient phase of social life. He is a retrograde, not a degenerate type" (88).

Da Cunha's argument is thus secretly a double one. On the one hand, on the face of it, this isolation was beneficial for "scientific" reasons: such organisms were not crushed by the weight of an incompatible and superior civilization and were given room to develop their own strengths and survival skills. On the other hand, the praise of isolation and the "intimacy" with the land that it bred in the *sertanejo* harbors the ghost of second argument, one that, under the necessity of defining the original essence of a nation, seeks, as Roberto Schwarz writes, to locate such an essence in the residue left after everything that is not indigenous has been eliminated or isolated. The untouched residue becomes the heart of the land. This notion, which starts to acquire form in the text that is itself composed of fragments, the *Caderneta de campo*, is what da Cunha is after. Nicolau Sevcenko will affirm that "the author perceives the populations of the interior as the model for a perfect consortium between man and land in Brazil, which would deliver it of the fallacies of cosmopolitism, 'this kind of colonial *regime* of the spirit which transforms the inhabitants of a country into virtual emigrants, living, barrenly, in the fictitious atmosphere of a borrowed civilization.'"[40]

The *sertanejo*, a retrograde, a ruin like the *sertão* he lives in and reflects, is, also like the *sertão*, a "fertile leftover." Da Cunha sees in the *sertanejo* the hope for a homogeneous Brazilian race. He insists, "This society, misunderstood and forgotten, was the vigorous core of our national life" (*Rebellion*, 78). Da Cunha mentions this notion twice in *Os sertões*, and he later elaborates it in response to Moreira Guimarães, who noted the contradiction between concerns about disunity of race in Brazil and portrayals of the *sertanejo* as the heart of a Brazilian nationality. Da Cunha responds with a dialectical proposition: "This means that in this indefinable compound—the Brazilian—I found something that was stable, a little bit of resistance like the integrating molecule of crystallizations under way. And it was natural that, admitting the bold and heartening conjecture that we are destined for national integration, I saw in those vigorous caboclos the nucleus of our future constitution, the living rock of our race."[41] As the nucleus of Brazil's future constitution, the *sertanejo* is inside perhaps not the actual nation but at least the nation's inevitable vector. Because of geogra-

phy, therefore, the *sertanejo* is both outside and inside Brazil—not simultaneously but successively. Da Cunha says that although Brazilians are united to
the *sertanejos* by the soil, the two are "wholly separated . . . by a co-ordinate of
history—time" (*Rebellion*, xxx). And yet time will heal this breach. This is da
Cunha's ultimate transculturating solution to the problem of Brazil's heterogeneity. As Sevcenko notes, this aspect of the text undermines any attempt to
characterize it as a dualistic confrontation between civilization and barbarism.
Os sertões is organized not by a clash between opposite terms but by a project of
integration between them: the incorporation of the *sertão* into national life and
the "reinvigoration of civilization through the ethical and social raw material of
the sertanejo."[42]

Da Cunha's representation of the army and its soldiers recapitulates this
argument; although da Cunha states that the Brazilian soldier does not live up
to the Prussian ideal, he clearly does not think the Brazilian soldier should do
so in every respect. In fact, he criticizes those army commanders who fail to
realize that their plans, strategies, and even clothing are ineffective in the Brazilian backlands. General Artur Oscar, who commanded the fourth expedition,
"could not imagine that the cool-headed strategist whose name he invoked . . .
might be willing to abandon these idealized precepts when brought face to face
with the realities of a backlands war—a roving war, with no fixed rules or rigid
plans to be upset with a thousand and one chance circumstances, by sudden
assaults at the turn of the road and ambushes everywhere" (*Rebellion*, 292). The
army instead needed to adapt to the realities of this new kind of war fought in
this new, unknown territory. The scouts, he writes, "should have gone through
the caatingas clad in the leathern armor of the sertanejos. . . . One or two corps
so clad and properly trained would have ended by imitating the astonishing
movements of the jagunços. . . . Bright-striped European dolmans and highly
polished boots are a good deal more out of place among the brushwood of the
caatingas" (283). The kind of adaptation he envisions differs significantly from
the degeneration that resulted when soldiers began imitating the worst and
most barbaric qualities of the Canudenses.[43] Da Cunha instead suggests they
imitate all that was intelligent and astonishing about the *jagunços'* relationship
to the environment and the way the rebels used their knowledge of the land
to fight. Lieutenant Colonel Menezes exemplifies the kind of combination he
imagines. Frail and with a "Chistlike face," Menezes came from "a backlands
family in the North, with close relatives among the fanatics of Canudos"; "this
fair-haired, frail-looking jagunço, with the physical and moral polish conferred

by modern culture, and endowed with a wit that matched his fearlessness, was the best guaranty of the army's safe-conduct. And he provided the expedition with a line of march which surprised even the sertanejos" (295). Menezes combined his origin in and knowledge of the backlands with the polish of moral culture and through this combination managed to produce a strategy for traversing the terrain that outsmarted even the *jagunços*.

In a sense, the army finally won precisely along these lines. Marshal Bittencourt, the secretary of state for affairs of war, was dispatched to Canudos along with more troops when it was feared that the army would once again lose to the Conselheiro's men. Da Cunha describes Bittencourt as a bureaucrat, someone whose skills lay in organization and other mundane affairs rather than heroics.

> While he was not the perfect type of military man, he was nonetheless addicted to the typical automatism of those machines composed of muscles and nerves which are so constructed as to react mechanically to the irresistible pressure of laws. All of this, however, was due not so much to a thorough disciplinary education as it was to his own inert and passive temperament, moving comfortably like a cog in a wheel within the complex machinery of rules and regulations. Outside of this he was a nonentity. Written orders with him were a fetish. He did not interpret them and he did not criticize them; he carried them out. (*Rebellion*, 394)

According to da Cunha, Bittencourt realized that the real enemy was the desert rather than the *jagunço* and put his mind to organizing regular supply trains. In doing so, he "transformed a huge, unplanned conflict into a regular campaign" (397). The campaign, therefore, was finally won not so much by becoming *jagunço* (by degenerating, as the soldiers spontaneously did) as by deploying the administrative and organizational apparatus that da Cunha had found woefully lacking in the earlier campaigns, though now acknowledging the realities of the terrain on which the battles were fought. The clear lesson, therefore, is that simply upholding modern models regarding, for example, military strategies and organization will not suffice absent any regard for the realities of Brazil, because that would simply continue to produce the fractures and heterogeneities that had led to the confrontations. Within this schema, the *jagunço* becomes key to the integration da Cunha envisions inasmuch as he is the model for the necessary intimacy with the land.

There are two things to note about this hypothesis. First, it is more urgent than the claim that the *jagunços* should have been incorporated into Brazil for their own good. They are, as it were, the supplement of the Brazilian nation-state, that without which it may always be fragmentary, divided, heterogeneous. Described in Žižekian terms, the *sertanejo* is the "irreducible trace of externality in the very midst of 'internality,' its condition of impossibility (a foreign body preventing the subject's full constitution) which is simultaneously its condition of possibility."[44] This aspect of the argument is clearly articulated by Gilberto Freyre's 1939 introduction to the collection of da Cunha's published articles. Da Cunha, he wrote, was "the voice that clamored in favor of the Brazilian desert: make right/straighten the paths of Brazil! . . . The paths between the cities and backlands. This was the great message of Euclydes: it was necessary to unite the sertão with the coast for the salvation—and not only for the convenience—of Brazil."[45]

Second, geography functions both literally and metaphorically within his argument. That is, by suggesting that geography may be at the core not only of Brazilian heterogeneity but also of the solution to the lack of a nation-state, da Cunha *displaces* and subsumes the problem of constituting new republican subjects into the problem of constituting a new territory. When da Cunha argues that Bittencourt won because he acknowledged the overriding necessity "to combat, not the jagunço, but the desert" (*Rebellion*, 396), he in a sense displaces the issue of integration of people (who may not want to be integrated) into an issue of conquering land. His professional training and duties surely predisposed him to such a perspective, since he "advised the technical work of environmental engineering which would be responsible for plowing new land, sanitation, the extinction of deserts, the definition of landmarks and geographical masses, gathering information about resources and establishing a variety of efficient lines of communication. 'Our engineering has the noble and useful destiny of rationally conquering our land.'"[46]

Significantly, da Cunha understood the relationship between humans and land to be dynamic. While the land has a determining influence on people, the converse is also true. Deserts, such as the Brazilian *sertão*, were made by man: "If he did not create the climate, he transformed it, made it worse" (*Rebellion*, 45). But if humans made the deserts, they can also unmake them. Da Cunha puts forward the example of the Romans in northern Africa, the "great colonizers" who were succeeded by the "barbarous heedlessness of the Arabians" (45). The Romans, "after the task of destroying Carthage had been completed, had put their shoulders to the incomparably more serious one of overcoming the antagonism of Nature" (46). They succeeded in pushing the desert back through a system of dikes, so that Tunisia "was transfigured and became once more the classic land of ancient agriculture. It was the granary of Italy" (47). France, he says, followed this example. "Thus is this historic region, freed of the inert Moslem's apathy, transformed, to resume once more that aspect which it bore of old. France is saving what remains of the opulent heritage of Roman civilization, following its long decline down the centuries" (47). The same, writes da Cunha the engineer, could be done with the *sertão*.

By identifying the desert, not the *jagunço*, as the central antagonist, so that the true struggle is to incorporate it by surveying, mapping, and domesticating it, by transforming the *sertão* into a fertile granary, da Cunha sidesteps the issue of effectively interpellating the Conselheiristas into a new political subjecthood. Turning land into geography effectively empties it of the people who inhabit it (and who scarcely dominate it in his opinion). By speaking for those who had previously been invisible and voiceless and pointing out their existence, da Cunha accomplishes rhetorically the task he set out for the Brazilian nation-state within a geological temporality, an act that Afrânio Peixoto significantly likened to a colonizing territorial expansion when, in 1911, he claimed: "Euclides da Cunha is the new *bandeirante* in this new 'entrada' in the soul of Brazilian nationality."[47] The Conselheiristas became Brazilian simply by virtue of their symbolic incorporation in his text. Da Cunha completes his erasure of everydayness by transferring the Canudos War into a problem of territory and land. Both moves work to prohibit, as Partha Banerjee suggests in *The Politics of Time*, the "coming face-to-face of the 'primitive' and the 'progressive,' the archaic and the portentious, the present and the past." What takes its place is representation. "The temporality of re-presentation, in other words, neutralizes the temporality of encounter, and therefore the temporality of collective practices. In the place of practice and politics, representation offers predictive knowledge, and in the place of contradiction and/or solidarity, it offers an anxious and brittle appearance of identity."[48]

Representation, therefore, is not the means through which the truth of Canudos is expressed, as many generations of critics would have it. It is not a mechanism that produces a portrait but a specific practice, a form of temporalization and an address that takes the place of other kinds of encounters. We therefore cannot assume that the city of Canudos was a protest against abandonment by the nation-state, that it harbored a demand for incorporation (symbolically or otherwise), and that this incorporation is equivalent to transforming a desert into a fertile granary. Yet the historian Nicolau Sevcenko seems to suggest just this when he remarks that da Cunha "did not champion the insurrections which he witnessed, understanding from the beginning their inefficiency and abhorring situations of violence. But he was able to *see* in the suicidal anguish of the rebels an agonizing protest against an unbearable situation of abandonment and penury."[49] The trope of da Cunha's sight rears its head again in Sevcenko's judgment. Reading the incidents concerning Canudos (and da Cunha as the medium of their message) as a protest against abandonment is deeply problematic. Abandonment by whom? To what? If measures such as increased taxation, the secularization of daily life, the census, and mapping numbered among the causes of the conflict, then the Conselheiristas seem to have been protesting not so much abandonment as the forced incorporation into a modern-state that they perceived to be an illegitimate power extending and deepening its structures of domination. To the extent that the Conselheiristas were combating precisely such an incorporation, da Cunha's solution would have sounded like a punishing sentence of condemnation.

CHAPTER FIVE

ANOTHER CANUDOS

> Once the world has been trimmed according to a particular intention, the rhetoric codified in the genre produces an ideology and a language, that is, it can reformulate the world by extracting from it only certain contents (which thus take the place of the whole of reality) and by constructing an expression appropriate to such a partiality. . . . The rhetoric of genre is, in short, a perspective that is limited but can reduce everything to itself and make everything in its own image.
>
> —M. M. Bakhtin and P. N. Medvedev, *The Formal Method in Literary Scholarship*

In *A imitação dos sentidos*, Leopoldo Bernucci notes that although works such as Afonso Arinos's *Os jagunços*, Dantas Barreto's *Ultima expedição a Canudos*, Alvim Martins Horcades's *Descrição de uma viagem a Canudos*, César Zama's *Libelo republicano*, and Manoel Benício's *O rei dos jagunços* had addressed the military campaign and Antonio Conselheiro's messianic movement before *Os sertões* appeared, da Cunha's text, not its predecessors, entered triumphantly into literary history. Why, he asks, didn't these other works acquire the literary or historical importance of *Os sertões*? Why does the public still ignore them despite their vehement critiques and the polemical tone of their pages?[1]

Bernucci later describes Afonso Arinos's *Os jagunços* as a minor, mediocre, and perishable text, answering his own question in terms of value and aesthetics.[2] Similarly, Silvia Maria Azevedo, who wrote the introduction to a recent edition of Manoel Benício's *O rei dos jangunços*, observes that "the clear eye with which he [Benício] registers such details does not prevent his newspaper articles, unlike da Cunha's, from being badly written, without stylistic preoccupations, an aspect that the journalist justifies by the precarious conditions in which he finds himself writing the dispatches."[3] Such judgments typify the slow transformation of da Cunha's text into a work of literature. As I argued in chapter 1, whereas the book initially received acclaim in terms that clearly linked it to a specific political, cultural, and social agenda for nationalism (one based on the inclusion of the local and regional), critics later excused da Cunha's outmoded positivism and racism as they elevated the text in aesthetic terms. If *Os sertões* is characterized as the "best" of the many texts written about Canudos, then how should we characterize the content of this excellence? What are the specific criteria according to which da Cunha's text is said to succeed?

The aesthetic values in question are governed by a version of transculturation. In other words, *Os sertões* is read as successful inasmuch as its form is deemed to express some facet of Brazilian reality, to respond to the pressure of the referent. Early on this reading manifested itself as, for example, the claim that *Os sertões* offered a model for stepping outside the hothouse in which Brazilian intellectuals were imprisoned and representing the people. Later this could mean that da Cunha's baroque prose reflected a mimesis of the extreme contrasts and contradictions of Brazil or, as in González Echeverría's reading, that his text joined its object in the moment it appeals to the sublime. From this perspective, Benício's *O rei dos jagunços* and Arinos's *Os jagunços* (both 1898) become interesting for the way they deviate from a transculturating norm, so that their formal options produce texts illegible under the name *Canudos*.

The Supremacy of Form

Well respected as a writer in his day, Afonso Arinos became a member of the Academia Brasileira de Letras in 1901, before da Cunha. Nonetheless, the first edition of his novel *Os jagunços* (published in installments during the last year of the conflict) ran to only 100 copies. The novel was reedited only in 1970 as part of Arinos's collected works.[4] Arinos was also a monarchist. Indeed, he was the editor for one of the monarchist newspapers ransacked during the conflict with Canudos (*O Comércio de São Paulo*). He was so disenchanted with the direction in which Brazil was moving that he relocated to Paris around 1904, when it became clear that restoration of the monarchy was no longer plausible.

The untimeliness of *Os jagunços* gives it its critical edge in the context of the conflict. Although Arinos inscribes Canudos within a narrative (and a geography) not its own, his version runs against the grain of the official story. Unlike da Cunha's text, which assumes an inexorable march of progress, *Os jagunços* is imbued with a nostalgia, a backward look for an older and better world that is patent in scenes such as the one in which the main character sits down with his adoptive mother to spin cotton into cloth: "In the midst of night's silence, that labor represented an indefinable something of past eras; it breathed of the tranquility and peace of saints, the crude and majestic simplicity of the sober, strong races that had erected the greatness of empires."[5] Arinos turns the conflict of Canudos into an allegory for a narrative concerning the breakdown of a past order, one that had been better not only for the elites but also for the people.

Arinos thus strikes at the heart of the new republic's claim to speak for and represent the people. In an interview published on December 20, 1915, in his hometown's newspaper, Arinos defended his monarchical ideals, arguing that "the past regime [the monarchy] . . . had its origin in the people and was founded freely by the people. When the last chief of state not born in Brazil was expelled from government, *the people chose the monarchy*, led by Evaristo da Veiga, a popular journalist with a penetrating political acumen" (emphasis added).[6] Unlike Nina Rodrigues, who equated the *sertanejos'* monarchist bent with their racial inferiority, Arinos insisted that supporting the monarchy had nothing to do with an argument about the racial inferiority of the Brazilian population. Indeed, he said, the Italian republics showed that the evolution of democracy required the return to monarchy. By advancing his argument through words and concepts held in common with the proponents of the new republic (such as "democracy" and "origin in the people"), Arinos tries to chip away at their monopoly on the corresponding signifieds. This strategy becomes explicit in his remark that the current, narrow meaning of the term *republic* was a modern development and that it had previously been used to mean government or even community more generally. In fact, Arinos said, "if we wanted to make it correspond to the Greek notion of democracy . . . , we would have to confess that this was only really practiced in Brazil under the Empire." In contrast, the republic "was imposed by a fraction of rebellious army officers and from that day on there had never been . . . free elections, so that our Republic could be many things, but not a democracy" (206–7). Arinos tempers such comments—offered twenty-six years after the inauguration of republican rule—by insisting that he and other monarchists have no desire to make trouble for the new government. They believe in law and order, he says, and would rather help the republican government if they could. Still, Arinos argues, explicitly in this interview and implicitly in the novel he wrote many years before, that the relationship between people and state could be interpreted differently.

Arinos's defense of the principle of representation and democracy provides an interesting counterpoint when read alongside an argument that Jeffrey Needell recently put forward in *The Party of Order: The Conservatives, the State and Slavery in the Brazilian Monarchy, 1831–71*, where he urges a serious consideration of the Conservative Party's defense of representative constitutionalism under the empire (traditional historiography has either dismissed its ideology as window dressing or emphasized only the authoritarian tradition of the Conservatives). The Conservative Party (or Party of Order) was formed in the late 1830s when the liberal opposition to Pedro I split into more moderate and more radical factions after his abdication in 1831. Needell argues that whereas the more moderate group (characterized by its detractors as "reactionaries") sought to recover the authority of the monarch and the state so as to defend the social order (threatened by violent social conflicts) and maintain the integrity of the nation (endangered by provincial revolts), this group also espoused the principle of representative, constitutional government. Their model, he says, was the liberal constitutional monarchism of the July Monarchy in France, and in particular the theorist François-Pierre-Guillaume Guizot. Guizot's supporters claimed to represent the "*juste milieu*," a government balanced between monarchy and republic, between reactionary nobility and revolutionary people. Guizot advocated a government with harmonious constituent powers, characterized by the deliberation of a select parliamentary elite who, through reason, would discover truth and justice and lead the nation.[7] Accordingly, the Conservatives' early ideologues insisted on the Chamber of Deputies' centrality to state policy and argued that the cabinet must enjoy the confidence not only of the crown but also of the Chamber's majority, which represented society. They also emphasized a balance between constitutional powers and the importance of elite representative deliberation, constitutional order, and ideological principles in good government. Needell argues that this vision of governance ultimately lost to that of Dom Pedro II, who trusted neither the political parties nor the perspectives of their spokespersons and wanted to foster a strong state under his control rather than one representing a party organically linked to the dominant oligarchies.

Needell describes the 1871 conflict over the Law of the Free Womb (passed in the first year of the Rio Branco cabinet) as a pivotal moment in the dynamic of representative governance versus a strong state in Brazil and argues that the conservatives were advancing an alternative abolitionist legislation that Brazilian historiography has completely ignored. According to Needell, the conservative elite was willing to accept a much more meaningful abolition reform that within a year would have freed some people already living (instead of granting freedom for children born eight years later, in 1879) and then would have done so annually until no slaves were left in chains. After a period of registration, slaves in certain categories (e.g., the married, the skilled and literate, and those over thirty-five or under fifteen years of age) would have become eligible for emancipation, and their owners reimbursed for value, according to a ranking scheme. A key feature of this alternative plan consisted of letting slaveholders participate in designating eligible captives, which would have avoided the blow to their moral authority that state intervention threatened. For Needell, this alternative plan shows that the conservatives opposed not abolition itself but abolition undertaken by the emperor at the expense of their authority.[8]

Whereas previous historiography has focused on the contradiction between a strong state used for enlightened reform and a strong state under the control of reactionary slaveholders, Needell argues that the differences represented instead "the contradiction of a strong state under the control of an autocrat versus a strong state associated with the developing political culture of representative government. This is not meant to suggest that one supplants the other; rather, what is argued is that both contradictions are present in the past under examination."[9] The defeat of the Conservatives, he says, may have represented less a victory of slaves over slaveholders than one of an authoritarian state over constitutional representative government. By 1871 Brazil had not a representative, constitutional government but an institutional farce, a "theatre of shadows," as it was described by a contemporary conservative critic. "It was this statist, authoritarian legacy, hardly covered by a thin sheet of institutional legitimization, which survived the Monarchy, a somber presence in Brazil's political culture ever since."[10] Whether or not one accepts Needell's argument that the planter elite were prepared to undertake a more meaningful abolition, his narrative of a decline in the culture of representative government resonates with Bieber's account of an increasingly centralized system of party politics and elections with decreasing autonomy of and participation by local populations and government. It also suggests that the republicans did not have a monopoly on the principle of representative government and, as Arinos asserted both in the interview and in his novel, that there were other ways to interpret the relationship between state and people. Os jagunços is in many ways an attempt to argue that the conflict represents not the defeat of barbarism but the defeat of an older and more just order.

Arinos's claim that the monarchy (and monarchists) bore a relationship to the common people of Brazil echoes the way his short stories and chronicles (*Os jagunços* was his only novel) revolve around the lands and people of his childhood in rural Minas Gerais. To the extent that the Brazilian Academy of Letters was divided between cosmopolitans and regionalists at the turn of the century, Arinos comes down on the side of the latter. The regionalists' anthropological vocation appears clearly in the first chapters of *Os jagunços*, which introduce a presumably uninitiated reader to the dances, celebration, songs, and customs of the *sertanejo*—although Antônio Oliveira Mello (the only critic to write a book on Arinos's life and work) points out that the details constructing the rural world of *Os jagunços* are drawn from Minas Gerais rather than the Bahian *sertão*, where it is supposedly located.[11] Critics cited such "local color," as well as "the sincerity of the narrative" and the "naturalism and exactitude of his observations," in praising *Os jagunços* when it was published.[12]

The presence of such "local color" led Oliveira Mello to describe Arinos's writing as "realist." Yet it is difficult to read Arinos's text as a "form of aesthetic experience that yet lays claim to a binding relationship to the real itself" (to use Fredric Jameson's definition of realism) in the wake of Angel Rama's theory of transculturation.[13] Arinos's text exemplifies instead the long-standing conundrum in Latin American literature that Gabriel García Márquez formulated as the "lack of conventional means to render our lives believable."[14] The problem is the heterogeneity between, on the one hand, the forms and conventions of literature—indeed, the historically specific concept of literature itself—and, on the other, the referent it attempts to represent. But the word *referent* will be misleading if one understands heterogeneity as simply marking literature's inability to grasp "the real." The referent includes the social, cultural, and economic forms of a society ("our lives"), so that certain notions of subjectivity, expressivity, temporality, and reality codified in literary forms may conflict with other worldviews expressed in other forms (which in Latin America may be indigenous, African, or simply popular). Transculturation, as I explained earlier, constitutes the attempt to solve this problem by positing the synthesis of two worlds as it was registered in literary forms, a phenomenon not unlike Bakhtin's "carnivalization" of literature. The contamination of Gabriel García Márquez's novels with characteristics of oral storytelling is a transculturating solution. Similarly, according to this perspective, José María Arguedas did not simply try to depict an indigenous referent when he wrote about the Andes but sought to change and transform the literary form through its contact with the cultural expressions of that indigenous referent. For Rama, Arguedas mined the novel form with Quechua linguistic and hermeneutical structures to conquer "one of the best defended bastions of the culture of domination."[15] But again, this solution left other questions unanswered. As Cornejo-Polar notes in his critique of transculturation, the model thus assumed "the construction of a syncretic plane that finally incorporates in a more or less unproblematical totality (in spite of the conflictive character of the process) two or more languages, two or more ethnic identities, two or more aesthetic codes and historical experiences. . . . This synthesis would be configured in the space of the hegemonic culture and literature; . . . at times the social asymmetry of the originating contacts would be obviated; and finally . . . , the discourses that have not influenced the system of 'enlightened' literature would be left at the margins."[16]

Manoel Benício operates much as does Arguedas to the extent that we can read his text as a struggle with form. Benício's text thus foregrounds the problem of finding the correct form to express a particular social reality. Arinos, however, sees no such problem inasmuch as he depicts a rural world in his novel but makes it legible through the coordinates established by a classical tradition that includes pastoral poetry and Romanticism. This leads the Brazilian critic Afrânio Coutinho to describe Arinos's novel as contradictory. For Coutinho, Arinos belongs with other nineteenth-century writers, such as José de Alencar, Gonçalves Dias, and Bernardo Guimarães, whose regionalism "supervalorizes the picturesque and local color even as it seeks to cover it up, attributing to it qualities, sentiments, values that do belong not to it but to the culture superimposed on it."[17] Tellingly, Coutinho also understands this strain of regionalism as a form of escape from the present to the past, a regionalism "idealized by sentiment and rendered artificial by the transposition of a desire of compensation and representation that we can call oneiric."[18] But Coutinho's negative judgment is measured against a transculturating ideal in which literature expresses rather than covers up the local world. The virtue of Cornejo-Polar's model is to suggest that if Latin American literature often fails to live up to such an ideal, the reason is not simply bad writing, or isolated personal failures, but rather the postcolonial fissures that continue to haunt Latin American social reality and cannot be overcome simply through writing.

The attempt to represent—through both proxy and portrait—a local reality strains against the deployment of forms that often seem singularly inappropriate to the task (and that seem to conceal rather than reveal that reality), and Arinos enacts this tension in a condensed fashion in an essay where he writes:

"We live!—they say though my mouth, just as the miserable English spoke through the mouth of Gwynplaine in the House of Lords! We live! We don't tune the strings of our souls to the orchestral baton of Bassiou or Mancinelli on concert nights! The press? We don't know any such thing! Brazil, government, politics, Republic—this is the language of parrots that we call Greek because we don't understand it."[19] This passage formulates the noncoincidence between a certain language (one that includes words such as *press, Brazil, government,* and *politics*) and the "lives" of the rural people. Yet there is also a performative contradiction here, inasmuch as the people are made to voice this impossibility in an impossible language (with references to figures from European high culture and a Greek they are said not to understand). At the same time, though Arinos says they have no access to his language, he (unlike Michelet) has access to theirs. He claims to speak for them, seemingly living out Michelet's fantasy of a seamless, homogeneous world. Whatever seams and differences exist, they do not pose a fundamental intractability to knowledge but can, Arinos believes, be translated into a language of universal humanism (accessible to him but not to them). This passage condenses the logic of Arinos's formal choices, which operates through his belief in literature as a universal translating machine.

Arinos's apparent belief in an unproblematic mediation goes hand in hand with his choice of national romance to tell his story of Canudos, a genre much used in Latin America throughout the nineteenth century. The first half of *Os jagunços* tells how the protagonist, Luís Pachola, decides to follow the Conselheiro. The narrative motor is provided by love. Conceição, a young girl, falls for Luís, who has come to her town for a festival with his employer, João Joaquim. Although Luís does not return her interest, Conceição is killed by a jealous suitor. This event marks a rupture in the life of Luís, who feels responsible for her death and decides he has to live in memory of her and in service to God. This vague sense of duty finds its form in following the Conselheiro. The second half of the novel takes us to Belo Monte, where Luís has settled with Conceição's mother, Joana, until violence befalls the community. Organizing the move to Canudos/Belo Monte around romance and family rather than political or religious motivations translates the motives of its inhabitants into a "universal language." This choice is repeated, to slightly different effects, in Benício's novel, as well as in Sándor Márai's *Veredicto em Canudos* (1969), Mario Vargas Llosa's *War of the End of the World*, and Sergio Rezende's film *Battle for Canudos* (1999). In all cases, romance and family ties offer the author/director and audience a seemingly unproblematic rhetorical bridge into the world of Canudos. When Doris Sommer analyzes these novels in *Foundational Fictions*, she emphasizes how the central pairs of star-crossed lovers were meant to furnish nineteenth-century readers with images of bridges across differences (since the young lovers always hail from different regions, parties, economic classes, or races), but the use of this conceit in the case of Canudos clearly shows that the plane on which the romantic or familial relations unfold never includes meaningful heterogeneities. Just as the language of romance works to cancel out political, economic, social, or religious differences, the text's allegorical drive reduces a world of multiplicities to a few "representative" individuals.

In one of the few published analyses of this text, the Brazilian critic Walnice Nogueira Galvão notes that Arinos chose to tell the story of Canudos at the level of the individual, in contrast to da Cunha, who, she says, makes the war intelligible by moving "from the general to the particular, seeking the determinants of the conflict in geography and racial elements." Arinos, however, "following a novelistic tradition, reveals the determinants—which are for him historical, rather than geographic or racial, in the widest sense of the term—in the particularity of a human destiny."[20] Using a distinction Foucault makes in his 1976 lectures (published as *Society Must Be Defended*), one could say that while da Cunha's text takes the perspective of biopolitics, Arinos's novel is an example of anatomo-politics, directed at individuals rather than humans as a population or species. Arinos's world is more homogeneous than da Cunha's because heterogeneity is not posed as a problem. The problem of the alignment, separation, and commonality of a series of bodies does not exist.

Nogueira Galvão thus misses the mark when she says that Luís Pachola's destiny reveals the "historical factors that transform an inhabitant of the sertão into a fanatic rebel." This statement typifies the continued hegemony of da Cunha's text, for it essentially translates Arinos's world into the terms of da Cunha's analysis. First, the rupture that bifurcates Pachola's life, and the novel, hardly maps onto the ontological change between categories or types of person (from inhabitant to rebel) that preoccupied da Cunha, since Arinos's world comprises individuals, not populations. Second, characterizing Pachola's transformation as one that moves him into the category of "rebel" misses the disciplinary dimension of Arinos's text. Pachola is an individual constructed through a discourse of service rather than liberty. His actions and choices render him exemplary of old-fashioned codes of honor, servitude, loyalty, and bravery. The novel paints him not as a rebel or fanatic but as a solitary, quiet, and noble figure who evokes Dumas's musketeers. Third, the reference to "historical factors" misreads the relationship between the level of the individual and that of larger external forces. Galvão's description of Pachola as a "rebel" translates him into a bourgeois world organized by notions of agency and will and therefore polarized between individual self-determination and determination by factors such as race, climate, and history. She correctly suggests that such external factors do not determine the individual, as da Cunha claims to be the case, but her wording seems simply to shift the cause of determination onto the level of history. Admittedly, one can hardly imagine Luís Pachola as an active agent, since his life is overtaken by external factors beyond his control (he is almost entirely passive—and impassive—before the girl's interest), but those external factors unfold on the level of the individual rather than the general or historical. A girl falls in love with him and is killed by a suitor. He perceives this event, Arinos tells us, as "a terrible blow [that] had interrupted the continuity of his existence, detaching him violently from the past, present and future" (98). His reaction to this blow is to accept it, to submit to the vicissitudes of destiny and to remain true to this event rather than attempt to reattach himself to the previous structure of his life. Pachola exemplifies submission rather than rebellion.

The word *rebel* also misses the alternative order within which Pachola is inscribed, for it casts Pachola simply in terms of his intransigence to the republican order da Cunha desires. Pachola's actions and choices, however, take place within a world clearly marked by older notions of nationhood, order, and the relationship between subject and sovereign. Indeed, the relationship between Pachola and the Conselheiro most closely resembles the relationship between subject and sovereign in an absolute monarchy, rather than the one imagined to hold in a constitutional monarchy, where notions of popular sovereignty already obtain (despite Arinos's affirmations in the 1915 interview). According to Foucault,

> the absolute monarchy's thesis was that the nation did not exist, or at least that if it did exist, it did so only to the extent that it found its condition of possibility, and its substantive unity, in the person of the king. The nation did not exist simply because there was a group, a crowd, or a multiplicity of individuals inhabiting the same land, speaking the same language and observing the same customs and laws. . . . What makes a nation is the fact that there exist individuals who, insofar as they exist alongside one another, are no more than individuals and do not form a unity. But they do all have a

certain individual relationship—both juridical and physical—with the real, living and bodily person of the king. It is the body of the king, in his physico-juridical relationship with each of his subjects, that creates the body of the nation.[21]

The relationship between Pachola and the Conselheiro takes this personal, direct form, for it is premised not on identity or representation but through *service*. The lack of a principle of identity or identification in this relationship is made all the more evident by the mystery and opacity of Arinos's Conselheiro. In this sense, the novel underscores the relationship itself rather than, to use Foucault's words, the "real, living, and bodily person" of the Conselheiro, for Arinos's Conselheiro does not have any density as an individual character. For Arinos, he is always a question mark or outline rather than the humanized character he becomes in Manoel Benício's text or the specimen of madness that da Cunha attempts to dissect in *Os sertões*: "What was the past of that man? Where did he come from? No one asked, and he never told them. He had been born again on the day that he felt himself moved by a divine mission; his life began on that day" (48). He is fundamentally unlike anyone else in the novel, too otherworldly to be united to his followers through a principle of identification (or to produce in them the kind of contagion described by nineteenth-century theorists of crowd psychology).

By representing the Conselheiro this way, the novel positions the reader as one of the Conselheiro's followers looking on him from afar and below. We cannot evaluate Pachola's relationship to the Conselheiro from an external point of view but are forced to live it as he does. For example, the novel suspends disbelief concerning the Conselheiro's prophetic visions and miracles, a remarkable approach in a context where positivism reigned and pronouncements regarding primitive superstition and religious fanaticism were thrown about to explain the causes of the conflict. Just as the novel provides readers no information about the Conselheiro's past, it offers no information that would lead us to shrug off his supposedly miraculous powers. When the Conselheiro disappears from his grave, for example, we are not told whether his body was moved, he had not really died, or, like Lazarus, he was resurrected.

But Arinos is not trying to write a fairy tale; rather, he wants to produce a perspective according to which the extraordinary is simply ordinary. Arinos situates the Conselheiro's beliefs well within the norm for the *sertão*: "His religion was none other than, in general terms, the Catholic religion" (133). Those

who don't see the Conselheiro's religion as part of Catholicism are simply out-
siders to this world. Thus, for example, when the Conselheiro and his followers first appear, we are told that someone other than João Joaquim and Luís
Pachola, "prepared as they were for all the surprises of a rural life, would have
fled, abandoning their place of rest, horrified by the strangeness of the prayers
and flagellations" (35–36). Arinos echoes da Cunha in suggesting that the
Canudos War resulted from a government and an elite that did not know their
own population and country. For da Cunha, however, this means that the government needed to incorporate and civilize these people and lands, whereas
Arinos's novel suggests that they could be left as they were. The city of Belo
Monte is explicitly described as an ordinary feature of the landscape, an integer
in the series of *sertanejo* life made up of cattle and agriculture: "Anyone who
went there would see calm everywhere, the normal life of the sertanejo people,
caring for their cattle and crops" (124).

I don't mean to suggest we read these moments innocently, as if Arinos
perceived a normality that da Cunha did not, for Arinos's project clearly harbors
a "normalizing" impulse. Where Arinos writes about the everyday, he seeks to
make Canudos legible not as a sign of disorder but as an element in an alternative order that could also be the fantasy of the rural landowner. Arinos thus
turns the inhabitants of Canudos into subjects of a history far from their own,
a move much like the one Guha criticizes when he takes Marxists to task for
turning rebels into examples of the universal proletariat in revolution or the
situation Spivak criticizes when she cautions against a new rhetoric that defends Third World women in the name of certain notions of democracy and
modernization. Nonetheless, describing Canudos/Belo Monte as normal ends
up denaturalizing the norms that governed the public discourse on the conflict.

Such an effect stands out most starkly when we read Arinos's text against
the prose of counterinsurgency that dominated public discourse on the conflict. For example, instead of foregrounding the dehumanization produced by
the code of counterinsurgency, Arinos inscribes Canudos within an epic code
of valuing and exalting the enemy. This philosophy emerges, for example, in
a scene involving an army official who is so impressed by the way the *jagunços*
fight that, "proud of being Brazilian before those Brazilians," he yells out, "Valiant people! Brave of the brave! What people in the world would not want to
have such soldiers?" (279–80).

The fact that Canudos/Belo Monte is essentially not insurgent in *Os jagunços* provides another example. Arinos portrays the events as an invasion of an

otherwise peaceful city. Da Cunha, of course, also saw it as a criminal invasion, but Arinos describes the causes as contingent, as if the battles could just as well not have taken place, whereas *Os sertões* projects a certain inevitability onto the war. As with Luís's personal life, the rupture between past and present, peaceful coexistence and war, results from external factors over which the inhabitants of Canudos have no control and that emerge at the individual rather than historical level. The first enemy is Luís's old boss, a man described as mean and miserly. João Joaquim dislikes the Conselheiro from the beginning, and even more so after the Conselheiro warns him that his cows are drowning, an act he reads as a curse. To avenge himself, João Joachim instigates the initial attacks against the city, and the city defends itself. In the novel, therefore, the events result from one man's personal flaws and hatreds, a narrative strategy that, like the use of love, translates possible economic and political differences into the language of human personality.

This attempt to reduce the conflict to more "normal" proportions finds a parallel in the way the novel assimilates the events to the level of nature. The novel's hypothesis is verbalized through Luís Pachola, who, saddened after killing men in the first battle, wonders why war happens, why men kill each other, and why he fought. His only answer is that all animals protect their home when invaded. As if to confirm his response, he runs into a beehive attacked by wasps: "There a battle was being fought and the earth was littered with the bodies of the bees, so hardworking and peaceful. Their house had been destroyed after a heroic defense, in which the little ones had lost their life" (164).[22] Arinos immediately and rather crudely spells out the scene's allegorical nature: "And he immediately began to think of the hive of Belo Monte, invaded by millions of soldiers, the houses flattened, the piles of dead bodies on the streets." The allegory serves not only to define and defend the perspective of Belo Monte's inhabitants as protecting their homes but to naturalize it, bringing it within the confines of an ordinary and not monstrous nature.

In another sense, however, this description also refuses to give the conflict a meaning. Arinos's world lacks any real conflict because it is seamless, a unity. Pachola moves to Canudos because a girl falls in love with him and is then killed; violence breaks out because of a petty man's revenge, just as wasps attack bees. Everyone speaks the same language. Arinos's strikingly smooth, coherent, and transparent vision undermines attempts to read the novel as an account of Canudos, for we have become used to understanding Canudos as a clash between the foreign and the autochthonous, between imported forms (of government, knowledge, and writing) and an American reality. Arinos's novel refuses such a perspective. It tells us that literary language is a universal translating machine in which nothing essential is lost. If the lives of the people of Canudos are sufficient and complete, without lacks, so too is his language.

The Failures of Form

Unlike Afonso Arinos, Manoel Benício was both a republican and present at the battles of the fourth expedition, working as a journalist for the *Jornal do Comércio*. Although he lived in Niterói, Rio de Janeiro, at the time, Benício had been born in Pernambuco, so that unlike both da Cunha and Arinos, he was familiar with the Northeast. In addition, Benício had already gained experience working as a war correspondent for the Rio de Janeiro newspaper *O Tempo* (1891) during the Revolta da Armada. Benício reached the scene of battle two months before da Cunha and remained there for little over a month (June 23–July 26). The brevity of his stay seems to have resulted from opinions that were not quite in line with reasons of state. Indeed, one of his main intentions was to critique Artur Oscar for what he believed were wrong-headed military tactics. The critique was not well received. On August 7 Artur Oscar sent a telegram to the minister of war declaring, "The information given by Manoel Benício, of the *Jornal do Comércio*, should not be believed. . . . Now . . . he invents jagunço forces numbering two hundred strong, to alarm the population."[23] The military commander's reaction against Benício went further. Alvim Martins Horcades writes that he was informed that "if the journalist for the Rio de Janeiro newspaper had not left Canudos three hours before he intended to, a hired hand would have gone there to beat him and perhaps even turn him into *nothing* for the *lies* that he had sent in his correspondence with the *Jornal do Comércio*."[24] Although Benício was at Canudos during July, his dispatches were published in the *Jornal do Comércio* only on August 3, the day after he arrived safely in Bahia and the day Marshal Bittencourt left for Bahia to coordinate the military operations. Benício's discord with the military's higher ranks leads Azevedo to describe his book as an "avenging work," like da Cunha's, but one marked with a personal flavor (a judgment that repeats the universal reach singularly granted da Cunha's text).[25] Although Benício was a republican, one cannot extract the story of his text from his relationship to the military campaign, which was by many accounts more fraught than was da Cunha's relationship to it at this early stage. The vexed relationship with authority encoded in these anecdotes about Benício and Artur Oscar is performed in *O rei dos jagunços* at the level of form, so that we can read the book as exemplifying the failure to find or constitute a form as a model of meaning. It is, in this regard, the counterface to Afonso Arinos's novel.

We can read this discomfort with form first through the generic hetero-geneity of *O rei dos jagunços*. This heterogeneity—which is perhaps its most striking feature—differs significantly from that of da Cunha's text. While *Os sertões* draws indiscriminately on sociology, geology, anthropology, history, and folklore in attempting to explain Canudos, all these discourses share a proxim-ity to the locus of enunciation of authority. *Os sertões* also includes passages or dialogues that tend toward a more literary cast, but these function largely on a secondary order as illustrations, subordinate to the discourses of knowledge (even if, as González Echeverría and Costa Lima point out, the text sometimes escapes its own strictures). Benício's *O rei dos jagunços*, however, oscillates more dramatically between fiction and nonfiction, between sections that resemble a novel and follow consistent plotlines and characters and others that attempt to render the conflict in a neutral discourse of truth. While the generic indeter-minacy of *Os sertões* seems to serve a project of mastery, that of Benício's text seems to literalize a certain schizophrenia to the extent that its often clumsy shifts in genres accompany a difference in perspectives—from a more dis-tanced outsider perspective to the simulated perspective of the Conselheiristas. It is this fracturing of perspectives that makes Benício's text fascinating.

Whereas Mikhail Bakhtin views the epic as the genre of official thought, for Benício, proximity to authority's locus of enunciation coincides with the sober, distanced third-person omniscient narrator of historiography, sociology, or anthropology that echoes da Cunha's text. In fact, the grid of intelligibility mobilized by this discourse of truth resembles that of da Cunha's text in several ways. For example, both texts cast the *sertanejo* population as inferior, barbaric, and irrational. As does da Cunha (and Afonso Arinos), Benício critiques the hysteria that produced rumors of a monarchist conspiracy behind Canudos. As does da Cunha (and Nina Rodrigues), he too claims that Canudos was not a political conflict: "The Conselheiro began to preach against the Republic not because he knew what a republic was, or because he was a monarchist or in the service of a monarchist conspiracy, but because the republic threatened his religion."[26] Benício attributes the conflict to social phenomena, making it the product of a disjuncture between the new political developments and the back-wardness of the people of the backland, a

> phenomenon of recomposition through which a people becomes different from what it once was over time.
>
> . . . The inferior layers, the crust of the nation, old and aged, fell like secre-tions through the passage of time into a reaction of ethnic elements.
>
> The commotion of Canudos, elimination . . . of what normally appears under religious form in the backward races and economic form in the more advanced ones, was a symptom of this social illness which resides in the center of Brazil. (200)

As does da Cunha, then, Benício embraces the new regime as a movement toward progress and seems to suggest that the solution to the problem should have been gradual incorporation into this new political life: "The conservative spirit of the hard-working peasants does not realize progress is happening or understand it only in evolutionary terms. They consider all political, economic and governmental reform as an artifice which will, for example, raise taxes or somehow restrict their freedom. The transformation of the old regime into the new, through revolutionary means, did not fit their moderate and conserva-tive spirit" (157). Benício here displays more sensitivity toward the *sertanejo* per-spective, registering their equation of change with greater control and loss of freedom. This same passage also raises the possibility that change could and perhaps should have been allowed to come naturally and slowly (as evolution rather than revolution). In this sense, Benício's text differs from da Cunha's in emphasizing the idea that the conflict was produced through a series of contin-gent circumstances, not through the inevitable unfolding of a logic of incom-mensurability. Benício describes the events with an eye attuned to the ever-expanding prose of counterinsurgency, noting, for example, that the clergy had soured on the Conselheiro as his prestige grew among the *sertanejos*, leading them to "denounce him as a criminal in Ceará and pressuring civil authorities to imprison him" (43). Benício's text thus focuses not on the *sertanejos'* back-wardness and ignorance but on the actions of those outside the community: "They may be crazy, but never criminal, if *imprudent circumstances hadn't produced* a degeneration of their professions of hatred against those that brutally at-tacked their faith and liberty" (65).

Still, these differences are minor. More significantly, Benício does not sustain the neutral, universalizing perspective that analyzes and judges the war from afar; instead, he attempts to represent the perspective of the inhabitants of Canudos under the guise of a novel. When describing his option for novelization, Benício says that he chose to give the book a "novelistic tone (preserving the strictest historical fidelity), thinking thus to soften the harshness of the subject and the tedium of the boring descriptions of someone who lacks style" (6). Yet this explanation does not explain anything, or at least, it fails to answer the most interesting question—namely, why only the Conselheiristas' perspective is novelized. Bakhtin's analysis of the connections between the genre of the novel and nonofficial forms of thought and speech seems fitting here. As if to prove Bakhtin right, Benício's chapters are dominated by tall tales, jokes, love stories, and intrigues rather than tragedy. Unlike Arinos, Benício allows no one story line to dominate. Rather, he gives us a patchwork of different moments in the lives of the community's residents. They are presented through their relationships to one another, through loves, family, intrigues, and hatreds. The model of the national romance appears in truncated form, for we move into Canudos following two sisters who are drawn there by love. As with Arinos, the language of human relationships thus acts as the conveyor belt that draws us into the world of the town. We likewise leave through the story of a young woman who escapes not the end of the fighting but the unwelcome advances of one of the main fighters. Unlike the figures of Arinos's world, these characters are not always presented sympathetically. Some are frankly ridiculous, sinister, or degenerate, more Balzac than Rabelais.

Benício's novelized sections are additionally Bakhtinian in their proximity to everydayness. Benício verbalizes the desire to generate a perspective that uncovers the everyday lives of the Conselheiro's followers when he invites readers to accompany him into the novelized world of Canudos: "While the fourth and last expedition is being organized let us study the daily manifestations of the instincts, habits, codes, morals and religion of the jagunços gathered in the saintly village" (244). This desire to consider, study, and decipher a culture produces a figure of the Conselheiro as a rather ordinary man, not the mysterious otherworldly figure we find in Arinos's novel. And unlike da Cunha's Conselheiro, he is brought into view not as exemplifying manifestations in biology and race but as embedded in family life. The novel introduces him through the story of his family (the tale of a famous *sertanejo* family feud), so that we first know him as a son, then a husband and father, and only later as the famous Conselheiro. As in many of the later Marxist interpretations of the war (as well as J. J. Veiga's novel *A casca da serpente*), a reduced emphasis on religion accompanies the representation of the Conselheiro as an essentially ordinary man. Religion holds no particular explanatory power in Benício's text. It neither marks the Conselheiro's atavism, as it does in da Cunha's text, nor serves as a screen for an alternative source of power, as in Arinos's. When religion surfaces in Benício's book, it takes on the lowly form of superstition and folklore. It is, in Benício's more anthropological account, simply one element among a series in the culture and everyday lives of Canudos's inhabitants, one term in a list that includes instincts, habits, codes, and morals. As in Arinos's novel, therefore, the invitation into the world of Canudos and the implication that its residents, too, live out daily lives full of regularities, contingencies, and transformations works against the erasure of common ground effected by the prose of counterinsurgency. Arinos appeals to the everyday, however, to make Canudos into an example of an alternative vision for Brazil, whereas Benício conjures up an ordinary Canudos for reasons more directly related to a problem of knowledge. Whereas da Cunha takes the truth of Canudos to lie in its intractability to power and universal knowledge (for it lies outside the voice of reason), Benício seems to suggest that the truth of Canudos can be found more easily, that it is ordinary and needs only to be made visible and sayable. Furthermore, his novel suggests that the *sertanejos'* perspective needs to be represented for the conflict to be understood and its story to be told.

But perhaps this statement does not get at the distinction I'm trying to make, for all these writers—da Cunha, Benício, and Arinos—purport to represent the voice of the *sertanejos*, providing both proxy and portrait. Yet da Cunha will follow a Micheletian model. He assumes a fundamental divide (Michelet names it death) between himself and those he represents, which allows him to see them as representative of something else. He peers unproblematically through or beyond them to that something else, so that they become symptoms of Brazil's problems. Because they stand on the other side of that divide—because they are subaltern, untimely, intractable—they have no real voices of their own. But this schema does not coincide with that of Benício's conundrum. Benício does not reduce the people of Canudos to windows through which to sight another, deeper truth; rather, he casts them as embodied characters with their own perspectives and voices. Because he takes them at face value, however, he must face the gulf between their perspectives and that of their supposed representatives: "That was where one could see the cold and dangerous courage of the sertanejos, convinced that they defended their sacred right to faith, to their goods and honor, threatened by the government of their country. And wasn't this conviction justified?" (292). Benício's text is an affirmation to this last question. This gulf between their convictions and that of the government cannot be dissolved. His text affords us no meeting place, no symbolic resolution. The fracturing in form mirrors this fracturing of perspectives. The option for novelization opens up the possibility that the Conselheiristas will find no place within the official genre of history or even within an anthropological mode of narration. According to Bakhtin, the rhetoric of genre reduces everything to itself and makes everything in its own image, so that "things enter the [pastoral] text only if they agree to be spoken of in the language of the world of shepherds, only if they know how to adapt to that imaginative system,"[27] but Benício seems to struggle to find the language or imaginative system that closes the distance between itself and the "things" he wants to enter the text. The book strives therefore to do something other than simply translate these things into the rules, codes, and language of more official discourses or genres. Unlike Afonso Arinos's rural denizens, who speak an exalted language with references to literary characters and conductors, Benício strains to make room for another language and voice within his text: "I organized this work in plain, Brazilian language, saturated with the syntax and words used by our sertanejos" (prologue). He seeks, in other words, to graft their voices directly onto his text, to produce the effect that he has simply stepped aside and allowed them to speak. In a dialogue between a husband and wife who leave Canudos near the end of the violence, Benício makes them articulate the abyss stretching between themselves and the government: "This will never end. One war ends and another one comes. We chose this forgotten corner of the earth, to live in peace and religion. But it hasn't turned out that way. This drives us crazy, and it would be so good, my dear, if we could spend the rest of our lives adoring God and our son, far away from the witchcraft of the governments" (290). Through this dialogue Benício gives voice to a Canudos that was a protest not against abandonment but against intrusion, the desire to live a peaceful, ordinary life in a small corner of the world, away from the reach of governments that did not and could not represent it.

Arinos, then, chips away at a certain principle of sovereignty's claim to represent the people, whereas Benício interferes with the articulation between a certain organization and genre of knowledge and its claim to truth. He raises, in other words, the possibility that there is no universal language (or form) into which everything can be translated without loss. In its clumsiness, his text also reveals some of the seams that bind truth and power. One of these concerns the place of writing. The official locus of enunciation is intimately bound up with a written archive and relies heavily on official sources, letters, and documents to tell the history of the Conselheiro and the campaigns against his community. One of the few non-novelized passages to use first-person narrative reveals this outside perspective's dependence on writing. In other words, this passage, where Benício transcribes or invents a soldier's journal, constitutes one of the few places where the perspective outside Canudos is transmitted through something other than an omniscient third-person narrator. Access is given through writing. Again, there is an archive one can troll for the official perspective, but how does one access the perspective of the Conselheiristas? And how does one give their perspective weight if the idea of truth remains intimately bound with the technology of writing? The same recourse is not possible with the world of Canudos. Indeed, the novelized sections of the book are saturated with orality, constituted largely by dialogues between the various characters. The book is split therefore between written and oral genres and perspectives. In a Bakhtinian way, then, just as Benício's novelized sections are made up of *sertanejo* voices, his text makes way for some of these other genres. *O rei dos jagunços* begins, for example, with this sentence: "Every cross that is found in the clearings of paths . . . stands for a crime, a murder performed out of revenge" (9). Such crosses, he says, give rise to *sertanejo* legends and heroic stories, which are later turned into songs. Modified, this sentence later finds its way into *Os sertões*, but by beginning his book this way, Benício announces that we, too, will be witnessing a legend or song, the story of another crime of vengeance. The text is framed from the simulated perspective of popular *sertanejo* culture. On the first page, the author characterizes the Canudos War as a crime and inscribes it not within the official book of history but within alternative forms and genres of memory.

This attempt to give voice or room to another perspective appears in an interesting scene where Benício addresses the practice of beheading prisoners, an element of the conflict that produced impassioned condemnations. Consider, for example, Alvim Martins Horcades, a Bahian medical student who went to provide aid during the last campaign. Like other Bahians, he participated in part to clear his region's name. Before he left Salvador, he wrote, "Canudos is not Bahia. Bahia is Salvador, the Medical School, the *Jornal de Notícias*, the symbols of civilization, not the 'rotting lugubrious Canudos.'"[28] His desire to prove his patriotism manifests itself in the eruptions of an exalted rhetoric. In general he finds the campaigns necessary and expresses no doubt that the nation is defending itself against a threat. Like da Cunha and others, he insists that Canudos was not a monarchist conspiracy but simply a collection of ignorant and fanatic people. Horcades nevertheless offered one of the most impassioned protests against beheading prisoners:

> Now, at the present time, when science has progressed and civilization is no longer unknown, in one of the parts of the world that considers itself civilized one does not confiscate, assassinate and murder as if one could thus extinguish completely the mania for revolutions! What a great example of civility and social progress! To take men with their arms tied as criminals, defenseless, in close proximity to their companions so as to increase the humiliation, lift their heads by their noses as if they were birds, and cut their throats with the murderous steel, letting the heads fall on the ground—it is the culmination of banditry practiced in cold blood as if it were a noble action! To kill a woman, simply because her companion was part of the insurgency—it is ultimate disgrace! To snatch away the life of little children, who had not yet felt the first signs of the corruption of humanity, unconscious brains who had not yet felt the vibrations of evil thoughts and which would have later contributed to solidify the enormous wall that sustains republican beliefs—it is the greatest of barbarisms and monstrous crimes that man can perpetuate![29]

Two points about this passage stand out. First, it is organized by a mounting level of criminality according to an ever-increasing state of defenselessness, from the chickenlike men to women to children. Second, the voice that condemns this criminality speaks from a locus of enunciation within a universalizing position of civilization and justice. The children are defenseless because they are *tabulae rasae* and have not yet had the chance to be written over with republican beliefs.

Da Cunha (like Benício) said nothing about the beheadings in his articles but added his voice to the chorus of critiques after the hostilities had ended. His critique bears many formal similarities to Horcades's. Like Horcades, for example, he condemns the beheadings in his own voice, in two sections entitled "Deposition by the Author" and "A Cry of Protest." The *sertanejos*, da Cunha writes, "by no means carried off the palm from our troops when it came to deeds of barbarism"; "this was not a campaign, it was a slaughterhouse."[30] Like Horcades, da Cunha organizes his text according to a mounting defenselessness. Unlike Horcades, however, he chooses to individualize the victims of the beheadings, thus suggesting that beheading crossed a line and became excessive when it involved killing a specific individual rather than a faceless mass of enemies in situations in which dialogue was possible. Not only was this specific rather than blind killing, undertaken coldly rather than in the heat of the battle, but it could also be seen as unnecessary. Da Cunha also ascribes particular meaning to the idea that the *jagunços* superstitiously believed that if they died by steel, their souls would not be saved. Beheading, then, was particularly cruel in exploiting this "naïve superstition" (*Rebellion*, 440).

There are three individuals cited in *Os sertões* in the passages where da Cunha discusses the beheadings. The first is a man da Cunha describes as "one of the few pure blacks that were there," someone whose appearance changes from that of a sickly orangutan to the more noble "ancient statue of a Titan" in the face of death (*Rebellion*, 441). After pausing on the "shameful antinomy" the black man presents, the conversion of roles whereby the *sertanejo* comes to represent nobility, da Cunha moves on to the other examples, two women, first commenting, "One concession at least [the soldiers] made to that respect which was due the human race: they did not slaughter the women and children. There was, however, a proviso attached to this: the prisoners must not give signs of being dangerous" (442). Interestingly, when da Cunha discusses these two female victims, his voice slides into an ironic simulation of the soldier's perspective. The first victim is the same woman who in his articles had twisted and turned, avoiding the soldiers questions with "How should I know?" Here da Cunha describes her as a forty-year-old "demon in petticoats," a "witch prophesying defeat" who is beheaded for her impudence and aggression (442). Although he says that the "timid ones were usually spared," da Cunha ends with a reference to an old, sick woman trailed by her two grandchildren and searching for food, a "sight to move even the hardest of hearts." But her comings and goings don't evoke pity. She represents instead a chastisement, "like the impertinent and persevering ghost of an old remorse" (443). Decapitation is infinitely preferable, according to the soldiers.

Like da Cunha, Benício individualizes the victims of the beheadings, but the way he handles the subject performs the difficulty in voicing a condemnation of these beheadings.[31] Da Cunha's condemnation oscillates between his own voice and a simulation of the soldiers' voices. For all the irony involved, the women end up appearing under the face of an intractability (they represent defiance or chastisement). Benício, however, puts his condemnation in the mouth of a Canudos schoolteacher who accuses the soldiers of taking the inhabitants' houses, clothes, and corn and then beheading the victims so that no one is left to curse them. After making this proclamation, the teacher is interrupted by an "imperious voice" that tells her to be quiet. Benício has her reply, "Be quiet? That's the last straw. You want to take away my voice too? Well, it is easy; cut off my head as you have done with my companions. . . . If you leave me alive you will regret it. I will talk, scream, tell the whole world of this supreme coward-ice and bestiality of beheading prisoners, women and children!" (393). And so they cut off her head. This dialogue, which takes place in one of the novelized sections of *O rei dos jagunços,* typifies how this text attempts to produce the per-spective of the Conselheiristas. Benício condemns the beheadings not from a neutral, universal perspective but from the outrage experienced by the Consel-heiristas who are subject to the beheadings. In this way, the passage explicitly brings up the problem of representation (as both portrait and proxy) and voice by staging a power (the voice of order and authority) that, rather than represent the people, denies them access to voice. Although the imperious voice presum-ably silences the woman's voice by cutting it off, Benício's written words stand in for the words she is not allowed to scream to the whole world.

Note that although Benício uses the novel—and its pretension to incor-porate other forms, such as legends and songs—to simulate the perspective of popular *sertanejo* culture, his text never manages to close in on the vantage point of the Conselheiristas, rendering his text truly dialogic. The novelistic genre is appropriated to produce the *effect* of a proximity he desires; it offers the reader a seemingly more transparent and immediate access to the reality of its subjects and their unmediated voices. This effect of transparency is ob-vious when, in one of Benício's novelized chapters, the Conselheiro is said to esteem a young follower "because he reminded him of the features and habits of a son whom he hadn't heard of in a while" (103). Fiction, therefore, provides the illusion of access. In contrast, the more historiographical sections include stretches where the Conselheiro appears and disappears according to his in-scription in the written record: "There were six years without notice of Maciel, when in 1873, he appeared in Itapicurú, in Bahia, wearing a rough cotton blue tunic" (41). Benício thus uses novelization to produce the kind of effect that Mario Vargas Llosa implements in *The Storyteller,* where he simulates counter-point to the main narrative voice by taking on the voice of the presumed story-teller of the Amazonian Machiguanga tribe. Indeed, Vargas Llosa employs this technique in *The War of the End of the World,* too, although there he conjures up not two but an entire labyrinth of perspectives and voices that never meet or enter into dialogue, thus suggesting that the Canudos War resulted from the blindness of conflicting ideologies. Yet the comparison to Vargas Llosa leads us back to the issue of *O rei dos jagunços*'s relationship to authority. Some critics have suggested that the clash between different worlds and perspectives in *The War of the End of the World* does not include an instance that explains the antagonisms globally, but this is part of Vargas Llosa's feint, an attempt to occupy a pragmatic, nonideological but ultimately universalizing position.[32] Benício's text is unable to do this.

This does not mean that the text forgoes a universalizing position. Indeed, the performance of other genres—the inclusion of novelized sections that simulate the perspective from Canudos, the way the book is framed as a *sertanejo* tale—accompanies a shift from a presumably universal to a perspectival position, thus implying that the Conselheiristas can occupy only a partial position, never a universal one. Like Rama's transculturators, the book tries to occupy the place of mediation between the two perspectives, as is indicated by the many parenthesis and footnotes defining *sertanejo* words for the non-*sertanejo* readers to whom the book is directed. Like Rama's transculturators, Benício's text evinces an instability of form that betrays the pressure of attempting such a mediation as well as the supposition that a change in form is necessary to do so. But the book undermines this universalizing position by showing itself unable to actualize it. It provincializes this supposedly universal position by suggesting all that it may not be able to capture. One example of this effect occurs when Benício accidentally uses a first-person pronoun when describing the conflict's last moments (these are essentially passages lifted from his newspaper articles, where he speaks in his own voice). At these moments the text reveals its locus of enunciation as that of someone who took part in the battle on the side of the soldiers. This slip shows us (in Foucault's words) a subject who is speaking in the midst of a war, someone who "is involved in the battle, has adversaries and is working toward a particular victory."[33] By slipping into first person precisely where the text is presumably performing a nonperspectival discourse (and the difference is marked in Benício's text by the shift in genres), Benício shows himself unable to write a text that establishes itself "between the adversaries, in the center and above them, imposing one general law on all and founding a reconciliatory order."[34]

Whereas Arinos's text displays the supremacy of form and its ability to let the world in only insofar as its speaks the language of the text, Benício's text shows form failing to impose itself as a legitimate language, for the book constantly shifts genre in its attempt to make the Canudos War legible. If neither text produces a Canudos that is recognizable as Canudos, then we may need to reflect on our deeply ingrained habit of reading *Canudos* as the name for a moment of mediation between form and world, the moment in which the pressure of the real produces a new form and a new language and compensates in this way for a reality that remains even today divided and disintegrated.

AFTERLIVES

Commemoration . . . fixes the dead in the past, where what the dead require is a place in the futures that were denied them. Only in remaining out of joint with the times to which the dead are lost is there any prospect of a redress that would not be concomitant with the desire to lay the dead to rest.

—David Lloyd, *Irish Times*

I have used the term *sentencing* to keep visible the relationship between power and representation. Those who have been sentenced to history have been inscribed in history, overtaken by it, condemned to take part in it, turned into its subjects. If power relations are (mis)translated into epistemological structures so that condemnations (one sort of sentence) become descriptions (another sort of sentence), what reconciliations can representation afford?

The community of Canudos was etched into the archive under a particular face that is intimately bound up with the representational politics of the modern nation-state and the place of intellectual mediation within that configuration. Canudos was turned into a symptom of larger problems in the postcolonial nation-state—an unknown people and territory, imported models of government—that ostensibly would be solved only when intellectuals, if not the state, perfected representational politics, aligning the state with its people and representing those people whose voices had not yet been captured. This structure cannot be undone. Canudos can never simply be Belo Monte. It is now the name of this surface of inscription.

But what of this sentence's afterlives? On the one hand, Canudos is some-times understood as having failed to survive except as it was absorbed into the modernizing drive; on the other hand, it is sometimes seen as "living on" in new and different ways. In *Irish Times* David Lloyd suggests that colonization erases the potentiality of a colonized people, denying them an orientation to-ward the future. To insist on the truncated potentialities of different cultural formations is not to indulge in mythic or utopian illusions, he argues, but sim-ply to "acknowledge that each cultural formation and moment envisages its own potential for transformation in its own materially available terms . . . in ways that cannot be contained by a single historical narrative or canonical path to development."[1] Lloyd urges us to understand those elements of a colonized culture incommensurable with modernity not as "melancholy survivals" but as forms of "living on" that do more than simply preserve belated practices, as "potentialities for producing and reproducing a life that lies athwart moder-nity."[2] This is a narrative of transformation, not recovery, since "to pass on is to be changed. And the changed live on in strange ways."[3]

I cite Lloyd here not to take up the challenge of investigating how inhabit-ants of the area lived on in changed ways after the Canudos War. Instead, I read Lloyd's remarks as a call to recognize how Canudos is either denied or granted a futuricity, how the dead are either laid to rest or summoned to take part of a future, and what this may tell us about the political projects evok-ing the name Canudos. To do so, I will pass through one final comparison of da Cunha, Benício, and Arinos and then consider two contemporary filmic it-erations on the theme: Sergio Rezende's *Battle for Canudos* (1999) and Antônio Olavo's *Paixão e guerra no sertão de Canudos* (1993).

Ends

In a famous passage near the end of *Os sertões*, da Cunha pictures five thou-sand soldiers fervently roaring before the last four survivors: "Canudos did not surrender. The only case of its kind in history, it held out to the last man. Conquered inch by inch, in the literal meaning of the words, it fell on Octo-ber 5, toward dusk—when its last defenders fell, dying, every man of them. There were only four of them left: an old man, two other full-grown men, and a child, facing a furiously raging army of five thousand solders."[4] At first glance this passage is exceptional for the visibility of the state's violence against Canu-dos, a visibility created by the grotesque contrast of four people, one old, one a child, standing before the rabid cheers of five thousand victorious soldiers.

This visibility is exceptional if one supposes that a prose of counterinsurgency is organized by the teleology of certain inevitable historical processes (progress, modernity, the state), making any violence done by or in these processes merely unfortunate but necessary fallout or residue. Their violence is therefore invisible as violence, while the violence of these others is glaringly visible. If we approach the passage according to this perspective, we can read da Cunha as subverting such a process. He would be seeing this violence as violence (once again the trope of da Cunha's sight rears its head).

But we should complicate such a reading by asking for da Cunha's particular investment in underscoring the violence at the end and for rendering this scene *as* an end. According to oral history undertaken since the 1950s, many inhabitants survived, several hundred or so. One local landowner even wrote to the baron of Geremoabo complaining that many women and children were being kept alive and would be an expense to the state (he suggested beheading them). He also complained about the troops' retreat, leaving residents unprotected from attacks by the two to three thousand *jagunços* still roaming about freely.[5] There were, then, enough elements to imagine survivors of different sorts. Indeed, various texts, both contemporary ones such as Benício's and Arinos's and more recent novels such as Sándor Márai's *Veredicto em Canudos* and J. J. Veiga's *A casca da serpente*, envision something other than complete destruction, imagining the Conselheiro or his followers as having survived and gone on to rebuild another Canudos elsewhere. This range of possibilities creates the sense that da Cunha's text is particularly invested in burying Canudos, in laying the dead to rest, and making sure it continues only insofar as it is absorbed and passed on as an element within the story of an emerging nation-state. Canudos can name only the past, never an orientation toward a future.

Whereas da Cunha's book ends with the end of Canudos, the corpse of the Conselheiro, and a lament that there is no Maudsley for "acts of madness and crimes on the part of nations,"[6] Benício's last chapter stages a series of encounters with the ruins of the community. First, soldiers find a child's skull and recoil. Next, two survivors of Canudos, Vilanova and Thiago, meet, talk, and move on. Their meeting suggests that witnesses to Canudos will pass on and survive. When Beatinho is being led away to have his head cut off, he sees Thiago escaping and thinks, "At least he, who had seen everything, would tell the world the supreme courage and disgrace of Canudos."[7] As if to prove Beatinho right, when Thiago meets up with Vilanova in the last chapter, he describes the town's final days to him (curiously, the historical Vilanova gave an oral deposition many years later), finishing by expressing a desire for revenge: "Who knows if we won't yet have a chance to take revenge on the cursed men who did this!"[8] The last figure is the strangest of all, a man we met at the beginning of *O rei dos jagunços* who had been raping his own daughter and who went mad when confronted and chastised by the Conselheiro. In the later scene, he is described as a Quixote-like figure on a mule: "A tall slim figure appeared like a Quixotic or fantastic being . . . , his feet dragging on the ground, naked, hat perched on his head!" Wandering lost through the ruins, he says, "I am Jararaca, the only animal that kills its young! And his hoarse, rough voice frightened the last birds of prey sifting the ruins of Canudos."[9] The figure of Jararaca is a maddened trace, a living reminder of the effect of the Conselheiro. He may also be a substitute voice for the republic—for it, too, killed its "children"—acting as a figure for a nation that is swallowed up in the vortex of Canudos (a reading several critics have argued for *Os sertões*) rather than founded on the subsumption of that disaster. By ending after the end of Canudos, Benício leaves open its various afterlives: the guilt of the soldiers, the desire for revenge on the part of the survivors and witnesses, the restless madness of a spectral figure who remains out of joint with the settled future of modernity.

Afonso Arinos, too, ends his book with survival rather than destruction. Before dying, the Conselheiro tells the main character to take a group of people out of Canudos. This way, he says, the soldiers will find only ashes, and the people of Canudos will have won.[10] Luís follows the Conselheiro's orders, so that he, Joana, and others escape. The book ends with a sequence that first describes the destruction of Canudos but then says it was not really the end. "It was the end," the book reads, but a few lines later we are told, "Not all the jagunços died in the furnace. Hiding there, some men, women and children had eluded the sight of the troops and escaped death."[11] These survivors are disoriented with the prospect of living after and outside Canudos, and their memories of lives before Canudos are tenuous. One of them comments that he got used to fighting and that he misses the sound of the bullets, the faces of the soldiers: "Little by little, their memory pieced together the life they had lived before Belo Monte and which seemed to them now so far away, so vague, like the vague scenery of dreamed landscapes. The jagunços found themselves in the position of those who doubted that there had been a world before or outside Belo Monte."[12] Arinos's survivors have "passed on" and changed in strange ways. They have to stitch together the dreamlike life before Canudos, Canudos itself, and its aftermath, producing a sense from that fragmented non-sense and finding a way to live on. Arinos ultimately ends with a rather biblical and open-ended line: "And the tribe marched to the desert."[13]

Comparing *Os sertões* to these other texts suggests that da Cunha wanted to wipe Canudos off the face of the earth. It is a symptom of da Cunha's desire to eliminate, if only symbolically, something he still secretly regarded as a threat. By killing off its inhabitants, da Cunha effectively isolates Canudos in time just as he had tried to isolate it in space. Nothing comes after it, other than his own book, the lullaby to lay them to rest. It provides a counterpart to the erasure of the everydayness of Canudos. Canudos is imaginable only as an extraordinary rupture that is then subsumed in the dialectical march of national history. Da Cunha's end textualizes the belief that this subsumption requires the destruction of Canudos as Canudos.

Moreover, this subsumption is necessary if the fantasy of community that motivated the Conselheiristas is to be translated to the level of the national imagined community. Although da Cunha subscribed to nineteenth-century crowd psychologists' unease regarding crowds, mobs, and multitudes, he struggles with the heterogeneity of Brazil and with the need to establish a common national imagined community and a common denominator. If the *jagunço* is to be the bedrock, the foundation, of Brazilian nationhood, then the unity of Canudos must be harnessed for Brazil. His book suggests that this process occurred in the campaigns against Canudos. Although the war turned the soldiers into *jagunços,* leading them to degenerate and become a multitude, a barbarous raging horde capable of cheering at the obscene victory over four miserable survivors, the book does not simply lay out a movement in which the army—and the republic—is sucked into the void of Canudos.[14] Rather than founder within the disaster of Canudos, the nation is founded on it. It becomes the occasion that produces the needed unity. In one of those dynamic transformations that mark the pages of *Os sertões* (desert-granary, Hercules-Quasimodo, orangutan-Titan), multitude is used to signify not only a human polyp but home. Salvador, the state capital of Bahia, receives the wounded soldiers with "deep emotion. As always happens, individual impressions were caught up in the collective reaction, which, with many persons experiencing the same feelings, thus became the exponent of individual sentiment; with all hearts beating as one, all were affected by the same contagion, the same suggestive images, and all individuals were merged in the ennobling anonymity of a pitying multitude, the like of which has seldom been seen in history. The vast city now became one huge home."[15]

The war elicits not only degeneration but also a noble unity. Furthermore, da Cunha confers particular significance to the fact that this unity takes place in Salvador, the old colonial capital of Brazil. When different men meet as the troops gather in Salvador, da Cunha calls it a reunification of that which had been scattered historically. The soldiers come from diverse regions and bear different temperaments, customs, and ethnic tendencies, and "the former capital," Salvador, "greeted with warm and glowing affection these wandering sons of hers—wandering for three whole centuries. Long dispersed, the various factors of our race, beautifully intermingled, were of a sudden returning to their point of departure."[16]

This combination of destruction and subsumption is repeated in Sergio Rezende's *A guerra de Canudos* (*The Battle for Canudos*) (1997), a remarkable feature since the film purports to splice da Cunha's version of Canudos with the other genealogy Arinos and Benício trace. The movie follows the story from the perspective of a poor family of *sertanejos*. The parents (Zé Lucena and Penha), alienated by the policies of the newly established republic (such as the imposition of taxes), are drawn to the Conselheiro's message and decide to follow him with their two young children. The oldest daughter, Luiza, refuses to join them and flees to a life of ill repute before marrying a young soldier who takes part in ensuing the military campaign. The movie bears consideration on several levels. First, it takes up the family romance in a slightly different vein, since there are really two families here. On the one hand, we have Luiza's original family, which is sundered by the conflict. This family stands as an allegory for the Brazilian national family; the Canudos War takes place inside an otherwise constituted and natural community, pitting sister against sister. On the other hand, the movie reimagines the constitution of a new family through the romance between the *sertaneja* and the soldier, which figures a coming together, a unification of differences, as in the nineteenth-century love stories Sommer analyses. Second, the movie incorporates much of the historiographical work that seeks to find lines of continuity between Canudos and the surrounding *sertão* and to show Canudos in its everyday, normal aspect. At least one reviewer notices precisely this aspect of the film, writing that the movie "partly succeeds" in placing the community within the larger context of life in the Northeast. It also, he writes, "helps to dispel the myth that the Conselheiro and his followers were a gang of radical, politically motivated millennial fanatics. Although Canudos was envisioned as a New Jerusalem and its inhabitants, who lived lives of austerity, were prepared to defend themselves, they were hardly fanatics."[17] The incorporation of such material serves to mark the movie as "progressive" (i.e., a film that incorporates the perspective of the defeated) but only to ultimately subsume it within a vision that is basically da Cunha's, a point particularly clear in the film's end. The final battle scene essentially re-creates da Cunha's scene of four fighters (one of them Luiza's father) standing against a raging army. Canudos is essentially razed. The only one left is Luiza, the film's main protagonist, who then chooses to migrate south. Framing the events through a woman's perspective lends a progressive sheen to a series of decisions whose concatenation is thus naturalized; to opt for change is to mi-grate not to Canudos but to the south. In effect, it trades one disfranchised population for another—women versus poor *sertanejos*, the right to choose an independent life and not follow patriarchal dictates versus the right to opt out of state-led modernization—and suggests that one of these minority positions points to the future while the other is effectively sealed off. An option to mourn and commemorate, but never to follow.

We can contrast Rezende's film—mainstream, well financed, and com-mercially successful—with a documentary produced by Antônio Olavo four years earlier: *Paixão e guerra no sertão de Canudos* (1993). Oral historians, musi-cians, and sociologists in present-day Canudos have been working to rescue local narratives that tell a story different from the canonical one, and Olavo's documentary contributes to this effort. This local perspective evokes the time that Prathama Banerjee distinguishes from the time of national history. It is, she says, a "spatialized time, which accumulated traces of all that passed over it. Its authenticity lay not in a chronological accuracy or a consistent sense of suc-cession of events or even of narrative resolutions, but in the admittance that the past and the present had the same location on the ground. The local historian knew the past because he lived in spatial intimacy to it."[18] Olavo organized his documentary as a counterpoint between two visual modes; the first consists of the kind of spatial intimacy to which Banerjee refers, a series of testimonies and narratives by older inhabitants of the region, some of whom were born be-tween 1893 and 1903. Although they were young children during the conflict, they grew up hearing the stories their elders told. The film's visual-oral me-dium enables Olavo to tap into an oral stream at the margins of the written rec-ord. In the context of dominant narratives of Canudos, Banerjee's "spatialized time" reconstitutes a ground between Canudos and now.

To a large extent this ground lies in the materiality of the storytellers' bod-ies, a materiality that the camera marks by lingering over their feet, hands, and eyes. The intense focus on these body fragments marks the inscription of time as well—their eyes are blind; their hands and feet, calloused and often covered with flies. Although near death, they are—on screen—still there. Olavo's camera thus stages itself as rescuing the last living memory of this battle as it lingers on the edge of erasure. But insofar as it adds itself to a living continuity, Olavo's camera interrupts da Cunha's attempt to erase Canudos beyond its inscription in his own text. Olavo shows us the living traces of ordinary men and women who remember the conflict not as a foundational event in a national history but as stories told by their fathers and mothers and their neighbors.

The documentary intervenes most forcefully by showing that these traces still exist, not by divulging the particular content of the stories being told. The documentary does not attempt to uphold a popular memory as containing "the truth" of Canudos but simply emphasizes the subsistence of popular memory. This is clear, for example, in a sequence that passes through three different versions of the Conselheiro's end. The first speaker, blind in one eye, tells us: "The Conselheiro said to him 'So many images and so many innocent, for those unbelievers to finish.' And then my father said, . . . 'You know that the Conselheiro will leave or he will die.' It became dark and the dawn did not come. There was no one who would see him anymore. No one knows what world he went to, nor if he died. When he went the next day they hunted Conselheiro and didn't find him. They didn't find him dead. He doesn't know. That is what he used to say." He wipes away his tears. The camera cuts to images of flowers, a *sertanejo* song playing in the background.

The camera then cuts to a man identified as Zé de Isabé, who is 100 years old, also blind, and comes from Riacho de Pedra, Bahia. The intense affect of the first speaker yields to a man who is sprightly and swings emphatically in a hammock. Whereas the first speaker's words convey an immeasurable loss that could be both the loss of his father and that of the Conselheiro, a loss that seems to leave behind little trace or certainty and whose closure is thus problematic, Zé's words and tones are energetic yet matter of fact: "I knew an old man named Santinho and he told me that he was Conselheiro's bodyguard. He was guarding him and the Conselheiro died. Three days passed. He said he would be resurrected. Three days passed. They couldn't stand the stench and they buried him with mats, he was stinking, and they put the images that he had and buried him. He didn't die from the shells. He fell ill and died."

The camera again cuts to flowers and the song and then cuts back to a third, more subdued speaker: "Conselheiro died inside of the church during that terrible bombardment. Balbino, who was guarding the church, said to me that a shell came, hit a corner of the church and exploded near the altar where the Conselheiro was. A shell fragment came . . . it opened his tunic and cut him sideways. He died instantly. That was how he died. He died on the twenty-second of September of 1897."

The documentary presents the three stories one after another without any further comment. Because the three versions contradict one another, their value lies not so much in the claims to truth or the authenticity of oral narrative as in the "spatial intimacy" to Canudos generated by these bodies and the personal relationships linking them to the community. Canudos is a part of their lives still, still present, neither pure past nor pure utopian future.

Just as he avoids setting up these stories as the repositories of the truth about the conflict, Olavo further avoids setting up himself as the transparent medium for this truth. Instead, he foregrounds the artificiality of his narrative: scenes in which a voice-over (curiously, by the actor who played the Counselheiro in Sergio Rezende's film) narrates incidents in the conflict punctuate the firsthand narratives. No documentary footage of the events exists, however, so Olavo fabricates substitutes; in scenes where the battle is described, for instance, we see ants scurrying about in confusion or mounds of earth falling. These images are meant to be allegorical (like Arinos's image of the bees), but the use of allegory rather than mimetic realism is more jarring in this film than it is in the novel, especially after the neorealistic images of old bodies talking. Darién Davis refers to this aspect when reviewing the film, saying that "many of the images of animals, water and landscapes are not adequately integrated into the narrative."[19] Indeed, the technique does interrupt rather than facilitate a move from image to referent. We feel that these images do not really "express" the "phenomena" to which they refer; the gap between ants scurrying about and men fighting and dying is too great for us to pass comfortably from one to the other. But perhaps this is deliberate, not a result of "inadequate integration." Whereas Michel Foucault and Gilles Deleuze sought to let the people speak for themselves, Olavo uses these moments to "thicken" his mediation, rendering it visible rather than transparent. The visual allegory thus separates his vision of the conflict—the vision of a Bahian (not *sertanejo*) intellectual, photographer, and filmmaker that cannot quite escape da Cunha's narrative but instead exists in tension with it—from the perspective of the old men and women who lived in the events' immediate aftermath.

Thus, although the documentary is organized around a "plot" (the narra-

tive of the military campaign), Olavo does not subsume all these stories into
the "unitary time and narrative of the nation." Whereas time—and temporalization—dominates the logic of the nation, space and spatiality inform the
local. The nation is the place of history, but the local is its archive. Olavo maintains the visibility of the disorder of scraps and fragments: "first-hand testimonies, personal memories, proverbs, tales, descriptions of local lands and ruins."[20] Although Olavo's film is oriented toward the past, toward the memories
of Canudos, the disorder and multiplicity of these scraps leaves open a gamut
of futures.

Olavo's documentary reaches for an explicitly local rather than national
locus of enunciation, a turn complemented by Canudos's recent emergence
as an element within a more global imaginary in the works of political philosophers such as Ernest Laclau, Slavoj Žižek, and Antonio Negri. Both possibilities, however, result from the perceived waning of the nation-state as the
horizon of the political. This does not mean that we are living in a nonrepre-
sentational world, but the possibility of another kind of politics is no longer
nonsensical. If hegemonic forms of conceptualization render other forms, other
imaginaries, "unreadable, inaudible and incomprehensible,"[21] then representational politics—the assumption that a "people" is represented by a particular
state form—may no longer be hegemonic in the same way. Canudos takes on
a different face in these circumstances. Turned into a datum in the life story of
the nation-state, engraved into history as the antagonist and counterface to the
modern state, this negativity becomes a condition of possibility for Canudos to
live on in new ways. In the concluding chapter to *GlobAL: Biopoder y luchas en una
América Latina globalizada,* Antonio Negri and Giuseppe Cocco write:

> [The] "commune" of Canudos, exterminated in the name of progress during
> the "war of the end of the world," reappears today in all of its potential as the
> anticipation of an irreducible alternative to modernity. . . . The potential of
> the exodus of Canudos has finally proven victorious over the projects of white
> colonialism. . . . In the history of Brazil there exists a magnificent paradigm
> of the rupture of continental European dominion, maintained and efficiently
> transfigured by the autonomous and bourgeois governments, inheritors of
> the 1800s. This consists in showing us how the potential of the exodus of
> Canudos has finally been victorious over the projects of white colonialism
> (whether of European or Brazilian origin). The potential of biopolitical mes-
> tizaje confronts the management of biopower . . . Canudos won![22]

This is a simultaneously familiar and fantastic vision. Canudos retains the utopian face that it acquired when it was turned into a rupture and hiatus, a no-place. This is the romantic line of the flight of pirates. But it is now also the name of a victory and of a future rather than an end. By ending with Negri and Cocco I do not mean to install them in the place previously given to Euclides da Cunha, to suggest that they somehow "see" Canudos correctly. What I hope their vision shows, however, is the extent to which Canudos was turned into and remains a surface on which political meaningfulness is negotiated. It is a place of judgment about the possibilities and limits of politics. A sentence.

NOTES

Introduction

1. Homi Bhabha, *The Location of Culture* (New York: Routledge, 1994), 172.

2. John Beverley, *Subalternity and Representation* (Durham: Duke University Press, 1999), 43.

3. Ranajit Guha, *Elementary Aspects of Peasant Insurgency in Colonial India* (New Delhi: Oxford University Press, 1983), 18.

4. Michel Foucault, *The Archeology of Knowledge and the Discourse on Language* (New York: Pantheon, 1972), 129.

5. Charles Taylor, *Altarity* (Chicago: University of Chicago Press, 1987), 195.

6. Qtd. in Walnice Nogueira Galvão, *No calor da hora: A guerra de Canudos nos jornais, 4a expedição* (São Paulo: Atica, 1974), 105. All translations are my own unless otherwise specified.

7. Contemporary texts on Canudos include chronicles by Machado de Assis, as well as Francisco Mangabeira, *Tragédia epica* (1900); José Aras, *Sangue de irmãos*; the so-called "Manifesto dos estudantes das escolas superiores da Bahia aos seus collegas e aos Republicanos dos outros estados" (1897); Marcos Evangelista da Costa Villela Júnior, *Canudos: Memórias de um combatente* (1988); César Zama, *Libelo republicano acompanhado de comentários sobre a guerra de Canudos*; Alvim Martins Horcades, *Descrição de uma viagem a Canudos* (1899); Aristides Augusto Milton, *A campanha de Canudos* (1902); J. P. Favilla Nunes, *Guerra de Canudos*; and the newspaper articles gathered in Walnice Nogueira Galvão's *No calor da hora*. The best collection of sources on Canudos can be found at the Núcleo Sertão in the library of the Universidade Federal da Bahia (UFBA) and on a CD-ROM archive at the Universidade Estadual da Bahia (UNEB). Of the great many fictionalized narratives of Canudos, the most well known may be Mario Vargas Llosa, *The War of the End of the World*. Other novelized versions of Canudos written by non-Brazilians include Lucien Marchal, *The Sage of Canudos*; Sándor Márai, *Veredicto em Canudos* (1969); and R. B. Cunninghame Graham, *A Brazilian Mystic: Being the Life and Miracles of Antonio Conselheiro* (1920). Novels

by Brazilian authors include J. J. Veiga, *A casca da serpente* (1989); Eldon Canário, *Cativos da terra*; Julio José Chiavento, *As meninas do Belo Monte* (1993); Paulo Dantas, *O Purgatório* (1954) and *O Menino-Jagunço* (1968); Ayrton Marcondes, *Canudos: As memórias de Frei João Evangelista* (1997); and Luiz Carlos Lisboa, *A guerra santa do gato* (2002). There is, finally, a vast quantity of popular verse on Canudos both from the time of the war and more recently. Two published examples are Gastão Neves, *Romancero de Canudos* (1991); and Edio Souza and Paulo Setubal, *ABC da guerra do absurdo* (1997).

8. Todd Diacon, "Peasants, Prophets, and the Power of a Millenarian Vision in Twentieth Century Brazil," *Comparative Studies in Society and History* 32.3 (1990): 488–514. See also Todd Diacon, *Millenarian Vision, Capitalist Reality: Brazil's Contestado Rebellion 1912–1916* (Durham: Duke University Press, 1991).

9. Lizir Arcanjo Alves, *Humor e sátira na Guerra de Canudos* (Salvador, Brazil: Empresa Gráfica da Bahia, 1997), 178.

10. Regina Abreu, *O enigma de "Os sertões"* (Rio de Janeiro, Funarte / Rocco, 1998), 265.

11. Robert Levine, *Vale of Tears: Revisiting the Canudos Massacre in Northeastern Brazil, 1893–97* (Berkeley: University of California Press, 1992), 20.

12. Abreu, *O enigma*, 19.

13. Edivaldo Boaventura, "Parque estadual de Canudos: Criação e evolução," *Revista Canudos* 1.1 (1997): 66.

14. Qtd. in Abreu, *O enigma*, 300.

15. David Lloyd and Paul Thomas, *Culture and the State* (New York: Routledge, 1998), 21.

16. Qtd. in Manoel Neto, "Canudos na boca do povo," *Revista Canudos* 2.2 (1997): 56.

17. Levine, *Vale of Tears*, 4.

18. Guha, *Elementary Aspects*, 333.

19. Michel de Certeau, *The Practice of Everyday Life* (Berkeley: University of California Press, 1984), 155.

20. Florencia Mallon, "The Promise and Dilemma of Subaltern Studies: Perspectives from Latin American History," *American Historical Review* 5 (1994): 1497.

21. Ibid.

22. There are several accounts of the group's trajectory. See, for example, Ileana Rodríguez's introduction ("Reading Subalterns across Texts, Disciplines, and Theories: From Representation to Recognition") to her edited collection *The Latin American Subaltern Studies Reader* (Durham: Duke University Press, 2001), 1–32; and Gareth Williams, "La deconstrucción y los estudios subalternos, o, una llave de tuerca en la línea de montaje latinoamericanista," in *Treinta años de estudios literarios/culturales Latinoamericanistas en Estados Unidos: Memorias, testimonios, reflexiones críticas*, ed. Hernán Vidal, 221–56 (Pittsburgh: International Institute of Iberoamerican Literature, 2008). See also Latin America Subaltern Studies Group, "Founding Statement," *boundary 2* 20 (Fall 1993): 110–21; and John Beverley, "Negotiating with the Disciplines: A Conversation on Latin American Subaltern Studies," *Journal of Latin American Cultural Studies* 6.2 (1997): 233–56.

23. Mallon, "Promise and Dilemma," 1506.

24. Gyan Prakash, "Subaltern Studies as Postcolonial Criticism," *American Historical Review* 99 (Dec. 1994): 1482.

25. Gyan Prakash, "The Impossibility of Subaltern History," *Nepantla* 1.2 (2001): 293.

26. Prakash, "Subaltern Studies," 1480.

27. Prakash, "Impossibility of Subaltern History," 1.

Chapter One: The Voice of Others

1. For many fans, Euclides da Cunha has the status of a national hero in a rather nineteenth-century Romantic fashion: the writer as the great genius. His biography, at least, certainly fits a Romantic register. Born in Rio de Janeiro in 1866, Euclides da Cunha was a "dislocated person . . . marked by the early loss of his mother, by his father's financial limitations, by his aloof character, by his stormy rebelliousness, by his emotional sterility, and by his severe morality" (Luiz Costa Lima, "In the Backlands of Hidden Mimesis," *Control of the Imaginary: Reason and Imagination in Modern Times* [Minneapolis: University of Minnesota Press, 1988], 152). Unable to pay for an engineering degree at the Escola Politécnica, he entered the military, studying engineering instead at the Escola Militar da Praia Vermelha, where he met Benjamin Constant and was strongly influenced by positivist and republican ideas. His relationship with the army was never to be tight, however. He was expelled from the military academy for an antimonarchical act of insubordination, and in 1894 he was exiled to a small city in Minas Gerais for being anti-Florianist, after which he left the army for good. In his adult life he worked mainly as a civil engineer, living a nomadic life from engineering job to engineering job, with periods of unemployment, all the while writing for several newspapers. *O Estado de São Paulo* hired him as a war correspondent during the final three weeks of the fourth Canudos expedition. After writing *Os sertões* he was admitted into the Instituto Histórico e Geográfico Brasileiro and the Academia Brasileira de Letras. In 1905 the Barão do Rio Branco sent him as the chief of the expedition to demarcate the borders between Peru, Bolivia, and Brazil in the Amazon, an expedition that led to a series of texts later published as *Peru X Bolívia* and *À margem da história*. In 1909, at age forty-three, he was killed in a duel with his wife's lover.

2. Walnice Nogueira Galvão and Oswaldo Galotti, eds., *Correspondência de Euclides da Cunha* (São Paulo: Editora da Universidade de São Paulo, 1997), 133.

3. Gayatri Spivak, *A Critique of Postcolonial Reason* (Cambridge, Mass.: Harvard University Press, 1999), 256–64.

4. Euclides da Cunha, *Rebellion in the Backlands*, trans. Samuel Putnam (Chicago: University of Chicago Press, 1944), 443.

5. Qtd. in Galvão and Galotti, *Correspondência*, 103.

6. This despite the enormous abundance of material produced on da Cunha. The bibliography Irene Monteiro Reis organized for the Instituto Nacional do Livro in 1971 listed 2,057 titles published about Euclides da Cunha, including books, articles, pamphlets, chapters, and so on (see Adelino Brandão, *Euclides da Cunha e a questão racial do Brasil: A antropologia de "Os sertões"* [Rio de Janeiro: Presença, 1990], 150). Brandão reels off a list of the various ways da Cunha has been read: "Euclides, the poet, Euclides, the prosaist; Euclides the artist of the written word; Euclides the novelist, the fictionalizer, the stylist; the academic, the military, the journalist; the professor of logic, the engineer, the mapmaker; the war correspondent, the reporter, the letter-writer; the regionalist writer,

the pre-modernist, the nationalist, the social philosopher, the political thinker and teacher, the socialist 'militant' and founder of working class newspapers and clubs, the nineteenth-century Brazilian 'prophet,' the humanist, the romantic realist, the 1889 revolutionary, the rebel cadet, activist for republicanism and for the abolition of slavery; the diplomat, the *sertanista*, the patriot and exemplary functionary; the impassioned liberal, the eternal defender of the *sertanejos* and of the dispossessed backlands populations; the defender of democratic and progressive theses. . . . Also, the 'determinist,' the 'racist' or 'fatalist,' or even the passionate, the imitator of Góngora, the baroque writer, the writer of 'exaggerated, irritating language' (Walnice Nogueira Galvão); the 'irritating writer' (Rachel de Queiroz); the man who 'wrote with a vine' (Joaquim Nabuco). . . . And parallels are made: Euclides and Machado, Euclides and Raul Pompéia, Euclides and Herculano, Euclides and Rui . . . [;] parallels are also made with foreigners: Euclides and Sarmiento, Euclides and Steinbeck, Euclides and Tolstoy, or, inversely, Monteiro Lobato and Euclides da Cunha, Guimarães Rosa and Euclides. . . . Or the drama of his life is painted anew, the true page of a 'great tragedy' (Monteiro Lobato), the 'Passional Drama' which ended his career and life, after the travails of his marriage, in a biography known for its apparently irrational moves" (20).

7. Olimpio de Sousa Andrade qtd. in Euclides da Cunha, *Caderneta de campo* (São Paulo: Editora Cultrix, 1975), 191.

8. Qtd. in Luiz Costa Lima, *Terra ignota: A construção de "Os sertões"* (Rio de Janeiro: Civilização Brasileira, 1997), 21.

9. Qtd. in Olimpio de Sousa Andrade's classic *História e interpretação de "Os sertões"* (São Paulo: EdArt, 1966), 358.

10. Patrícia Cardoso Borges, "A interpretação d'os Sertões, ontem e hoje," in *"Os sertões" de Euclides da Cunha: Releituras e diálogos*, ed. José Leonardo do Nascimento (São Paulo: Editora Universidade Estadual Paulista, 2002), 193.

11. Ibid., 200.

12. Ibid., 194.

13. Silviano Santiago, *Nas malhas da letra* (Rio de Janeiro: Editora Rocco, 2002), 107.

14. Borges, "A interpretação," 201.

15. Marco Antonio Villa, *Canudos: O povo da terra* (São Paulo: Editora Atica, 1995), 7.

16. José Augusto Cabral Barreto Bastos, *Incompreensível e bárbaro inimigo: A guerra simbólica contra Canudos* (Salvador, Brazil: Editora da Universidade Federal da Bahia, 1995).

17. Ibid., 21.

18. Ibid., 22.

19. Ibid., 25.

20. Leopoldo Bernucci, *A imitação dos dentidos: Prógonos, contemporâneos e epígonos de Euclides da Cunha* (São Paulo: Editora da Universidade de São Paulo, 1995), 21.

21. Ibid., 27. Similarly, Regina Abreu, who analyzes the canonization of *Os sertões* as a weathervane of intellectual developments in Brazil, returns to the issue of da Cunha's present value at the end of her book by citing Gilberto Freyre's assessment that da Cunha had lucidly perceived the social and cultural dimensions of the tragic violence as the manifestation of a clash between two cultures in Brazil, "even though his scientistic

prejudices—principally those regarding race—perturbed his analysis and his interpretation of some of the facts of Brazilian social formation, *which his keen eyes were able to perceive,*
as they sought the roots of Canudos" (Regina Abreu, *O enigma de "Os sertões"* [Rio de
Janeiro: Funarte / Rocco, 1998], 391; emphasis added).

22. Roberto González Echevarría, *Myth and Archive: A Theory of Latin American Narrative*
(Cambridge: Cambridge University Press, 1990), 130.

23. Costa Lima, *Terra ignota,* 172.

24. See, e.g., Brandão, *Da Cunha e a questão racial.*

25. See Costa Lima, "Imitação e Contagio" and "Euclides e a Ciência," in *Terra ignota,*
59–124.

26. Qtd. in Spivak, *Critique of Postcolonial Reason,* 255.

27. Ibid., 257.

28. David Lloyd and Paul Thomas, *Culture and the State* (New York: Routledge,
1998), 13.

29. Waren Montag, "Beyond Force and Consent: Althusser, Spinoza, Hobbes," in
Postmodern Materialism and the Future of Marxist Theory, ed. Antonio Callari and David F.
Ruccio (Hanover, N.H.: University Press of New England / Wesleyan University Press,
1996), 97.

30. Alfred Radcliffe-Brown, preface to Meyers Fortes and Edward Evans-Pritchard,
eds., *African Political Systems* (London: Kegan Paul International, 1987), xxii.

31. Ibid.

32. Philip Abrams, "Notes on the Difficulty of Studying the State," *Journal of Historical
Sociology* 1.1 (1988): 82.

33. Slavoj Žižek, *The Sublime Object of Ideology* (New York: Verso, 1989), 28.

34. Lloyd and Thomas, *Culture and the State,* 44.

35. Žižek, *Sublime Object,* 149.

36. Lloyd and Thomas, *Culture and the State,* 4.

37. Kirsten Schultz, *Tropical Versailles: Empire, Monarchy, and the Portuguese Royal Court in
Rio de Janeiro, 1808–1821* (New York: Routledge, 2001), 235 (further citations of this work
are made parenthetically in the text).

38. Constitutionalism, however, did not mean the same thing in both places, as
Schultz carefully points out. Her book is written somewhat against the narrative that
turns the transfer of the Portuguese court into the beginning of a larger process in which
both independence and the conservative form it takes in Brazil (with a monarchy instead
of republic) are foregone conclusions. Schultz argues that the meanings of empire and
monarchy, and their attending political culture, were not transferred wholesale along with
the court but instead were changed through the process, not only by the officials of the
exiled court, but also by the residents of Rio de Janeiro. To the extent that Schultz is trying
to avoid the blind spots produced by a teleological nationalist narrative, she dwells on the
multiple alternative frameworks proposed during the process, the attempts on both sides
of the Atlantic to rebuild "a political framework that appeared to be crumbling before their
eyes" in articulation with ideas of constitutionalism (6). Constitutionalism was therefore
given a variety of different meanings. In Portugal, for example, it featured a reaction

against Brazil's more central position within the Portuguese empire, but in Brazil, it was perceived as another step in cementing this new order (236).

39. Schultz writes that unlike the Spanish monarchy, the Portuguese crown had failed to effectively establish the presence of the king as a legal person, or *persona ficta*. In the Spanish monarchy, the institution of the viceroyalty served to sustain the fiction of the king's simultaneous presence throughout the kingdom, but in Portuguese America governors were seen only as administrators (154). This produced the sense that Brazil was not part of a kingdom, as were the Spanish Indies, but a conquest and colony. This changed with arrival of the king. The historian Diogo Curto explains that the possibility of directly witnessing the spectacle of the royal audience demonstrated "the possibility of direct access" both to the king's person and to the "immediate practice of exemplary justice" (qtd. in Schultz, 156). This was true not only for exiled courtiers and wealthy residents and visitors but also for the poor. Dom João VI's advisers encouraged the continuation of this institution in Brazil as politically expedient, arguing that it projected an image of paternal authority, of a political family where even "the poor and destitute" were tied to their "Sovereign who is also their Father." In addition, it showed that this relationship transcended the hierarchies of empire and corresponded, as Anthony Pagden has said of its Spanish counterpart, to a "multicultural society" (Schultz, 160). Although slaves had formerly been excluded from the community of vassals in Rio, they were also accorded access—albeit limited access—to the king. As Schultz describes, this created the vexing and unresolved problem of defining the relationships between the slave, slave own-ers, and the monarch, a problem that anticipated many of the quandaries Canudos again raised concerning how to imagine a relationship between populations deemed inferior and that which was supposed to represent them (166). See Scultz's chapter entitled "Tropical Versailles" for a fuller discussion of the way the practice of petitioning created a new, unique political identity for slaves.

40. Marco Morel, "La génesis de la opinión pública moderna y el proceso de indepen-dencia (Rio de Janeiro, 1820–1840)," *Los espacios públicos en Iberoamerica* (Mexico City: Fondo de Cultura Económica, 1998), 310.

41. Keith Michael Baker, *Inventing the French Revolution: Essays on French Political Culture in the Eighteenth Century* (New York: Cambridge University Press, 1990), 198.

42. Ibid., 196.

43. In *Inventing the French Revolution,* Baker disagrees with Jürgen Habermas's approach to public opinion as a sociological phenomenon. He argues that the nature of a discrete social referent among specific groups and classes remains ill defined and that "one can understand the conflicts of the Pre-Revolution as a series of struggles to fix the sociologi-cal referent of the concept in favor of one or another competing group" (186). Even if such a discrete social referent could be located in France, it would be infinitely more difficult for Brazil, where, as some critics argue, the creation of a public sphere was "frustrated" by political, economic, and social traditionalism (see Schultz, 117). Consequently, Baker's suggestion that we understand the "public" not as an actually existing sociological referent but as a political invention is particularly useful for the case of Brazil (see Baker, 172).

44. Qtd. in Baker, *Inventing the French Revolution,* 188.

45. Ibid., 193.

46. Qtd. in ibid.

47. Qtd. ibid., 195.

48. Morel, "Génesis de la opinion," 304.

49. This was true not only of the 1820s in Rio de Janeiro but also of the years at that century's end. One need only think of Gabriel Tarde's distinction between "crowd" and "public," the latter defined as "a dispersion of individuals who are physically separated and whose cohesion is entirely mental," a phenomenon that "could begin to arise only after the first great development in the invention of printing" (Tarde, "The Public and the Crowd," *On Communication and Social Influence (Selected Papers)* [Chicago: University of Chicago Press, 1969], 277, 279). Tarde identifies the second half of the eighteenth century as the moment when a political public arose and absorbed all other publics (literary, philosophical, scientific, religious) and the French Revolution as the moment when journalism (and hence the public) truly began. The crowd, he says

> is the social group of the past . . . [;] it is incapable of extension beyond a limited area. . . . But the public can be extended indefinitely, and since its particular life becomes more intense as it extends, one cannot deny that it is the social group of the future. Thus three mutually auxiliary inventions—printing, the railroad, and the telegraph—combined to create the formidable power of the press, that prodigious telephone which has so inordinately enlarged the former audiences of orators and preachers. I therefore cannot agree with that vigorous writer, Dr. LeBon, that our age is the "era of the crowds." It is the era of the public or of publics, and that is a very different thing. (281)

Although this essay was published the same year as *Os sertões* (1901), da Cunha might have agreed, for his text is peppered with phrases such as "the public opinion of the nation, finding its expression in the press" (372).

50. Judy Bieber, *Power, Patronage, and Political Violence: State Building on a Brazilian Frontier 1822–1889* (Lincoln: University of Nebraska Press, 1999), 45.

51. Ibid., 45–46.

52. Richard Graham, *Patronage and Politics in Nineteenth-Century Brazil* (Stanford, Calif.: Stanford University Press, 1990), 3.

53. Ibid., 148.

54. Bieber, *Power, Patronage,* 158 (further citations to this work are made parenthetically in the text).

55. Qtd. in Judy Bieber, "A 'Visão do Sertão': Party Identity and Political Honor in Late Imperial Minas Gerais, Brazil," *Hispanic American Historical Review* 81.2 (2001): 316.

56. Giorgio Agamben, *Homo Sacer: Sovereign Power and Bare Life* (Stanford, Calif.: Stanford University Press, 1998), 177.

57. Ibid., 179.

58. Ibid., 178.

59. Jean-Jacques Rousseau, "Of the Social Contract," *The Social Contract and Other Later Political Writings* (Cambridge: Cambridge University Press, 1997), 114.

60. For an extended discussion of Rousseau's critique of the theater and his approval of the festival, or fête, see Lloyd and Thomas, "Rousseau, Transparency, and the Fate of the Fête," in *Culture and the State*, 35–46.

61. Ibid., 46.

62. Qtd. in Baker, *Inventing the French Revolution*, 250.

63. Ibid., 249.

64. Qtd. in Schultz, *Tropical Versailles*, 262.

65. Roland Barthes, *Michelet* (Berkeley: University of California Press, 1992), 101–2.

66. Ibid., 102–3.

67. Ibid., 27, 101–2.

68. Ibid., 199.

69. Ibid., 188.

70. Lloyd and Thomas, *Culture and the State*, 3 (further citations will be made parenthetically in the text).

71. Qtd. in Julio Ramos, "'Saber Decir': Literatura y modernización en Andrés Bello," *Nueva Revista de Filología Hispánica* (Mexico) 35.2 (1987): 687.

72. Julio Ramos, *Desencuentros de la modernidad en América Latina* (Mexico City: Fondo de Cultura Económica, 1989), 8.

73. Doris Sommer, *Foundational Fictions: The National Romances of Latin America* (Berkeley: University of California Press, 1991): 17–18.

74. Qtd. in José Murilo de Carvalho, *A formação das almas: O imaginário da república no Brasil* (São Paulo: Editora Schwarcz, 1990), 33.

75. Nicolau Sevcenko, *Literatura como missão: Tensões sociais e criação cultural na Primeira República* (São Paulo: Editora Brasiliense, 1983), 218.

76. Qtd. in Roberto Schwarz, *Misplaced Ideas: Essays on Brazilian Culture* (London: Verso, 1992), 9.

77. Ibid., 10.

78. Abreu, *O enigma*, 262.

79. Durval Muniz de Albuquerque, *A invenção do nordeste e outras artes* (São Paulo: Cortez Editora, 1999), 53.

80. Ibid., 40.

81. Ibid., 54.

82. Abreu, *O enigma*, 340.

83. Ibid., 323.

84. Ibid., 328.

85. Ibid., 327.

86. Ibid., 349. According to Abreu, new paradigms for explaining Brazilian reality (new methods of sociology and rereadings of Brazilian literature through the lens of *modernismo*) and new editorial projects did not emerge until the 1960s. This also corresponded with the military dictatorship's attempt to stop the Semanas Euclidianas. The tendency thereafter was the increased regionalization and specialization of scholarship related to da Cunha, so that today "Euclidianistas" are local intellectuals, as Abreu points out, who don't participate in the networks and codes of the great cities or in institutions with national

visibility: "they don't seem to have enough intellectual capital to compete in the hegemonic intellectual field" (355). Still, this doesn't mean that da Cunha has been displaced. Consider, for example, the continued difference between, on the one hand, literary critics based in Rio and São Paulo, who enjoy relatively greater access to the most prestigious intellectual institutions in Brazil and international circuits and who tend to read Canudos largely through the lens of *Os sertões*, and, on the other, the more "regional" intellectuals in the Northeast, who work on Canudos through local lore and oral memory and who don't have the same kind of access to the hegemonic intellectual arena.

87. Lloyd and Thomas, *Culture and the State*, 13; emphasis added.

88. Schwarz, *Misplaced Ideas*, 22–23.

89. Idelber Avelar, *The Untimely Present: Postdictatorial Latin American Fiction and the Task of Mourning* (Durham: Duke University Press, 1999), 28.

90. Fernando Ortiz, *Contrapunteo cubano del tabaco y el azúcar* (Madrid: Edito CubaEspaña, 1999), 90.

91. Ibid., 90. Violence is not completely absent in Angel Rama's version, but it is deemphasized. For example: "The deculturation that made the incorporation of this ideological corpus in regionalist cultures possible would be violent. Yet, paradoxically, it helped open up enriching paths" (Angel Rama, *Transculturación narrativa en América Latina* [Mexico City: Siglo Veintiuno, 1982], 52).

92. Ortiz, *Contrapunteo cubano*, 88.

93. Over the last decade various writers have used the concept of transculturation in ways that seek to preserve the hybridizations or contaminations implied while divesting it of its teleological assumptions. For example, Walter Mignolo criticizes the term for implying a biological/cultural mixture of people, but he accepts a teleological, noncultural sense of the word when it is used for what he calls border thinking. This is a transculturation arrested in the middle of becoming, provided one knows that the "becoming" is not oriented, like a compass, to one direction alone. Border thinking entails thinking beyond dichotomies produced by "Occidentalism," a work not in fusion but in "contrapuntal analysis" (Mignolo, *Local Histories/Global Designs: Coloniality, Subaltern Knowledges and Border Thinking* [Princeton: Princeton University Press, 2000], 208), underscoring the impurities of transculturation. John Kraniauskas suggests that whatever "national-populist and culturally elitist complicities" transculturation may betray, they hardly exhaust the potential critical content of what he calls the *work* of transculturation, which includes also "labour processes within an international political economy" and "displacements in the notion of culture associated with 'development'" ("Translation and the Work of Transculturation," *Traces* 1:96). John Beverley's analysis of texts surrounding the Tupac Amaru rebellion includes a discussion of transculturations that do not overcome subalternities; see "Transculturation and Subalternity: The 'Lettered City' and the Túpac Amaru Rebellion," in *Subalternity and Representation* (Durham: Duke University Press, 1999), 41–64. Alberto Moreiras likewise proposes the possibility of a critical or unoriented transculturation in "The End of Magical Realism: José María Arguedas's Passionate Signifier," in *The Exhaustion of Difference* (Durham: Duke University Press, 2001), 184–207.

94. Beverley, *Subalternity and Representation*, 10.

95. Qtd. in Rama, *Transculturación narrativa*, 37.

96. Ibid., 54.

97. Ibid., 43.

98. José María Arguedas, *The Fox from Up Above and the Fox from Down Below* (Pittsburgh: University of Pittsburgh Press, 2000), 269.

99. Antonio Cornejo-Polar, "El indigenismo andino," In *America Latina: Palavra, literatura e cultura*, vol. 2, *Emancipação do discurso*, ed. Ana Pizarro (São Paulo: Memorial, 1993), 722.

100. Antonio Cornejo-Polar, *Los universos narratives de José María Arguedas* (Buenos Aires: Editorial Losada, 1973), 156.

101. Terry Eagleton, *Literary Theory: An Introduction* (Minneapolis: University of Minnesota Press, 1983), 8.

102. Costa Lima, *Terra ignota*, 16.

103. Abreu, *O enigma*, 326.

104. Adilson Citelli, *Roteiro de leitura: "Os sertões" de Euclides da Cunha* (São Paulo: Editora Atica, 1996), 38.

105. Franklin de Oliveira, *Euclydes: A espada e a letra: Uma biografia intelectual* (Rio de Janeiro: Editora Paz e Terra, 1983), 37.

106. See, e.g., Andrade, *A história e interpretaçao de "Os sertões"*; Citelli, *Roteiro de leitura*; Oliveira, *Euclydes: A espada e a letra*; Herbert Parentes Fortes, *Euclides: O estilizador de nossa história* (Rio de Janeiro: Edições Gumercindo Rocha Dorea, 1959); and Gilberto Freyre, *Atualidade de Euclides da Cunha* (Rio de Janeiro: Casa do Estudante do Brasil, 1940).

Chapter Two: A Prose of Counterinsurgency

Epigraph: The original text reads: Antônio Carola: "Ali naquele canto ele [Antônio Conselheiro] . . . falava ao povo. Era um velho seco, barbudo, rezador que fazia gosto." Cited in David Ribeiro de Sena, "Canudos: Ficção e Realidade," *A História de Canudos*, http://www.portfolium.com.br/Sites/Canudos/conteudo.asp?IDPublicacao=93.

1. According to Oliveira Castro, of Quixeramobim, the Conselheiro married a cousin, a daughter of Francisca Maciel and Miguel Carlos, who was not named Brasilina (Edmundo Moniz, *A guerra social de Canudos* [Rio de Janeiro: Civilização Brasileira, 1978], 21).

2. According to the oral testimony of Honorório Villanova, a merchant in Canudos, the Conselheiro's response was "How could I have killed my mother if I was mistreated by my stepmother?" ["Como posso ter assasinada minha mãe se fui maltratado pela minha madrasta?"] (Honorio Vilanova [and Nertan Macedo], *Memorial de Vilanova: Depoimento do último sobrevivente da Guerra de Canudos* [Rio de Janeiro: Edições O Cruzeiro, 1964], 70).

3. Ranajit Guha, *Elementary Aspects of Peasant Insurgency in Colonial India* (New Delhi: Oxford University Press, 1983), 4.

4. Ibid., 4.

5. Gyan Prakash, "Subaltern Studies as Postcolonial Criticism," *American Historical Review* 99 (Dec. 1994): 1482.

6. Dipesh Chakrabarty, "Marx after Marxism: History, Subalternity, and Difference," *Marxism beyond Marxism* (New York: Routledge, 1996), 58.

7. Euclides da Cunha is usually read as exemplifying this position. As a positivist he associates the religiosity of Canudos with its barbarity. Sara Castro-Klarén, however, provocatively argues that religious discourse and models secretly inform and organize da Cunha's text:

> Both the lexicon and iconography [of *Os sertões*] are framed within a new scientific discourse which pretends to distance itself from the Christological, but which in fact it needs in order to convey its full meaning so that the meaning of the discourse on the land in *Os Sertões* is fundamentally affective . . . [T]he imaginary displayed by da Cunha in his unforgettable depiction of the *caatinga* as a strange place produced by abnormal, unsuspected climatic conditions scientifically understood and described does not draw its signifying power from the scientific discourse, but rather from the very old and naturalized discourse of the body of the early Church. (Castro-Klarén, "In-forming the Body of Man in the *Caatinga*," *Colorado Review of Hispanic Studies* 3 [2005]: 106–7)

8. Rui Facó, *Cangaceiros e fanáticos: Gênese e lutas*, 2 ed. (Rio de Janeiro: Editôra Civilização Brasileira, 1965), 55.

9. Another example in which religion is—in a sense—written out of the story is J. J. Veiga's novel *A casca da serpente* (Rio de Janeiro: Bertrand Brasil, 2001 [1989]), in which the Conselheiro survives the end of the war and rebuilds a Canudos markedly different from the first, since he has changed with the experience of war and shed his skin for a new one. The changes include a decreased emphasis on religion and prayer.

10. Marco Antonio Villa makes much the same point from a more sympathetic political perspective: "Religion, which is an epistemological obstacle for Marxists, ends up discarded and overlooked. The point is that, instead of functioning as the opium of the people, religion made it possible for the dominated to construct societies without parallels in the Western revolutionary tradition, tributary of the French Revolution" (Villa, "Em busca de um mundo novo," *Revista Canudos* 1 [1997]: 33). Religion appears in Guha's *Elementary Aspect* as an example of an immature form of rebel consciousness: "It was this consciousness, an unquestionably false consciousness if ever there was one, which also generated a certain kind of alienation: it made the subject look upon his destiny not as a function of his own will and action, but as that of forces outside and independent of himself. The thinking which filled the void created thus by the displacement of the subject was, in its most general sense, religious—that is, to put it in Marx's words, 'a product of self-alienation' . . . [;] what was political came thus be regarded as religious" (268).

11. Mario Vargas Llosa, *The War of the End of the World* (New York: Avon Books, 1981), 109.

12. Mario Vargas Llosa, *Contra Viento y Marea* (Barcelona: Seix Barral, 1986), 218.

13. Dipesh Chakrabarty, "Provincializing Europe: Postcoloniality and the Critique of History," *Cultural Studies* 6.3 (1992): 351.

14. Ranajit Guha, "The Prose of Counter-Insurgency," in *Selected Subaltern Studies*, ed. Ranajit Guha and Gayatri Spivak (Oxford: Oxford University Press, 1988), 59.

15. Qtd. in Oleone Coelho Fontes, *O treme-terra: Moreira Cesar, a republica e Canudos* (Petrópolis, Brazil: Vozes, 1996), 186.

16. Robert Levine, *Vale of Tears: Revisiting the Canudos Massacre in Northeastern Brazil, 1893–97* (Berkeley: University of California Press, 1992), 31. Vicente Dobroruka lists the following characteristics of "traditional" Catholicism: it displayed mystical tendencies; its leaders were often not part of the Church hierarchy; and it was medieval, social (impregnating all spheres of public life), and familial (Dobroruka, *Antonio Conselheiro, o beato endiabrado de Canudos* [Rio de Janeiro: Diadorim, 1977], 54).

17. José Calasans, *Cartografia de Canudos* (Salvador, Brazil: Secretaria da Cultura e Turismo do Estado da Bahia / Empresa Gráfica da Bahia, 1997), 13.

18. Dobroruka, *Antonio Conselheiro*, 55.

19. Alexandre Otten, "A influência do ideário religioso na construção da comunidade de Belo Monte," *Luso-Brazilian Review* 30.2 (1993): 87.

20. See Roderick Barman, "The Brazilian Peasantry Reexamined: The Implications of the Quebra-Quilo Revolt, 1874–75," *Hispanic American Historical Review* 57.3 (1977): 401–24.

21. José Augusto Cabral Barreto Bastos, *Incompreensível e bárbaro inimigo: A guerra simbólica contra Canudos* (Salvador, Brazil: Editora da Universidade Federal da Bahia, 1995), 127. See also Cândido da Costa e Silva's "O peregrino entre os pastores" (*Cadernos da Literatura Brasileira: Euclides da Cunha* 13–14 [2002]: 201–32) for an analysis of the Conselheiro's relations and conflicts with the Church at this time through a detailed reading of letters (including those of Fiorentini) found in the archive of Salvador's parish.

22. Qtd. in Bastos, *Incompreensível e bárbaro inimigo*, 128.

23. Ibid., 129.

24. Ibid., 128.

25. Costa e Silva, "O peregrino," 213.

26. Euclides da Cunha, for example, described him as a "second-century heresiarch in the modern world" (da Cunha, *Rebellion in the Backlands*, trans. Samuel Putnam [Chicago: University of Chicago Press, 1944], 136).

27. Bastos, *Incompreensível e bárbaro inimigo*, 133.

28. Ibid., 131.

29. There are four parts to the "Predicas e Discursos de António Conselheiro": (1) twenty-nine sermons on "storms that rise in Mary's heart"; (2) ten sermons on the Ten Commandments; (3) texts extracted from the Bible (on the Ten Commandments and the life and sayings of Jesus); and (4) miscellaneous sermons including ones (a) on the cross, on the Mass, on confession, on the miracles of Jesus, on the construction of Solomon's temple, on receiving the key to the church of Saint Anthony, patron saint of Belo Monte, and on the parable of the sower; (b) on the Republic: the Jesuits, civil marriage, the Imperial family, and the liberation of the slaves; and (c) a farewell (Antonio Vicente Mendes Maciel, *Antonio Conselheiro e Canudos (revisão histórica): A obra manuscrita de Antonio Conselheiro e que pertenceu a Euclides da Cunha*, ed. Ataliba Nogueira [São Paulo: Companhia Editora Nacional, 1974]). There is some discussion as to whether Conselheiro wrote the manuscript himself or dictated it (or portions of it) to his scribe, the Leão de Natuba.

30. Otten, "A influência," 79.

31. For a comparison of the Conselheiro and Padre Cícero and a discussion of the way both were intimately tied into—rather than isolated from—national ecclesiastical and political power structures of imperial and republican Brazil, see Ralph Della Cava, "Brazilian Messianism and National Institutions: A Reappraisal of Canudos and Joaseiro," *Hispanic American Historical Review* 48.3 (1968): 402–20.

32. Bastos, *Incompreensível e bárbaro inimigo,* 133.

33. Costa e Silva, "O peregrino," 209–11.

34. Ibid., 220.

35. Bastos, *Incompreensível e bárbaro inimigo,* 131. In an earlier letter in 1876, the vicar of N. S. do Livramento do Barracão, João da Silva Paranhos, demonstrates an energetic call for intervention, complaining that the Conselheiro not only spreads superstition but also, and perhaps more important, shows a lack of respect for rightful priests: "I approach Your Excellency so that you may take prompt and energetic measures in conjunction with the Police Chief in order to remove from this parish a man who claims to be a holy man and who, accompanied by three women and one or more followers, wanders the center of the province of Bahia, without stating his purpose, and even causing some damages. He disquiets the conscience of the people in questions of faith—unfortunately divided in terms of doctrine these days—preaching superstitions on the roads and in villages and not giving the respective priests the respect that is their due" (qtd. in Bastos, *Incompreensível e bárbaro inimigo,* 130; emphasis added).

36. Bastos, *Incompreensível e bárbaro inimigo,* 129.

37. Da Cunha, *Rebellion,* 118.

38. Otten, "A influência," 77.

39. Ibid. Although undertaken in a radically different context, one of the more striking formulations of this democratizing potential is Eric Auerbach's analysis of the New Testament's radical step toward the mimesis of everyday reality, in which for the first time ordinary people and their daily lives and conversations take on transcendental importance: "What we see here is a world which on the one hand is real, average, identifiable as to place, time and circumstances, but which on the other hand is shaken in its very foundations, is transforming and renewing itself before our eyes. For the New Testament authors who are their contemporaries, these occurrences on the plane of everyday life assume the importance of world-revolutionary events" (Auerbach, *Mimesis: The Representation of Reality in Western Literature* [Princeton: Princeton University Press, 1974 (1946)], 43). Auerbach argues that this shift in which anybody could from then on be the subject of historical representation was a consequence of the positing of the equality of all persons—as children of God—in Christian doctrine.

40. Claudio Lopes Maia, *Canudos: Um povo entre a utopia e a resistencia* (Goiânia, Brazil: Centro Popular de Estudos Contemporâneos, 1999), 52.

41. Euclides da Cunha, *Rebellion,* 139.

42. Consuelo Novais Sampaio, ed., *Canudos: Cartas para o barão* (São Paulo: Editora da Universidade de São Paulo, 2001), 131.

43. Ibid., 31.

44. Ibid., 25.

45. Ibid., 18.

46. Barão de Geremoabo, "Carta do Barão de Geremoabo publicada no Jornal de Notícias—Bahia—nos dias 4 e 5 de março de 1987 (anexo II)," appendix to João Arruda, *Canudos: Messianismo e conflito social* (Fortaleza, Brazil: Edições Universidade Federal do Ceará / Secult, 1993), 177.

47. Ibid., 173.

48. In 1821–30 sugar accounted for 30 percent of Brazilian exports; by 1900 it had fallen to only 5 percent. Meanwhile, coffee production, developed in the early nineteenth century, took off in the 1890s. In 1901 Brazil produced nearly three-quarters of the total world supply. The development of new processes in the production of both sugar and coffee, moreover, created a gulf between those with the money to implement them and those who still relied on older methods (Thomas Skidmore and Peter Smith, *Modern Latin America* [New York: Oxford University Press, 1992], 153). These changes took place in a context marked by the spread of industrial capitalism (from 175 industries in 1874 to 600 ten years later), the early formations of an internal market, and the shift from slave to wage labor, as well as the increasing use of immigrant labor in the South. Even though slavery was abolished in 1888, this shift had been taking place over a number of years with the individual liberation of slaves. According to Herbert Klein's statistics, sixteen years before abolition, freemen were 74 percent of people of color (ctd. in Thomas Skidmore, "Toward a Comparative Analysis of Race Relations since Abolition in Brazil and the United States," *Journal of Latin American Studies* 4.2 [1972]: 23).

49. In 1893, for instance, São Paulo had only three senators, while Bahia and Pernambuco had six each (Emília Viotti da Costa, *Da monarquia à república: Momentos decisivos* [São Paulo: Editora Universidade Estadual Paulista, 1998], 273–74).

50. Otten, "A influência," 80.

51. Mike Davis sees the combination of droughts, famine, intense social conflict, and millenarian movements that marked the Nordeste at this time as part of a larger, global phenomenon that similarly affected China, India, and North Africa and that resulted from the "fatal meshing" of the world climate system (El Niño), the late Victorian world economy, and new imperialism (Davis, *Late Victorian Holocausts: El Niño Famines and the Making of the Third World* [London: Verso, 2001], 12). Roughly 30 million people are thought to have died in the three waves of droughts that in 1876–9 and 1896–1900 swept what would become the Third World; Davis argues that they died "not outside the 'modern world system,' but in the very process of being forcibly incorporated into its economic and political structures" (9).

52. Geremoabo, "Carta," 174–75.

53. Sampaio, *Canudos*, 103.

54. Della Cava, "Brazilian Messianism," 411.

55. Sampaio, *Canudos*, 79–80.

56. One example of this interpretation is a *cordel* poem entitled "Antônio Conselheiro e a Guerra de Canudos," whose last verse ends with "Twenty-five thousand men / Died in that War / For that barren land / At the base of mountain ranges / Today we have a group / With the same goals / The Landless Movement" ["Vinte e cinco mil homens / Morreram

naquela Guerra / Pela aquela terra seca / naquele sopé de serra / Hoje temos entidade / Com mesma finalidade / "Movimento dos Sem Terra"] (Fortaleza, Brazil: Tupynamquim Editora, January 2002), 32.

57. Geremoabo, "Carta," 178.

58. Levine, *Vale of Tears,* 141.

59. Qtd. in Walnice Nogueira Galvão, *No calor da hora: A guerra de Canudos nos jornais, 4a expedição* (São Paulo: Atica, 1974), 141.

60. Ibid., 155.

61. Qtd. in Sampaio, *Canudos,* 102.

62. Ibid.

63. Maia, *Canudos,* 58.

64. Lizir Arcanjo Alves, *Humor e sátira na guerra de Canudos* (Salvador, Brazil: Empresa Gráfica da Bahia, 1997), 25.

65. Ibid., 27.

66. Ibid., 66.

67. Ibid., 65.

68. Ibid., 66–67.

69. Galvão, *No calor da hora,* 15.

70. Qtd. Galvão, *No calor da hora,* 53.

71. Nelson Werneck Sodré, *História da imprensa no Brasil* (Rio de Janeiro: Editora Mauad, 1998), 315.

72. Samuel de Oliveira, e.g., complained, "The newspapers don't have any circulation. Those that publish in this capital inhabited by a million people don't print more than 50,000 copies" (qtd. in Nicolau Sevcenko, *Literatura como missão: Tensões sociais e criação cultural na Primeira República* [São Paulo: Editora Brasiliense, 1983], 89). In 1900 José Veríssimo calculated that "according to official statistics the number of those who could not read in Brazil in 1890 was 12,213,356 in a population of 14,333,915. That is, only 16 or 17 of every hundred Brazilians or inhabitants of Brazil could read" (ibid., 88).

73. Machado de Assis, "Crônica: 14 de Fevereiro de 1897," *A Semana. Obras Completas de Machado de Assis,* vol. 3 (Rio de Janeiro: W. M. Jackson, 1957), 412.

74. Ibid., 413. Assis prophetically suggests,

> After this sect of the Canudos is over and done with, perhaps we'll find that these events contain a book about the fanaticism of the sertanejos and the figure of the Messias. Another Coelho Neto, if he has his talent, might write a century from now an interesting chapter, studying the fervor of the barbarians and the laziness of the civilized, who let them grow when it would have been easier to have dissolved them with a police patrol, since the simple monk did not do anything. Who knows? Perhaps a devotee, relic of the Canudos, will celebrate the centenary of this sect. (416)

75. Candace Slater, *Stories on a String: The Brazilian Literatura de Cordel* (Berkeley: University of California Press, 1982), 3.

76. Ibid., 9–10.

77. Ibid., 4.

78. José Calasans, ed., *Canudos na literatura de cordel* (São Paulo: Editora Atica, 1984), 23 (emphasis added).

79. Ibid., 26.

80. Ibid., 27.

81. Peter Beattie, *The Tribute of Blood* (Durham: Duke University Press, 2001).

82. Beattie makes the point that "soldiers are often depicted as the State's minor henchmen who often oppress more sympathetic victims of State coercion: ethnic and racial minorities, slaves, ritual organizations, labor unions, and women, among other groups. In Brazil . . . soldiers were also direct 'victims' of State coercion" (*Tribute of Blood*, 126).

83. Ibid., 113.

84. Ibid., 59.

85. Calasans, *Canudos na literatura de cordel*, 28.

86. Ibid.

87. Moreira César's reputation for ferocity caused some of the landowners around Canudos to lament what they foresaw as an unnecessary massacre: "To take care of Antônio Conselheiro, whom I know personally, it is not necessary to send Colonel Moreira César, a wicked and bloody man, who will cover the soil of our beloved backlands with corpses" ["Para dar cabo de Antônio Conselheiro, a quem conheço pessoalmente, não era preciso mandar aí o coronel Moreira César, homem malvado, sanguinário por índole, o qual vai talar de cadaveres o solo do nosso querido sertão"] (Sampaio, *Canudos*, 142).

88. Nobody knows who killed Moreira César. Popular lore is rich with different versions, among them that he was shot either by a *jagunço* or by a soldier of his own army for his brutal disciplining of his soldiers. An example: "Moreira César / Who killed you? / Was it a bullet from Canudos / Sent by the Conselheiro?" ["Moreira César / Quem foi que te matou? / Foi a bala de Canudos / Que o Conselheiro mandou?"] (qtd. in Calasans *Cartografia de Canudos*, 91).

89. Maria de Lourdes Monaco Janotti, *Os subversivos da república* (São Paulo: Editora Brasiliense, 1986), 140. The newspaper *A República* had accused Gentil de Castro of helping Canudos, leading him to initiate legal proceedings for calumny. *A República*'s editor-in-chief insisted, "Mr. Coronel Gentil de Castro, leader of the monarchist chiefs, responsible for the political movement being prepared, has sent arms and munitions to those who perturb our country's public peace" (qtd. in Janotti, *Os subversivos*, 137).

90. Lizir Arcanjo Alves, *Humor e sátira na guerra de Canudos* (Salvador: Empresa Gráfica da Bahia, 1997), 58.

91. Ibid., 91.

92. Janotti, *Os subversivos*, 137. According to one editorial in *O Estado de São Paulo*,

> The insurrectional movement in the Bahian backlands is monarchist. It is not necessary to ask if it was always so, because even if it wasn't initially, we republicans, we ourselves who took it as our enemy, turned it into a monarchist movement. For monarchists and republicans the movement of the Conselheiro's fanatics is today a movement to restore the monarchy—it is so for them because

they may take advantage of the agitation which dominates the interior of Bahia; for us because of our need to repress this agitation. Whether or not it was monarchist at the beginning, what is certain is that today it is so, and as such it has to be faced and fought. (Janotti, *Os subversivos*, 145)

93. Another article, for instance, ridiculed accusations that the Conselheiro was monarchist because, it claimed, he couldn't comprehend the notion of a "republic" or of "Brazil" (in Galvão, *No calor da hora*, 95–96). Rui Barbosa insisted that the monarchists "would not brave the infinite obstacles of the backlands to ally themselves to the insanity of Antônio Maciel" (ibid., 96). Such defenses, however, reinforced the "backwardness" and "insanity" of the Conselheiristas and the incompatibility of these characteristics with the monarchists.

94. For Nelson Werneck Sodré, many of the changes of the army and its outlook were associated with the emergence of a middle class in Brazil in the nineteenth century. He affirms that "Florianism corresponded to the spontaneous and not always very clear desires of the middle class. The middle class articulated themselves around the figure of Floriano Peixoto, resisting the ever rising pressure of the oligarchy and leaning on the energetic measures he took to maintain order and consolidate the regime. . . . Once the monarchy was defeated, and the obsolete machinery of the State reformed, once the alterations that interested the dominant class had been introduced, there was no longer any need to accept the increasingly uncomfortable alliance [with the military]" (qtd. in Clovis Moura, *Introdução ao pensamento de Euclides da Cunha* [Rio de Janeiro: Editora Civilização Brasileira, 1964], 56).

95. Beattie, *Tribute of Blood*, 95.

96. This was not true of everyone in the army: higher officials were drawn from the higher classes, and many tended to be promonarchist.

97. In a famous letter dated 1887, Floriano Peixoto wrote: "I saw the solution to the class question; without a doubt it exceeded everyone's expectations. This fact proves the rottenness of this poor country and the necessity of a military dictatorship to extirpate it. Being the liberal that I am I can't desire military rule for my country, but everyone knows . . . that only the military can purify the blood of a social body which, like ours, is corrupted" (qtd. in Viotti da Costa, *Da monarquia*, 402.

98. Moniz argues that Moreira César was chosen to command the third expedition as part of a carefully laid plan in which, after the *jagunços* were beaten, he would return as a "national hero, his prestige redoubled, and would be able to undertake an important role in the political plans of the Florianistas against the government of Prudente de Morais, whom Floriano Peixoto rejected for being civilian" (Moniz, *A guerra social*, 134).

99. Odorico Tavares, *Canudos: 50 anos depois* (Salvador, Brazil: Fundação de Cultura do Estado, 1947), 48.

100. "If we pause on top of the hill which faces the lake covering Canudos, we can imagine the inundation of the village with its simple houses, its white church and its dead. Everything and everyone covered by water. Canudos immersed like Claude Debussy's underwater cathedral, whose bells toll slowly with the rise and fall of the tide. Likewise, at

sunset, in a burst of clairvoyance, we can also hear, below the barely perceptible, undulating movement of the waters, the intermittent memories" (Edivaldo Boaventura, *O parque estadual de Canudos* [Salvador, Brazil: Secretaria da Cultura e Turismo, 1997], 68).

Chapter Three: The Event and the Everyday

1. Euclides da Cunha, *Canudos: Diário de uma expedição* (Rio de Janeiro: Livraria José Olympio Editora, 1939), 107.

2. Ibid., 86.

3. Nina Rodrigues described the Conselheiro as unusual in several respects: "His disdain for mundane preoccupations drives him to ignore all hygienic care for the body. He tries to detach himself as much as possible from the contingency of mortals. Antonio Conselheiro does not sleep, he does not eat or barely eats. His life is a continuous prayer and he lives continuously with God, probably in a state of hallucination" (Raimundo Nina Rodrigues, *As coletividades anormais* [Brasília: Edições do Senado Federal, 2006], 46). R. B. Cunninghame Graham's *Brazilian Mystic*, a book that some have described as essentially a plagiarism of *Os sertões*—it appeared roughly twenty-five years before the English-language translation by Samuel Putnam in 1944—describes the community with a rather dead-pan version of the unordinary life of Canudos: "No such ideas entered the heads of the Jagunços, who sang their hymns with fervour, passed hours in church, and fornicated briskly, drinking as much raw rum as they could come by (as there was no fast on the drink), and waiting patiently for the destruction of mankind" (Graham, *A Brazilian Mystic, Being the Life and Miracles of Antonio Conselheiro* [New York: Dodd, Mead, 1920], 111).

4. To my knowledge, the first to develop the theme of Machado de Assis's articles on Canudos was the historian Clímaco Días, to whom I'm very much indebted; see Días, "Canudos: Poesia e mistério de Machado de Assis," *Revista Canudos* 1.1 (1997): 92–95.

5. Márai's temporal distance from da Cunha (post-1968) is actively thematized in the novel, for the (English-speaking) narrator is an old man who lived through the Canudos War as a soldier but then went on to witness the two world wars and the "barbarities" of the civilized world. He writes his memoirs as he is about die. The intent is clearly to add to and correct the story that da Cunha told because he didn't live enough, didn't see enough, to write this other side. The narrator's memoirs revolve around a conversation he witnesses on October 5, the last night of the conflict, between Marshal Bittencourt and a woman who comes to him with a message from the Conselheiro. After a transformative bath—she is initially described as a grotesque "*sertaneja*" in much the same manner as da Cunha describes the women in Canudos but then becomes a real "woman"—she is asked to tell her story. The woman is an aristocrat from some English-speaking European country (possibly Ireland or Scotland) who followed her husband, a doctor, into Canudos. She reports that he abandoned everything, an empty life, to find out about "social diseases," to discover why, as in cancer, one "cell" could suddenly go crazy and contaminate others, why people abandon everything, including "social contracts" (religion, she says, isn't the motivation, since it too is a "social contract"). When she got to Canudos, her husband was already dead, and although Canudos was hard, she says that she slept well there and eventually realized that it was "reality" and that everyone

would go to Canudos. It was a place not of disorder but of another order, not a system but a live order. The message she delivers is simple: the Conselheiro is not dead (the famous photograph of the Conselheiro in a grave was simply a photo of another man), and a bell will toll to indicate when he leaves Canudos. She also tells Bittencourt that there will be more Canudoses (and that there had already been many Canudoses). She and her two companions are decapitated, but the encounter is described as surprising and changing Bittencourt (portrayed, in imitation of da Cunha, as a typical bourgeois bureaucrat). He learns that there is something stronger than power and that, despite the force on his side, he didn't win (Sándor Márai, *Veredicto em Canudos* [São Paulo: Editora Schwarcz, 2001], 144).

6. For example, Edmundo Moniz writes, "Although Antonio Conselheiro was politically outdated with regards to the Republic, not understanding the historical significance of the bourgeois revolution as an advance, on the social plane he was ahead of the Republic and Monarchy both. Antonio Conselheiro opposed a socialist community to the bourgeois state backed by landowners" (Moniz, *A guerra social de Canudos* [Rio de Janeiro: Civilização Brasileira, 1978], 68).

7. Slavoj Žižeck, "Heiner Mueller out of Joint," available at http://www.lacan.com/mueller.htm (accessed Mar. 29, 2010).

8. Dain Borges, "Salvador's 1890's: Paternalism and Its Discontents," *Luso-Brazilian Review* 30.2 (1993): 47.

9. Maurice Blanchot, "Everyday Speech," *Yale French Studies* 73 (1987): 19.

10. Henri Lefebvre, *Critique of Everyday Life,* vol. 2, *Foundations for a Sociology of the Everyday* (New York: Verso, 2002), 337, 357.

11. Lefebvre, "The Everyday and Everydayness," *Yale French Studies* 73 (1987): 9.

12. Qtd. in Henri Lefebvre, *Critique of Everyday Life,* vol. 1 (New York: Verso, 1991), 1.

13. Machado de Assis isn't the only one to suggest Canudos as a place of critique to this kind of modern everyday. At one point in Sándor Márai's *Veredicto em Canudos*, the English-speaking woman mentions that the inhabitants of Canudos are afraid of the new order: "They began to fear losing something. . . . Individuality, what each one was. . . . In this [new] order man dries up inside, he ceases to become what he is. . . . He has to become like everyone else. . . . This is the great danger" (139). Cunninghame Graham also includes comments that suggest a Canudos defined as the opposite of a modern, bourgeois life: "A people in this state is moved more easily to acts of heroism and of self-abnegation than those who pass an ordinary life, marrying and giving in marriage, buying and selling and setting down accounts by double entry" (*Brazilian Mystic,* 113).

14. Lefebvre, *Critique,* vol. 1, 7.

15. Ibid., 9.

16. Michel de Certeau, *The Practice of Everyday Life* (Berkeley: University of California Press, 1984), 201.

17. Ibid.

18. Ibid., 107.

19. Antonio Gramsci, *The Antonio Gramsci Reader: Selected Writings 1916–1935* (New York: New York University Press, 2000), 205.

20. Ibid., 205.

21. Derek Sayer, "Everyday Forms of State Formation: Some Dissident Remarks on Hegemony," *Everyday Forms of State Formation* (Durham: Duke University Press, 1994), 375.

22. Ibid., 374.

23. Louis Althusser, "Ideology and Ideological State Apparatuses (Notes towards an Investigation)," *Essays on Ideology* (London: Verso, 1993), 42.

24. Ibid.

25. Gramsci, *Gramsci Reader*, 211.

26. Ibid., 218.

27. Ibid., 232.

28. Ibid.

29. For more on the religious question, see Roderick Barman, "The Brazilian Peasantry Reexamined: The Implications of the Quebra-Quilo Revolt, 1874–75," *Hispanic American Historical Review* 57.3 (1977): 413–14.

30. Armando Souto Maior, *Quebra-Quilos: Lutas socais no outono do Império* (São Paulo: Companhia Editora Nacional, 1978). Although sparse, a few other studies touch on the Quebra-Quilos riots. See, in addition to Roderick Barman's essay "The Brazilian Peasantry Reexamined," Joan Meznar, "The Ranks of the Poor: Military Service and Social Differentiation in Northeast Brazil, 1830–1875," *Hispanic American Historical Review* 72.3 (1992): 335–51; and Peter Beattie, *The Tribute of Blood* (Durham: Duke University Press, 2001).

31. Souto Maior, *Quebra-Quilos*, 122.

32. Barman, "Brazilian Peasantry," 416.

33. Ernesto Laclau, *Emancipation(s)* (New York: Verso, 1996), 42.

34. Qtd. in Souto Maior, *Quebra-Quilos*, 84.

35. Martin Lienhard, *La voz y su huella: Escritura y conflicto étnico-social en América Latina 1492–1988* (Hanover, N.H.: Ediciones del Norte, 1992), 79.

36. Benedict Anderson, *Imagined Communities: Reflections on the Origin and Spread of Nationalism* (London: Verso, 1991), 26.

37. The first attempt, which took place from 1822 to 1840, was a continuation of the institutionalization associated with Dom João's stay in Rio, 1808–1822. This moment included projects such as the creation of a school of fine arts and the foundation of elite higher education, as well as historical and geographical institutions. All these institutions were beholden to French models, which identified patronage of the arts as one of the state's reponsibilities and thus sought to establish the cultural infrastructure of a new nation-state. It was succesful, says Needell, but circumscribed in its effect (it matched an elitist vision of society and culture as designed for and by a literate, urban, and wealthy minority). The second moment comprised the previously described failed attempts of the Rio Branco cabinet, 1871–75. The third era (which corresponds to the Belle Epoque) began in the late 1890s with the republic's stabilization after the political violence and financial turmoil following the fall of the monarchy (Jeffrey Needell, "The Domestic Civilizing Mission: The Cultural Role of the State, 1808–1930," *Luso-Brazilian Review* 36.1 [1999]: 1–18).

38. Ibid., 5.

39. Qtd. in Barman, "Brazilian Peasantry," 411.

40. Ibid.

41. A more complete list of exemptions includes the following categories: men who lived with and supported an "honest" sister or mother; widowers raising children; fishermen; employees of important factories; ranchers with more than fifty head of cattle; owners, managers, or representatives of farms or rural businesses with more than ten employees (exempt in peacetime); and policemen, priests, and graduates of or students in medical or law schools (exempt even in wartime) (Beattie, *Tribute of Blood*, 73–75).

42. Ibid., 148.

43. Ibid., 85.

44. Brazilian society as a whole had long associated military service with slavery. In 1828 General Cunha Mattos had declared in the Chamber of Deputies that "the worst disgrace in all the universe is to be a recruit in Brazil. It is a real punishment: a common soldier is considered a miserable slave." He asserted that "everyone wants to defend his homeland, but no one wants to be treated worse than the most vile slave," and concluded on another occasion that "military law is as severe as that of slavery; or slaves are perhaps more free than soldiers on certain occasions" (qtd. in Meznar, "Ranks of the Poor," 345). Meznar points out that the parallels between army service and slavery sharpened whenever recruitment efforts intensified and that the free poor were particularly intent on maintaining their difference from slaves.

45. Barman, "Brazilian Peasantry," 412.

46. Souto Maior, *Quebra-Quilos*, 166.

47. Even Barman writes, "Since such forms of action did not aim at taking control or giving positive direction to the body politic, they can be described as pre-political," although he notes that it is not clear that such lack of "political consciousness" should be deplored and that the lack does not mean that such action was inefficient or ineffective ("Brazilian Peasantry," 423).

48. Souto Maior, *Quebra-Quilos*, 2.

49. Robert Levine, *Vale of Tears: Revisiting the Canudos Massacre in Northeastern Brazil, 1893–97* (Berkeley: University of California Press, 1992), 90. Barman, too, argues that taxes—imposed particularly by local and provincial governments—increased during the 1870s as a consequence of increased expenditures. He notes that many of these fell on the activities of the marketplace, including taxes on each head of cattle entering the town's slaughterhouse, larger fees for purchasing peddler's licenses, and the "imposto de chão," a tax on every load of grain and vegetables sold on market day (Barman, "Brazilian Peasantry," 415). By many accounts, the Conselheiro's first clash with authorities occurred over this "imposto de chão."

50. Guha, *Elementary Aspects*, 9.

51. Barman, "Brazilian Peasantry," 422.

52. Magnus Mörner, *Region and State in Latin America's Past* (Baltimore: Johns Hopkins University Press, 1993), 67.

53. Souto Maior, *Quebra-Quilos*, 56.

54. Manoel Benício, *O rei dos jagunços: Chronica histórica e de costumes sertanejos sobre os acontecimentos de Canudos* (Brasília: Senado Federal, 1997), 94–95.

55. Ibid., 162.

56. Needell, "Domestic Civilizing Mission," 6.

57. Nicolau Sevcenko, *Literatura como missão: Tensões sociais e criação cultural na Primeira República* (São Paulo: Editora Brasiliense, 1983), 42.

58. Honório Vilanova, echoing the Conselheiro, justifies the Conselheiro's anti-Republican sentiment as defensive: "If the Pilgrim preached against the Republic, it's because the Republic was against religion" (Honório Vilanova (and Nertan Macedo), *Memorial de Vilanova: Depoimento do último sobrevivente da Guerra de Canudos* [Rio de Janeiro: Edições O Cruzeiro, 1964], 70). The Conselheiro expresses the same sentiment to the leader of a mission that went to Canudos before the war in an attempt to convince him to submit to Church authority. When queried on the armed guard that protected him, the Conselheiro replied (according to the Capuchin brother):

> I have these men with me for my defense, because Your Reverence knows that the police attacked me and tried to kill me in a place called Maceté, and there were deaths on either side.
>
> Under the monarchy I let myself be arrested, because I recognized the government; but not today because I don't accept the Republic.
>
> [E para minha defesa que tenho comigo êstes homens armados, porque V. Revma. há de saber que a polícia atacou-me e quis matar-me no lugar chamado Maceté, onde houve mortes de um e de outro lado.
>
> No tempo da monarquia deixei-me prender, porque reconhecia o govêrno; hoje não, porque não reconheço a República."] (Frade Capuchinho João Evangelista, "Relatório apresentado ao Arcebispo da Bahia sobre Antônio Conselheiro pelo Frade Capuchinho João Evangelista de Monte-Marciano [anexo I]," *Canudos: Messianismo e conflito social* [Fortaleza, Brazil: Edições Universidade Federal do Ceará / Secult, 1993], 164)

59. António Vicente Mendes Maciel, *Antônio Conselheiro e Canudos (revisão histórica): A obra manuscrita de António Conselheiro e que pertenceu a Euclides da Cunha,* ed. Ataliba Nogueira (São Paulo: Companhia Editora Nacional, 1974), 175.

60. Ibid.

61. Qtd. in Maciel, 179–80

62. Euclides da Cunha, *Rebellion in the Backlands,* trans. Samuel Putnam (Chicago: University of Chicago Press, 1944), 163.

63. Vicente Dobroruka, *Antonio Conselheiro, o beato endiabrado de Canudos* (Rio de Janeiro: Diadorim, 1977), 159.

64. Qtd. in Maciel, *António Conselheiro,* 178.

65. Maria de Lourdes Monaco Janotti, *Os subversives da república* (São Paulo: Editora Brasiliense, 1986), 93.

66. Qtd. in Maciel, *António Conselheiro,* 181.

67. Ibid.

68. Cited in Alexandre Otten, "A influência do ideário religioso na construção da comunidade de Belo Monte," *Luso-Brazilian Review* 30.2 (1993): 86.

69. Judith Butler, Ernesto Laclau, and Slavoj Žižek, *Contingency, Hegemony, Universality: Contemporary Dialogues on the Left* (New York: Verso, 2000), 83.

70. Levine, *Vale of Tears*, 145.

71. Incidentally, it may be that the Conselheiro had attempted to found another city in 1890 or 1891; he situated this town, called Bom Jesus, in abandoned farms 217 km from Salvador, but for reasons unknown it did not flourish (Rodrigo Lacerda, "Sobrevoando Canudos," in *Canudos: Palavra de Deus, sonho da terra,* ed. Benjamin Abdala Jr. and Isabel M. M. Alexandre [São Paulo: Editora Serviço Nacional de Aprendizajem Comercial São Paulo / Boitempo Editorial, 1997], 26).

72. Roberto Ventura, "A Nossa Vendéia: Canudos, o mito da Revolução Francesa e a constituição de identidade nacional-cultural no Brasil," *Revista de Crítica Literaria Latinoamericana* 24 (1986): 114.

73. Euclides da Cunha, *Os sertões* (Rio de Janeiro: Ediouro, 1998), 170. The English-language translation renders the number incorrectly as five hundred rather than fifty huts; see da Cunha, *Rebellion*, 143.

74. Cited in Consuelo Novais Sampaio, "Repensando Canudos: O jogo das oligarquias," *Luso-Brazilian Review* 30.2 (1993): 105.

75. José Calasans, *Cartografia de Canudos* (Salvador, Brazil: Secretaria da Cultura e Turismo do Estado da Bahia / Empresa Gráfica da Bahia, 1997), 51. According to the story, while living in Belo Monte, Mota was falsely accused of treason by competing merchants, and he and his family were massacred on the orders of João Abade, against orders by the Conselheiro.

76. Levine (*Vale of Tears,* 167) provides the information on the school. Many scholars suggest that the word *favela* applied to the shantytowns of major cities in the twentieth century originates in a hill alongside Canudos called o Morro da Favela. Favelas began to sprout at the end of the nineteenth century after a series of urban reforms in Rio made the center too expensive and inaccessible; returning soldiers from the Canudos War are supposed to have been among the first to find housing inaccessible (Dobroruka, *Antonio Conselheiro,* 24).

77. Calasans, *Cartografia de Canudos,* 55.

78. Ibid., 53.

79. Little work has been done on the presence of indigenous groups in Canudos, but three articles worthy of note are Maria Lúcia Mascarenhas, "Rio de sangue e ribanceira de corpos," in *Canudos* (*Cadernos do CEAS*), ed. Alfredo Souza Dórea (Salvador, Brazil: Centro de Estudos e Ação Social, 1997), 59–72; Mascarenhas, "Toda nação em Canudos, 1893–1897: Índios em Canudos (memória e tradição oral da participação dos Kiriri e Kaimbes na guerra de Canudos)," *Revista Canudos* 2.2 (1997): 68–84; and Edwin Reesink, "A tomada do coração da aldeia: A participação dos índios de massacará na Guerra de Canudos," in *Canudos* (*Cadernos do CEAS*), ed. Alfredo Souza Dórea (Salvador, Brazil: Centro de Estudos e Ação Social, 1997), 73–95.

80. Qtd. in Calasans, *Cartografia de Canudos,* 84.

81. Lacerda, "Sobrevoando Canudos," 28.

82. Dobroruka, *Antonio Conselheiro*, 212.

83. Levine, *Vale of Tears*, 65.

84. Da Cunha, *Rebellion*, 149. In "O cosmo festivo: A propósito de um fragmento de 'A terra,'" José Leonardo do Nascimento argues that da Cunha sees evolution as the march from homogeneity to heterogeneity and that this explains both his critique of Canudos as a homogeneous mass and his critique of the way fanaticism in the army transforms the human into a human-machine, human-object. He derives this argument from an analysis of the contrast between da Cunha's descriptions of drought as homogeneous and descriptions of abundance with rains as scenes of heterogeneity (Nascimento, ed., *"Os sertões" de Euclides da Cunha: Releituras e diálogos* [São Paulo: Editora Universidade Estadual Paulista, 2002], 173–90).

85. Vilanova, *Memorial de Vilanova*, 67 ("Gostei tanto da ordem ali observada que resolvi ficar. Canudos era um pedaço de chão bem-aventurado. Não precisava nem mesmo de chuva. Tinha de tudo. Até rapadura do Caririri" [first quotation]; "Não havia precisão de roubar em Canudos porque tudo existia em abundância, gado e roçado, provisões não faltavam" [second quotation]).

86. Ibid. ("Era um formigueiro de gente, zelosa e ordeira nos seus bons costumes, onde não havia uma só mulher prostituta. Do balcão eu via em derredor a quietude e a paz em que findavam os dias. Reina o Peregrino. A sua palavra era ouro de lei").

87. Ibid., 68 ("só uma vez ou outra aparecia pela igreja. Não gosta muito de reza" [first quotation]; "Os homens, repito, não eram tanto de freqüentar os ofícios. As mulheres, sim, iam quase tôdas ao santuário ou à latada, onde rezavam e ouviam pregação" [second quotation]).

88. Ibid., 67 ("Grande era o Canudos do meu tempo. Quem tinha roça tratava da roça na beira do rio. Quem tinha gado tratava do gado. Quem tinha mulher e filhos tratava da mulher e dos filhos. Quem gosta de reza ia rezar. De tudo se tratava porque a nenhum pertencia e era de todos, pequenos e grandes, na regra ensinada pelo Peregrino").

89. Evangelista, "Relatório," 165.

90. Da Cunha, *Os sertões*, 149.

91. Calasans, *Cartografia de Canudos*, 58. In letters collected by Favila Nunes, a sergeant named Jacinto Ferreira da Silva sends word to Rumão Suares dos Santos: "and come here to buy my 3 houses because I am Awaiting you so we can be neighbors" ["i venha para comprar as 3 casas minhas que estou a sua Espera para sermos vizinhos"] (Calasans, *Cartografia de Canudos*, 58).

92. Honório tells the following story:

> The Pilgrim asked then what profit we expected to make with the sale of the merchandise. And my brother Antônio responded:
> "20 percent."
> "We'll buy everything if you lower it to 15."
> My brother accepted the offer and the Pilgrim had them pay us the proposed amount. And my brother liked Canudos so much that he decided to stay there. From Vila Nova da Rainha I would send my brother the merchandise that he

requested. Canudos began to obtain its supplies from Vila Nova and so it was that Antonio, and later I myself, came by the name that we now use—Vilanova.

[O Peregrino indagou, então, qual era o lucro que esperava obter com a venda da mercadoria trazida. Compadre Antônio respondeu:
— "O lucro é de vinte por cento."
— "Pois faça um abate para quinze e nós ficamos com tudo."
Compadre Antônio aceitou a oferta e o Peregrino mandou pagar a quantia proposta. E tanto gostou meu irmão de Canudos que ali decidiu ficar. De Vila Nova da Rainha eu ia despachando ao compadre as mercadorias que êle pedia. Canudos começou a abastcer-se de Vila Nova e foi assim que Antônio, tanto quanto eu, mais tarde, ganhamos o apelido que conservamos—Vilanova.] (Vilanova, *Memorial de Vilanova*, 38)

93. Evangelista, "Relatório," 162.

94. Ibid., 167 ("Ora, isto não é jejum: é comer a fartar").

95. Qtd. in Reesink, "A tomada do coração," 86 ("Minha mãe . . . queria ir, espiar a beleza que tava em Canudos. . . . Ela achava que aquilo era bonito que dizia que ali era um rio de leite e uma ribanceira de cuscus"). These visions are echoed in popular poetry, such as the following verses:

> A thousand rumors spread
> throughout the backlands
> King Sebastian was living
> In Belo Monte
> Oil ran from the hills
> The rivers flowed with milk
> And stones turned into bread
>
> [Espalharam mil boatos
> por todo aquele sertão
> Em Belo Monte já estava
> O Dom Rei Sebastião
> Dos montes corria azeite
> A água do monte era leite
> As pedras convertiam-se em pão].
> (From a text by José Aras, cited in José Calsans, *No tempo de Antônio Conselheiro* [Salvador, Brazil: Livraria Progresso Editora, 1959], 53)

96. Mascarenhas, "Toda nação em Canudos," 69. For an extended discussion of the image of a Canudos of plenty, see Patricia de Santana Pinho, "Revistando Canudos hoje no imaginário popular," *Revista Canudos* 2.2 (1997): 173–203.

97. Odórico Tavares, *Canudos: 50 anos depois* (Salvador, Brazil: Fundação de Cultura do Estado, 1947), 48 ("No tempo do Conselheiro, não gosto nem de falar para não passar por mentiroso, havia de tudo, por estes arredores. Dava de tudo e até cana-de-açúcar de se descascar com a unha, nascia bonitona por estes lados. Legumes em abundância e chuvas à vontade. . . . Esse tempo, parece mentira").

98. Qtd. in Calasans, *Cartografia de Canudos,* 59.

99. Reesink, "A tomada do coração," 86 ("Não gostei daquele lugar não. . . . Foi o lugar mais idiota que eu já vi, não sei como que esse pessoal brigaram naquele lugar. Porque ali para ninguém errar uns nos outros, porque estava tudo descoberto como um gado, um lote de gado no campo. . . . Como que vivia aquele pessoal lá?").

100. Italo Calvino, *Invisible Cities* (New York: Harcourt Brace Jovanovich, 1972), 105.

101. José J. Veiga, *A Casca da serpente* (Rio de Janeiro: Bertrand Brasil, 2001), 158–59.

Chapter Four: *Os Sertões*

1. For a more extended discussion of the relationship between da Cunha and Victor Hugo, see Leopoldo Bernucci, *A imitação dos sentidos: Prógonos, contemporâneos e epígonos de Euclides da Cunha* (São Paulo: Editora da Universidade de São Paulo, 1995).

2. Euclides da Cunha, *Canudos: Diário de uma expedição* (Rio de Janeiro: Livraria José Olympio Editora, 1939), 12–13 (further citations of this work will appear parenthetically in the text as *Diário*). A version of this passage makes its way into the last quarter of *Os sertões*, where da Cunha notes that disabled soldiers recovering in Bahia talked to others about their experiences in Canudos and that

> their tales were true in essence, even though marred by exaggerations. Out of them strange episodes were woven; and, as a result, the jagunço now began to appear as a being apart, terratological and monstrous, half-man and half-goblin; violating all biological laws by displaying an inconceivable power of resistance; daringly attacking his adversary, yet himself unseen, intangible, slipping away invisible through the caatinga, like a cobra; gliding or tumbling down the sides of steep cliffs like a specter; yet lighter than the musket that he bore; lean, dried up, fantastic, melting into a sprite, weighing less than a child, his bronzed skin stretched tightly over his bones, rough as the epidermis of a mummy. The popular imagination from then on ran riot, in a drunken delirium of stupendous happenings, woven out of fantasies. (Da Cunha, *Rebellion in the Backlands*, trans. Samuel Putnam [Chicago: University of Chicago Press, 1944], 386)

In this later version, da Cunha distances himself even more from these representations, presenting them as stories told by the soldiers, even though they are "true in essence."

3. See Marco Antonio Villa, *Canudos: O povo da terra* (São Paulo: Editora Atica, 1995), 248–60.

4. Euclides da Cunha, *Caderneta de Campo* (São Paulo: Editora Cultrix, 1975), 18.

5. Ibid., 19.

6. Lélis Piedade, *Histórico e relatório do Comitê Patriótico da Bahia (1897–1901),* 2d ed., ed. Antônio Olavo (Salvador, Brazil: Portfolium, 2002), 183.

7. Ibid., 174.

8. Da Cunha, *Caderneta,* 148.

9. Lima Barreto, "O falso Henrique V," *Contos reunidos* (Belo Horizonte, Brazil: Crisálida, 2005), 97.

10. Nicolau Sevcenko, *Literatura como missão: Tensões sociais e criação cultural na Primeira República* (São Paulo: Editora Brasiliense, 1983), 210.

11. Da Cunha, *Rebellion*, 277 (further citations of this work will appear parenthetically in the text as *Rebellion*).

12. Da Cunha was also prey to such speculations in his articles: "General Artur Oscar … showed me some of the bullets littering the ground after the shoot-out last night. They are made of steel, some are similar to the bullets of the Mannlicher, but they are unknown. They are undoubtedly projectiles of modern arms that we do not possess. All of this leads one to believe that this conflagration in the backlands has deeper roots" (da Cunha, *Diário*, 67). The teleological logic of developmentalism to which da Cunha subscribed means that the enemy who was before primitive and barbaric appears, under the shadow of success, to take on the overtones of aliens of an ultramodern sort, slinging weapons that even the Brazilian state does not possess.

13. "Not being blood brothers, the inhabitants found a moral consanguinity which gave them the exact appearance of a *clan*, with their chieftain's will as the supreme law, while justice lay in his irrevocable decisions. Canudos, indeed, was a stereotype of the dubious form of social organization that prevailed among the earliest barbarian tribes" (*Rebellion*, 148).

14. Raimundo Nina Rodrigues, *As coletividades anormais* (Edições do Senado Federal: Brasília, 2006), 89.

15. Ibid., 86.

16. Ibid., 51.

17. Ibid., 52.

18. See Gabriel Tarde, "The Public and the Crowd," *On Communication and Social Influence (Selected Papers)* (Chicago: University of Chicago Press, 1969), 277–94.

19. In *Time and the Other* Fabian argues that the relationship of anthropology to its subject has always been organized in significant correlations of oppositions, such as Here-There and Now-Then, which he interprets as distancing techniques between the subject and object of ethnographic practice and views as resulting from the overarching colonial production of distance between the West and everywhere else. Whereas "evolutionist time" (which establishes other cultures at earlier stages on a temporal axis) dominated in previous eras, Fabian argues that ethnography is marked by "encapsulated time." In both cases, however, what obtains is a "denial of coevalness": "By that I mean a persistent and systematic tendency to place the referent(s) of anthropology in a Time other than the present of the producer of anthropological discourse" (Johannes Fabian, *Time and the Other: How Anthropology Makes Its Object* [New York: Columbia University Press, 2002], 31).

20. Prathama Banerjee, *Politics of Time: "Primitives" and History-writing in a Colonial Society* (New Delhi: Oxford University Press, 2006), 149.

21. César Zama, *Libelo republicano acompanhado de comentários sobre a guerra de Canudos* (Salvador, Brazil: Universidade Federal da Bahia, 1989), 23.

22. Peter Beattie, *The Tribute of Blood* (Durham: Duke University Press, 2001), 6.

23. Zama, *Libelo republicano*, 28.

24. "What they were being called upon to do now was what other troops had done—to stage an invasion of a foreign territory. For it was all a geographic fiction" (da Cunha, *Rebellion*, 406).

25. Roberto Ventura, "'A Nossa Vendéia': Canudos, o mito da Revolução Francesa e a constituição de identidade nacional-cultural no Brasil (1897–1902)," *Revista de Crítica Literaria Latinoamericana* 24 (1986): 111.

26. Jens Anderman, *The Optic of the State: Visuality and Power in Argentina and Brazil* (Pittsburgh: University of Pittsburgh Press, 2007), 2.

27. Sevcenko, *Literatura como missão*, 232.

28. Ibid., 81–82.

29. Beattie, *Tribute of Blood*, 11.

30. "After having lived for four hundred years on a vast stretch of seaboard, where we enjoyed the reflections of civilized life, we suddenly came into an unlooked-for inheritance in the form of the Republic. Caught up in the sweep of modern ideas, we abruptly mounted the ladder, leaving behind us in their centuries-old semidarkness a third of our people in the heart of our country. Deluded by a civilization which came to us second hand; rejecting, blind copyists that we were, all that was best in the organic codes of other nations, and shunning, in our revolutionary zeal, the slightest compromise with the exigencies of our own national interests, we merely succeeded in deepening the contrast between our mode of life and that of our rude native sons, who were more alien to us in this land of ours than were the immigrants who came from Europe. For it was not an ocean which separated us from them but three whole centuries" (da Cunha, *Rebellion*, 161).

31. David Lloyd and Paul Thomas, *Culture and the State* (New York: Routledge, 1998), 3.

32. Before the publication of da Cunha's book, the word *sertões* referred to backlands generically. It became associated with the desertlike backlands of the Northeast after his book (Regina Abreu, *O enigma de "Os sertões"* [Rio de Janeiro: Funarte / Rocco, 1998], 193).

33. As is well known, da Cunha was passionately interested in the French Revolution, and Michelet's monumental history of the French Revolution influenced him enormously, but historians and critics have paid less attention to the determining influence of Taine, who described mobs that "exhibited nearly all the characteristics that Sighele, Tarde and Le Bon were later to include in their 'scientific' analyses" (Susanna Barrows, *Distorting Mirrors: Visions of the Crowd in Late Nineteenth-Century France* [New Haven, Conn.: Yale University Press, 1981], 85). For a brief discussion of Taine's influence on da Cunha, see Edgar Salvadori de Decca and Maria Lucia Abaurre Gnerre, "Prefigurações literárias da barbárie nacional em Euclides da Cunha, Machado de Assis e Lima Barreto," in *"Os sertões" de Euclides da Cunha: Releituras e diálogos*, ed. José Leonardo Nascimento (São Paulo: Editora Universidade Estadual Paulista, 2002), 132–34.

34. Luiz Costa Lima, *Terra ignota: A construção de "Os sertões"* (Rio de Janeiro: Civilização Brasileira, 1997), 123.

35. Antoine Seel, "Por trás das palavras: Fluxos e ritmos en *Os Sertões*," in *"Os sertões" de Euclides da Cunha: Releituras e diálogos*, ed. José Leonardo Nascimento (São Paulo: Editora Universidade Estadual Paulista, 2002), 162.

36. Costa Lima, *Terra ignota*, 191.

37. Ibid.

38. Nina Rodrigues, *As coletividades,* 49.

39. Ibid., 49.

40. Sevcenko, *Literatura como missão,* 145.

41. Cited in Olímpio de Sousa Andrade, *História e interpretação de "Os Sertões,"* vol. 2 (São Paulo: EdArt, 1966), 309.

42. Sevcenko, *Literatura como missão,* 220.

43. The soldiers came to resemble the *jagunços* in a spontaneous, undirected way. "There was no longer any trace of military formation in their ranks. For the most part, through a process of adaptation, they had come to adopt the garb of the sertanejos" (da Cunha, *Rebellion,* 379).

44. Slavoj Žižek, "Class Struggle or Postmodernism," in Judith Butler, Ernesto Laclau, and Slavoj Žižek, *Contingency, Hegemony, Universality: Contemporary Dialogues on the Left* (New York: Verso, 2000), 117.

45. Gilberto Freyre in da Cunha, *Diário,* xii.

46. Sevcenko, *Literatura como missão,* 141.

47. Qtd. in Costa Lima, *Terra ignota,* 20.

48. Banerjee, *Politics of Time,* 239.

49. Sevcenko, *Literatura como missão,* 224.

Chapter Five: Another Canudos

1. Leopoldo Bernucci, *A imitação dos sentidos: Prógonos, contemporâneos e epígonos de Euclides da Cunha* (São Paulo: Editora da Universidade de São Paulo, 1995), 41.

2. Ibid., 82.

3. Silvia Maria Azevedo, "*O rei dos jagunços* de Manuel Benício: Um estudo introdutório," *"O rei dos jagunços" de Manuel Benício: Entre a ficção e a história* (São Paulo: Editora da Universidade de São Paulo, 2003), 16.

4. Walnice Nogueira Galvão, *Saco de gatos* (São Paulo: Duas Cidades, 1976), 76.

5. Afonso Arinos, *Os jagunços,* 3d ed. (Brasília: Philobiblion, 1985), 132 (further citations of this work will appear parenthetically in the text).

6. Evaristo da Veiga (1799–1837) was one of the more celebrated political polemicists of the day, a deputy for Minas Gerais, and an editor of and writer for the leading opposition periodical, *Aurora Fluminense.* According to Needell, although he was a "liberal firebrand," he supported the reformist majority rather than the radical minority of the liberal opposition in their split after the abdication of Pedro I, therefore supporting many of the original founders of what would come to be the Party of Order (Jeffrey Needell, *The Party of Order: The Conservatives, the State, and Slavery in the Brazilian Monarchy, 1831–1871* [Stanford, Calif.: Stanford University Press, 2006], 43).

7. Needell, *Party of Order,* 78.

8. Ibid., 311.

9. Ibid., 321.

10. Ibid.

11. Oliveira Mello, *De volta ao sertão: Afonso Arinos e o regionalismo Brasileiro* (Rio de Janeiro: Livraria Editora Cátedra, 1981), 126. "Although *Os Jagunços* is about the Canudos War, written daily to be published in installments in the *Comércio de São Paulo*, the first part is authentically rooted in Minas Gerais. Arinos neither participated in the war nor went to the war front like Euclides da Cunha. That is why he uses the customs and characters of his surroundings" (ibid.). This includes characters such as Joaquim Pachola (based on a cowhand in the area in which he grew up) as well as geography and toponyms.

12. Qtd. in Azevedo, "*O rei dos jagunços*," 31.

13. Fredric Jameson, "Reflections on the Brecht-Lukács Debate," *The Ideologies of Theory: Essays 1971–1986*, vol. 2, *The Syntax of History* (Minneapolis: University of Minnesota Press, 1989), 135.

14. Gabriel García Márquez, 1982 Nobel Prize lecture, "The Solitude of Latin America," available at http://nobelprize.org/nobel__prizes/literature/laureates/1982/marquez-lecture-e.html.

15. Angel Rama, *Transculturación narrativa en América Latina* (Mexico City: Siglo Veintiuno Editores, 1982), 211.

16. Antonio Cornejo-Polar, "*Mestizaje*, Transculturation, Heterogeneity," in *The Latin American Cultural Studies Reader*, ed. Ana del Sarto, Alicia Rios, and Abril Trigo (Durham: Duke University Press, 2004), 117.

17. Qtd. in Antônio Oliveira Mello, *De volta ao sertão: Afonso Arinos e o regionalismo Brasileiro* (Rio de Janeiro: Livraria Editora Cátedra, 1981), 62.

18. Qtd. in ibid.

19. Alfonso Arinos, "Nacionalização e arte," qtd. in ibid., 122.

20. Galvão, *Saco de gatos*, 85.

21. Michel Foucault, *Society Must Be Defended* (Picador: New York, 2003), 217.

22. The idea that the Canudenses were simply defending their home is not absent from *Os sertões*, but it takes on a different valence within that text, which emphasizes how the *jagunços* were out of place in Brazil of that time: "He [the *jagunço*] was not in the proper sense of the word an 'enemy,' which is an extermporized term, an exquisite euphemism, to take the place of 'notorious bandit' as he was called in that form of martial literature known as orders of the day. The sertanejo was merely defending his invaded home, that was all" (Euclides da Cunha, *Rebellion in the Backlands*, trans. Samuel Putnam [Chicago: University of Chicago Press, 1944], 368).

23. Qtd. in Azevedo, "*O rei dos jagunços*," 20. With the death of Moreira César, Artur Oscar became the candidate of the Jacobin wing of the army, and they planned a coup to assassinate Prudente de Morais on November 5, 1897. The attack was made, but in the confusion Bittencourt was mortally wounded. Public opinion turned suddenly in favor of Prudente de Morais and against the Jacobins (Azevedo, "*O rei dos jagunços*," 23).

24. Qtd. in Azevedo, "*O rei dos jagunços*," 19.

25. Azevedo, "*O rei dos jagunços*," 22. See http://www.portfolium.com.br/Sites/Canudos/conteudo.asp?IDPublicacao=158 for more on Benício and Alvim Martins Horcades.

26. Manoel Benício, *O rei dos jagunços: Chronica histórica e de costumes sertanejos sobre os*

acontecimentos de Canudos (Brasília: Senado Federal, 1997), 158 (further citations will be made parenthetically in the text). In *O Comércio de São Paulo* (1897) Arinos will write, "It was a fanatical movement which grew until it became a public threat, thanks to the force with which it was opposed from the beginning. Ultimately the movement gained such importance that it really took on a political nature; but the ones who gave it this political nature were neither the fanatics nor their chiefs but the Republican Government" (qtd. in Oliveira Mello, *De volta ao sertão*, 148).

27. Mikhail M. Bakhtin and Pavel N. Medvedev, *The Formal Method in Literary Scholarship* (Cambridge, Mass.: Harvard University Press, 1985), 116.

28. Qtd. in Azevedo, *"O rei dos jagunços,"* 28.

29. Alvim Martins Horcades, *Descrição de uma viagem a Canudos* (Bahia: Editora da Universidade Federal da Bahia, 1996), 104–5.

30. Da Cunha, *Rebellion,* 439, 443 (further citations are made parenthetically in the text as *Rebellion*).

31. Azevedo, *"O rei dos jagunços,"* 18.

32. Antonio Cornejo-Polar, *"La guerra del fin del mundo," Revista de Crítica Literaria* 20 (1984): 219–21.

33. Foucault, *Society Must Be Defended,* 52.

34. Ibid., 53.

Afterlives

1. David Lloyd, *Irish Times: Temporalities of Modernity* (Dublin: Field Day, 2008), 18.

2. Ibid., 29.

3. Ibid., 37.

4. Euclides da Cunha, *Rebellion in the Backlands*, trans. Samuel Putnam (Chicago: University of Chicago Press, 1944), 475.

5. Consuelo Novais Sampaio, ed., *Canudos: Cartas para o barão* (São Paulo: Editora da Universidade de São Paulo, 2001), 221–22.

6. Da Cunha, *Rebellion,* 476.

7. Manoel Benício, *O rei dos jagunços: Chronica histórica e de costumes sertanejos sobre os acontecimentos de Canudos* (Brasília: Senado Federal, 1997), 401.

8. Ibid., 460.

9. Ibid., 407–8.

10. Alfonso Arinos, *Os jagunços,* 3d ed. (Brasília: Philobiblion, 1985), 288.

11. Ibid., 311.

12. Ibid., 317.

13. Ibid., 319.

14. Juan Pablo Dabove, *Nightmares of the Lettered City* (Pittsburgh: University of Pittsburgh Press, 2007), 227–28.

15. Da Cunha, *Rebellion,* 382.

16. Ibid., 392.

17. Darién Davis, Review of *A guerra de Canudos, American Historical Review* 104.5 (Dec.

1999): 1808.

18. Prathama Banerjee, *Politics of Time: "Primitives" and History-writing in a Colonial Society* (New Delhi: Oxford University Press, 2006), 171.

19. Davis, Review, 1808.

20. Banerjee, *Politics of Time*, 172.

21. David Lloyd and Paul Thomas, *Culture and the State* (New York: Routledge, 1998), 21.

22. Antonio Negri and Giuseppe Cocco, *GlobAL: Biopoder y luchas en una América Latina globalizada* (Buenos Aires: Paidós, 2006), 235–36.

BIBLIOGRAPHY

Abrams, Phillip. "Notes on the Difficulty of Studying the State." *Journal of Historical Sociology* 1.1 (1988): 58–89.

Abreu, Modesto de. *Estilo e personalidade de Euclides da Cunha: Estilística d' "Os sertões."* Coleção *Vera Cruz*, vol. 52. Rio de Janeiro: Civilização Brasileira, 1963.

Abreu, Regina. *O enigma de "Os sertões."* Rio de Janeiro: Funarte / Rocco, 1998.

Agamben, Giorgio. *The Coming Community*. Minneapolis: University of Minnesota Press, 1993.

———. *Homo Sacer: Sovereign Power and Bare Life*. Stanford, Calif.: Stanford University Press, 1998.

Aguiar, Durval Vieira de. *"Monte Santo." Descrições prácticas da provincia da Bahia*, 74–77. Bahia: Diário da Bahia, 1888.

Alberdi, Juan Bautista. *Bases y puntos de partida para la organización política de la República Argentina*. Buenos Aires: Centro de Estudios de America Latina, 1979.

Althusser, Louis. "Ideology and Ideological State Apparatuses (Notes towards an Investigation)." *Essays on Ideology*, 1–60. London: Verso, 1993.

———. *Machiavelli and Us*. London: Verso, 1999.

Althusser, Louis, and Étienne Balibar. *Reading Capital*. New York: Verso, 1968.

Alves, Lizir Arcanjo. *Humor e sátira na guerra de Canudos*. Salvador, Brazil: Empresa Gráfica da Bahia, 1997.

Anderman, Jens. *The Optic of the State: Visuality and Power in Argentina and Brazil*. Pittsburgh: University of Pittsburgh Press, 2007.

Anderson, Benedict. *Imagined Communities: Reflections on the Origin and Spread of Nationalism*. London: Verso, 1991.

Andrade, Olímpio de Sousa. *História e interpretação de "Os sertões."* Vol. 2. São Paulo: EdArt, 1966.

Arguedas, José María. *The Fox from Up Above and the Fox from Down Below.* Pittsburgh: University of Pittsburgh Press, 2000.

Arinos, Afonso. *Os jagunços.* 3d ed. Brasília: Philobiblion, 1985.

Arruda, João. *Canudos: Messianismo e conflito social.* Fortaleza, Brazil: Edições Universidade Federal do Ceará / Secult, 1993.

Assis, Machado de. "Crônica: 14 de fevereiro de 1897." *A Semana. Obras Completas de Machado de Assis,* 31 vols., 3:413–18. Rio de Janeiro: W. M. Jackson, 1937.

Auerbach, Erich. *Mimesis: The Representation of Reality in Western Literature.* Princeton: Princeton University Press, 1974 [1946].

Avelar, Idelbar. *The Untimely Present: Postdictatorial Latin American Fiction and the Task of Mourning.* Durham: Duke University Press, 1999.

Azevedo, Sílvia Maria. "*O rei dos jagunços* de Manuel Benício: Um estudo introdutório." "*O rei dos jagunços" de Manuel Benício: Entre a ficção e a história,* 11–38. São Paulo: Editora da Universidade de São Paulo, 2003.

Baker, Keith Michael. *Inventing the French Revolution: Essays on French Political Culture in the Eighteenth Century.* New York: Cambridge University Press, 1990.

Bakhtin, Mikhail, and Pavel N. Medvedev. *The Formal Method in Literary Scholarship.* Cambridge, Mass.: Harvard University Press, 1985.

Banerjee, Prathama. *Politics of Time: "Primitives" and History-writing in a Colonial Society.* New Delhi: Oxford University Press, 2006.

Barelt, Dawid Danilo. "Cerco Discursivo de Canudos." In *Canudos (Cadernos do CEAS),* edited by Alfredo Souza Dórea, 37–46. Salvador, Brazil: Centro de Estudos e Ação Social, 1997.

Barman, Roderick. "The Brazilian Peasantry Reexamined: The Implications of the Quebra-Quilo Revolt, 1874–75." *Hispanic American Historical Review* 57.3 (1977): 401–24.

Barreto, Lima. "O falso Henrique V." *Contos reunidos,* 90–100. Belo Horizonto, Brazil: Crisálida, 2005.

Barros, Luitgarde Oliveira Cavalcanti. "Do Ceará, três santos do nordeste." *Revista Canudos* 1.1 (1997): 37–54.

Barrows, Susanna. *Distorting Mirrors: Visions of the Crowd in Late Nineteenth-Century France.* New Haven, Conn.: Yale University Press, 1981.

Barthes, Roland. *Michelet.* Berkeley: University of California Press, 1992.

———. *The Rustle of Language.* Berkeley: University of California Press, 1986.

Bastos, Abguar. *A visão histórico-sociológica de Euclides da Cunha.* São Paulo: Editora Nacional, 1986.

Bastos, José Augusto Cabral Barreto. *Incompreensível e bárbaro inimigo: A guerra simbólica contra Canudos*. Salvador, Brazil: Editora da Universidade Federal da Bahia, 1995.

Baxi, Upendra. "Discussion: 'The State's Emissary': The Place of Law in Subaltern Studies." In *Subaltern Studies*, vol. 7, edited by Partha Chatterjee and Gyanendra Pandey, 247–64. London: Oxford University Press, 1992.

Beattie, Peter. *The Tribute of Blood*. Durham: Duke University Press, 2001.

Benício, Manoel. *O rei dos jagunços: Chronica histórica e de costumes sertanejos sobre os acontecimentos de Canudos*. Brasília: Senado Federal, 1997.

Benjamin, Walter. *Illuminations*. New York: Schocken, 1968.

——. *Reflections: Essays, Aphorisms, Autobiographical Writings*. New York: Schocken, 1978.

Bernucci, Leopoldo. *A imitação dos sentidos: Prógonos, contemporâneos e epígonos de Euclides da Cunha*. São Paulo: Editora da Universidade de São Paulo, 1995.

Beverley, John. "Negotiating with the Disciplines: A Conversation on Latin American Subaltern Studies." *Journal of Latin American Cultural Studies* 6.2 (1997): 233–56.

——. *Subalternity and Representation: Arguments in Cultural Theory*. Durham: Duke University Press, 1999.

Bhabha, Homi. *The Location of Culture*. New York: Routledge, 1994.

Bieber, Judy. *Power, Patronage, and Political Violence: State Building on a Brazilian Frontier, 1822–1889*. Lincoln: University of Nebraska Press, 1999.

——. "A 'Visão do Sertão': Party Identity and Political Honor in Late Imperial Minas Gerais, Brazil." *Hispanic American Historical Review* 81.2 (2001): 309–42.

Blanchot, Maurice. "Everyday Speech." *Yale French Studies* 73 (1987).

——. *Writing the Disaster*. Lincoln: University of Nebraska Press, 1995.

Boaventura, Edivaldo. *O parque estadual de Canudos*. Salvador, Brazil: Secretaria da Cultura e Turismo da Bahia, 1997.

——. "Parque estadual de Canudos: Criação e evolução." *Revista Canudos* 1.1 (1997): 65–80.

Borges, Dain. "Salvador's 1890's: Paternalism and Its Discontents." *Luso-Brazilian Review* 30.2 (1993): 47–57.

Borges, Patrícia Cardoso. "A interpretação d'*os Sertões*, ontem e hoje." In *"Os sertões" de Euclides da Cunha: Releituras e diálogos*, edited by José Leonardo do Nascimento, 191–204. São Paulo: Editora Universidade Estadual Paulista, 2002.

Brandão, Adelino. *Euclides da Cunha e a questão racial no Brasil: A antropologia de "Os sertões."* Rio de Janeiro: Presença, 1990.

Burns, E. Bradford, ed. *Perspectives on Brazilian History*. New York: Columbia University Press, 1967.

Butler, Judith, Ernesto Laclau, and Slavoj Žižek. *Contingency, Hegemony, Universality: Contemporary Dialogues on the Left*. New York: Verso, 2000.

Calasans, José, ed. *Canudos na literatura de cordel.* São Paulo: Editora Atica, 1984.

———. "Canudos não Euclidiano: Fase anterior ao início da Guerra do Conselheiro." In *Canudos: Subsídio para a sua reavaliação histórica,* edited by José Augusto Vaz Sampaio Neto, 1–21. Rio de Janeiro: Fundação Casa de Rui Barbosa, 1986.

———. *Cartografia de Canudos.* Salvador, Brazil: Secretaria da Cultura e Turismo do Estado da Bahia / Empresa Gráfica da Bahia, 1997.

———. *A Faculdade Livre de Direito da Bahia (subsídios para sua história).* Salvador, Brazil: Universidade Federal da Bahia, 1984.

———. *No tempo de Antônio Conselheiro.* Salvador, Brazil: Livraria Progresso Editora, 1959.

———. *Quase biografias de jagunços: O sequito de Antonio Conselheiro.* Salvador, Brazil: Centro de Estudos Baianos, Universidade Federal da Bahia, 1986.

Calvino, Italo. *Invisible Cities.* New York: Harcourt Brace Jovanovich, 1972.

Carvalho, Gilmar de. *Madeira matriz: Cultura e memória.* São Paulo: Annablume Editora, 1999.

Carvalho, José Murilo de. "Brazil 1870–1914: The Force of Tradition." *Journal of Latin American Studies* 24 (1992): 145–62.

———. *A formação das almas: O imaginário da república no Brasil.* São Paulo: Editora Schwarcz, 1990.

———. *Teatro de sombras: A política imperial.* São Paulo: Editora Revista dos Tribunais, 1988.

Castro-Klarén, Sara. "In-forming the Body of Man in the *Caatinga.*" *Colorado Review of Hispanic Studies* 3 (2005): 99–116.

Certeau, Michel de. *Heterologies: Discourse on the Other.* Minneapolis: University of Minnesota Press, 1986.

———. *The Practice of Everyday Life.* Berkeley: University of California Press, 1984.

———. *The Writing of History.* New York: Columbia University Press, 1988.

Chakrabarty, Dipesh. "Discussion: Invitation to a Dialogue." In *Subaltern Studies,* edited by Ranajit Guha, 364–76. London: Oxford University Press, 1985.

———. "Marx after Marxism: History, Subalternity, and Difference." In *Marxism beyond Marxism,* edited by Saree Makdisi, Cesare Casarino, and Rebecca Karl, 55–70. New York: Routledge, 1996.

———. "Provincializing Europe: Postcoloniality and the Critique of History." *Cultural Studies* 6.3 (1992): 337–57.

———. *Provincializing Europe: Postcolonial Thought and Historical Difference.* Princeton: Princeton University Press, 2000.

———. *Rethinking Working-Class History: Bengal 1890–1940.* Princeton: Princeton University Press, 1989.

Chaterjee, Partha. *The Nation and Its Fragments: Colonial and Postcolonial Histories.* Princeton: Princeton University Press, 1993.

———. "The Nation and Its Peasants." In *Mapping Subaltern Studies and the Postcolonial*, edited by Vinayak Chaturvedi, 8–23. London: Verso, 2000.

Chaturvedi, Vinayak, ed. *Mapping Subaltern Studies and the Postcolonial*. London: Verso, 2000.

Citelli, Adilson. *Roteiro de leitura: "Os sertões" de Euclides da Cunha*. São Paulo: Editora Atica, 1996.

Clastres, Pierre. *Societies against the State: Essays in Political Anthropology*. New York: Zone, 1989.

Coelho Fontes, Oleone. *O treme-terra: Moreira César, a república e Canudos*. 2 ed. Petrópolis, Brazil: Vozes, 1996.

Cohen, Jean, and Andrew Arato. *Civil Society and Political Theory*. Cambridge, Mass.: MIT Press, 1995.

Cornejo-Polar, Antonio. *Arte, literatura, crítica latinoamericanas*. Caracas: Universidad Central de Venezuela, 1982.

———. "*La guerra del fin del mundo*." *Revista de Critica Literaria* 20 (1984): 219–21.

———. "El indigenismo andino." In *América Latina: Palavra, literatura e cultura*, vol. 2, edited by Ana Pizarro, 719–38. São Paulo: Memorial, 1993.

———. "*Mestizaje*, Transculturation, Heterogeneity." In *The Latin American Cultural Studies Reader*, edited by Ana del Sarto, Alicia Rios, and Abril Trigo, 116–19. Durham: Duke University Press, 2004.

———. *Los universos narrativos de José María Arguedas*. Buenos Aires: Editorial Losada, 1973.

Costa e Silva, Cândido da. "O peregrino entre os pastores." *Cadernos de Literatura Brasileira: Euclides da Cunha*, special issue, 13–14 (Dec. 2002): 201–32.

Costa Lima, Luiz. "In the Backlands of Hidden Mimesis." *Control of the Imaginary: Reason and Imagination in Modern Times*, 152–86. Minneapolis: University of Minnesota Press, 1988.

———. *Terra ignota: A construção de "Os sertões."* Rio de Janeiro: Civilização Brasileira, 1997.

Critchley, Simon. *Ethics, Politics, Subjectivity*. New York: Verso, 1999.

Cullenberg, Stephen. "Althusser and the Decentering of the Marxist Totality." In *Postmodern Materialism and the Future of Marxist Theory*, edited by Antonio Callari and David F. Ruccio, 120–49. Hanover, N.H.: University Press of New England / Wesleyan University Press, 1996.

Cunha, Euclides da. *À margem da história*. Pôrto, Portugal: Editôra Lello Brasileira, 1967.

———. *Caderneta de campo*. São Paulo: Editora Cultrix, 1975.

———. *Canudos: Diário de uma expedição*. Rio de Janeiro: Livraria José Olympio Editora, 1939.

———. *Rebellion in the Backlands*. Translated by Samuel Putnam. Chicago: University of Chicago Press, 1944.

———. *Os sertões*. Rio de Janeiro: Ediouro, 1998.

Dabove, Juan Pablo. *Nightmares of the Lettered City: Banditry and Literature in Latin America 1816–1929*. Pittsburgh: University of Pittsburgh Press, 2007.

Dantas, Paulo. *Os sertões de Euclides e outros sertões*. São Paulo: Conselho Estadual de Cultura / Comissão de Literatura, 1969.

Davis, Darién. Review of *A guerra de Candudos*. *American Historical Review* 104.5 (Dec. 1999): 1807–9.

Davis, Mike. *Late Victorian Holocausts: El Niño Famines and the Making of the Third World*. London: Verso, 2001.

Decca, Edgar Salvadori de, and Maria Lucia Abaurre Gnerre. "Prefigurações literárias da barbárie nacional em Euclides da Cunha, Machado de Assis e Lima Barreto." In *"Os sertões" de Euclides da Cunha: Releituras e diálogos*, edited by José Leonardo Nascimento, 127–47. São Paulo: Editora Universidade Estadual Paulista, 2002.

Deleuze, Gilles. *Cinema 1: The Movement Image*. Minneapolis: University of Minnesota Press, 1986.

———. *Cinema II: The Time Image*. Minneapolis: University of Minnesota Press, 1986.

———. "Postscript on the Societies of Control." *October* 59 (1993): 3–7.

Della Cava, Ralph. "Brazilian Messianism and National Institutions: A Reappraisal of Canudos and Joaseiro." *Hispanic American Historical Review* 48.3 (1968): 402–20.

Derrida, Jacques. *Deconstruction and the Possibility of Justice*. New York: Routledge, 1992.

———. *The Politics of Friendship*. New York: Verso, 1997.

———. *Spectres of Marx: The State of the Debt, the Work of Mourning and the New International*. Trans. Peggy Kamuf. New York: Routledge, 1994.

———. "Violence and Metaphysics: An Essay on the Thought of Emmanuel Levinas." *Writing and Difference*, 79–195. Chicago: University of Chicago Press, 1978.

Diacon, Todd. *Millenarian Vision, Capitalist Reality: Brazil's Contestado Rebellion 1912–1916*. Durham: Duke University Press, 1991.

———. "Peasants, Prophets, and the Power of a Millenarian Vision in Twentieth Century Brazil." *Comparative Studies in Society and History* 32.1 (1990): 488–514.

Días, Clímaco. "Canudos: Poesia e mistério de Machado de Assis." *Revista Canudos* 1.1 (1997): 91–104.

Dobroruka, Vicente. *Antonio Conselheiro, o beato endiabrado de Canudos*. Rio de Janeiro: Diadorim, 1977.

Dolar, Mladen. "Beyond Interpellation." *Qui Parle* 2 (1993): 75–96.

Eagleton, Terry. *Literary Theory: An Introduction*. Minneapolis: University of Minnesota Press, 1983.

Estudantes das escolas superiores da Bahia. *Manifesto dos estudantes das escolas superiores da Bahia aos seus colegas e aos republicanos dos outros Estados*. Salvador, Brazil: Typographia do "Correo de Notícias," 1897.

Evangelista, Frade Capuchinho João. "Relatório apresentado ao Arcebispo da Bahia sobre Antônio Conselheiro pelo Frade Capuchinho João Evangelista de Monte-Marciano." In João Arrudas, *Canudos: Messianismo e conflito social,* appendix 1. Fortaleza, Brazil: Edições Universidade Federal do Ceará / Secult, 1993.

Fabian, Johannes. *Time and the Other: How Anthropology Makes Its Object*. New York: Columbia University Press, 2002.

Facó, Rui. *Cangaceiros e fanáticos: Gênese e lutas*. 2d ed. Rio de Janeiro: Editôra Civilização Brasileira, 1965.

Fausto, Boris. "Society and Politics." In *Brazil: Empire and Republic 1822–1930,* edited by Leslie Bethell, 257–308. Cambridge: Cambridge University Press, 1989.

Ferreira, Jerusa Pires. "Canudos—as vozes perdidas." In *Canudos: Palavra de Deus, sonho da terra,* edited by Benjamin Abdala Jr. and Isabel M. M. Alexandre, 137–46. São Paulo: Editora Serviço Nacional de Aprendizajem Comercial São Paulo / Boitempo Editorial, 1997.

Fortes, Herbert Parentes. *Euclides: O estilizador de nossa história*. Rio de Janeiro: Edições Gumercindo Rocha Dorea, 1959.

Fortes, Meyers, and Edward E. Evans-Pritchard, eds. *African Political Systems.* London: Kegan Paul International, 1987.

Foucault, Michel. *The Archaeology of Knowledge and the Discourse on Language*. New York: Pantheon, 1972.

———. *Society Must Be Defended*. Picador: New York, 2003.

Freyre, Gilberto. *Atualidade de Euclydes da Cunha*. Rio de Janeiro: Casa do Estudante do Brasil, 1943.

Furtado, Celso. "Quatro expedições a Canudos." *Cadernos de Literatura Brasileira: Euclides da Cunha,* special issue, 13–14 (Dec. 2002): 118–23.

Galvão, Walnice Nogueira. "Um ausência: Euclides da Cunha." In *Os pobres na literatura brasileira,* edited by Roberto Schwarz, 31–53. São Paulo: Editora Brasiliense, 1983.

———. "O epos da modernização." *Luso-Brazilian Review* 31.1 (1994): 1–15.

———, ed. *Euclides da Cunha*. São Paulo: Atica, 1984.

———. *No calor da hora: A guerra de Canudos nos jornais, 4a expedição*. São Paulo: Atica, 1974.

———. *Saco de Gatos*. São Paulo: Duas Cidades, 1976.

Galvão, Walnice Nogueira, and Oswaldo Galotti, eds. *Correspondência de Euclides da Cunha*. São Paulo: Editora da Universidade de São Paulo, 1997.

Ganguly, Keya. *States of Exception: Everyday Life and Postcolonial Identity*. Minneapolis: University of Minnesota Press, 2001.

Geremoabo, Barão de. "Carta do Barão de Geremoabo publicada no *Jornal de Notícias*—Ba-hia—nos dias 4 e 5 de março de 1987." In João Arruda, *Canudos: Messianismo e conflito social,* appendix 2. Fortaleza, Brazil: Edições Universidade Federal do Ceará / Secult, 1993.

González Echevarría, Roberto. *Myth and Archive: A Theory of Latin American Narrative.* Cambridge: Cambridge University Press, 1990.

Graham, R. B. Cunninghame. *A Brazilian Mystic, Being the Life and Miracles of Antonio Conselheiro.* New York: Dodd, Mead, 1920.

Graham, Richard. *Patronage and Politics in Nineteenth-Century Brazil.* Stanford, Calif.: Stanford University Press, 1990.

Gramsci, Antonio. *The Antonio Gramsci Reader: Selected Writings 1916–1935.* New York: New York University Press, 2000.

Greenfield, Gerald Michael. "Sertão and Sertanejo: An Interpretive Context for Canudos." *Luso-Brazilian Review* 30.2 (1993): 35–46.

Gugelberger, Georg, ed. *The Real Thing: Testimonial Discourse and Latin America.* Durham: Duke University Press, 1996.

Guha, Ranajit. *Dominance without Hegemony: History and Power in Colonial India.* Cambridge, Mass.: Harvard University Press, 1997.

———. *Elementary Aspects of Peasant Insurgency in Colonial India.* New Delhi: Oxford University Press, 1983.

———. "The Prose of Counter-Insurgency." In *Selected Subaltern Studies,* edited by Ranajit Guha and Gayatri Spivak, 45–88. Oxford: Oxford University Press, 1988.

Guha, Ranajit, and Gayatri Spivak, eds. *Selected Subaltern Studies.* Oxford: Oxford University Press, 1988.

Guillory, John. *Cultural Capital.* Chicago: University of Chicago Press, 1993.

Gutiérrez, Angela Maria Rossas Mota de. "Notícia sobre cem anos de ficção canudiana." *Revista Canudos* 1.1 (1997): 9–22.

Hall, Stuart. "Signification, Representation, Ideology: Althusser and the Post-Structuralist Debates." *Critical Studies in Mass Communication* 2.2 (1985): 91–114.

———. "The State in Question." In *The Idea of the Modern State,* edited by David Held, Stuart Hall, and Gregor McLennan, 1–28. Milton Keynes, U.K.: Open University Press, 1984.

Hardman, Francisco Foot. "Tróia de taipa: De como Canudos queima aqui." In *Canudos: Palavra de Deus, sonho da terra,* edited by Benjamin Abdala Jr. and Isabel M. M. Alexandre, 57–66. São Paulo: Editora Serviço Nacional de Aprendizagem Comercial São Paulo / Boitempo Editorial, 1997.

Hardt, Michael. "The Withering of Civil Society." *Social Text* 14.4 (1995): 27–44.

Hegel, Georg. *The Philosophy of History.* New York: Dover, 1956.

Hentschke, Jens. *A luta abolicionista-republicana no Brasil e a Grande Revolução Francesa—um estudo da história das ideias.* Rostock: Universität Rostock / Instituto Latino-Americano, 1989.

Horcades, Alvim Martins. *Descrição de uma viagem a Canudos.* Bahia: Editora da Universidade Federal da Bahia, 1996.

Jameson, Fredric. "Reflections on the Brecht-Lukács Debate." *The Ideologies of Theory: Essays 1971–1986.* Vol. 2, *The Syntax of History,* 133–97. Minneapolis: University of Minnesota Press, 1989.

Janotti, Maria de Lourdes Monaco. *Os subversives da república.* São Paulo: Editora Brasiliense, 1986.

Kothe, Flávio R. *A proclamação da república e a literatura.* Rostock: Universität Rostock / Instituto Latino-Americano, 1990.

Kraniauskas, John. "Translation and the Work of Transculturation." *Traces* 1:95–108.

Lacerda, Rodrigo. "Sobrevoando Canudos." In *Canudos: Palavra de Deus, sonho da terra,* edited by Benjamin Abdala Jr. and Isabel M. M. Alexandre, 21–42. São Paulo: Editora Serviço Nacional de Aprendizajem Comercial São Paulo / Boitempo Editorial, 1997.

Laclau, Ernesto. *Emancipation(s).* New York: Verso, 1996.

———. *New Reflections on the Revolutions of Our Time.* London: Verso, 1990.

Laclau, Ernesto, and Chantal Mouffe. *Hegemony and Socialist Strategy: Towards a Radical Democratic Politics.* London: Verso, 1985.

Latin America Subaltern Studies Group. "Founding Statement." *boundary 2* 20 (Fall 1993): 110–21.

Lefebvre, Henri. *Critique of Everyday Life.* Vol. 1. New York: Verso, 1991.

———. *Critique of Everyday Life.* Vol. 2, *Foundations for a Sociology of the Everyday.* New York: Verso, 2002.

———. "The Everyday and Everydayness." *Yale French Studies* 73 (1987): 7–11.

Lessa, Renato. *Invenção republicana: Campos sales, as bases e a decadencia da Primeira Republica brasileira.* São Paulo: Vertice, 1988.

Levine, Robert. "The Singular Brazilian City of Salvador." *Luso-Brazilian Review* 30.2 (1993): 59–69.

———. *Vale of Tears: Revisiting the Canudos Massacre in Northeastern Brazil, 1893–97.* Berkeley: University of California Press, 1992.

Lienhard, Martin. "Los comienzos de la literatura 'latinoamericana': Monólogos y diálogos de conquistadores y conquistados." *América Latina: Palavra, literatura e cultura,* vol. 1A, edited by Ana Pizarro, 41–62. São Paulo: Memorial, 1993.

———. *La voz y su huella: Escritura y conflicto étnico social en América Latina.* Lima: Editorial Horizonte, 1992.

Lloyd, David. *Irish Times: Temporalities of Modernity*. Dublin: Field Day, 2008.

Lloyd, David, and Paul Thomas. *Culture and the State*. New York: Routledge, 1998.

Lukács, Georg. *Theory of the Novel*. Cambridge, Mass.: MIT Press, 1971.

Maciel, António Vicente Mendes. *António Conselheiro e Canudos (revisão histórica): A obra manuscrita de António Conselheiro e que pertenceu a Euclides da Cunha*. Edited by Ataliba Nogueira. Brasiliana, vol. 355. São Paulo: Companhia Editora Nacional, 1974.

Madden, Lori. "The Canudos War in History." *Luso-Brazilian Review* 30.2 (1993): 5–22.

———. "The Canudos War in Marxist Discourse." In *Toward Socio-Criticism: "Luso-Brazilian Literatures,"* edited by Roberto Reis, 189–96. Tempe: Center for Latin American Studies, Arizona State University, 1991.

———. "Evolution in the Interpretations of the Canudos Movement: An Evaluation of the Social Sciences." *Luso-Brazilian Review* 28.1 (1991): 59–75.

Maia, Cláudio Lopes, et al. *Canudos: Um povo entre a utopia e a resistência*. Cadernos do Centro Popular de Estudos Contemporâneos. Goiânia, Brazil: Centro Popular de Estudos Contemporâneos, 1999.

Mallon, Florencia. "The Promise and Dilemma of Subaltern Studies: Perspectives from Latin American History." *American Historical Review* 5 (1994): 1491–1515.

Mangabeira, Francisco. *Tragédia epica*. Bahia: Imprenta Moderna de Prudência de Carvalho.

Márai, Sándor. *Veredicto em Canudos*. São Paulo: Editora Schwarcz, 2001.

Marx, Karl. *Early Writings*. New York: Vintage, 1975.

Mascarenhas, Maria Lúcia F. "Rio de sangue e ribanceira de corpos." In *Canudos (Cadernos do CEAS)*, edited by Alfredo Souza Dórea, 59–72. Salvador, Brazil: Centro de Estudos e Ação Social, 1997.

———. "Toda nação em Canudos, 1893–1897: Índios em Canudos (memória e tradição oral da participação dos Kiriri e Kaimbes naguerra de Canudos)." *Revista Canudos* 2.2 (1997): 68–84.

Massote, Fernando. "Por quê Canudos?" *Revista Canudos* 2.2 (1997): 130–39.

Mazzotti, José Antonio. "Indigenismos de ayer: Prototipos perdurables del discurso criollo." In *Asedios a la heterogeneidad cultural: Libro de homenaje a Antonio Cornejo Polar*, edited by José Antonio Mazzotti and Juan Zevallos Aguilar, 77–99. Philadelphia: Asociación Internacional de Peruanistas, 1996.

Meihy, José Carlos Sebe Bom. "Meu empenho foi ser o tradutor do universo sertanejo (entrevista com José Calazans)." *Luso-Brazilian Review* 30.2 (1993): 23–33.

Mello, Dante de. *A verdade sobre "Os sertões": Análise reivindicatória da Campanha de Canudos*. Rio de Janeiro: Biblioteca do Exército Editôra, 1958.

Meznar, Joan. "The Ranks of the Poor: Military Service and Social Differentiation in Northeast Brazil, 1830–1875." *Hispanic American Historical Review* 72.3 (1992): 335–51.

Mignolo, Walter. *The Darker Side of the Renaissance: Literacy, Territoriality, and Colonization.* Ann Arbor: University of Michigan Press, 1995.

———. *Local Histories/Global Designs: Coloniality, Subaltern Knowledges, and Border Thinking.* Princeton: Princeton University Press, 2000.

Miller, Nicola. *In the Shadow of the State.* London: Verso, 1999.

Moniz, Edmundo. *A guerra social de Canudos.* Rio de Janeiro: Civilização Brasileira, 1978.

Montag, Warren. "Beyond Force and Consent: Althusser, Spinoza, Hobbes." In *Postmodern Materialism and the Future of Marxist Theory,* edited by Antonio Callari and David F. Ruccio, 91–108. Hanover, N.H.: University Press of New England / Wesleyan University Press, 1996.

Moraña, Mabel. "El boom del subalterno." *Revista de Crítica Cultural* 15 (1997): 48–53.

Moreiras, Alberto. "The Aura of Testimonio." *The Real Thing: Testimonial Discourse and Latin America,* 192–224. Durham: Duke University Press, 1996.

———. *The Exhaustion of Difference: The Politics of Latin American Cultural Studies.* Durham: Duke University Press, 2001.

Morel, Marco. "La génesis de la opinión pública moderna y el proceso de independencia (Rio de Janeiro, 1820–1840)." *Los espacios públicos en Iberoamerica,* 300–320. Mexico City: Fondo de Cultura Económica, 1998.

Mörner, Magnus. *Region and State in Latin America's Past.* Baltimore: Johns Hopkins University Press, 1993.

Morse, Richard. "Political Foundations." *Man, State, and Society in Latin American History,* 72–79. New York: Praeger, 1972.

Moura, Clovis. *Introdução ao pensamento de Euclides da Cunha.* Rio de Janeiro: Editora Civilização Brasileira, 1964.

Muniz de Albuquerque, Durval. *A invenção do nordeste e outras artes.* São Paulo: Cortez Editora, 1999.

Nancy, Jean-Luc. *The Inoperative Community.* Minneapolis: University of Minnesota Press, 1991.

Nascimento, José Leonardo, ed. *"Os sertões" de Euclides da Cunha: Releituras e diálogos.* São Paulo: Editora Universidade Estadual Paulista, 2002.

Needell, Jeffrey. "The Domestic Civilizing Mission: The Cultural Role of the State, 1808–1930." *Luso-Brazilian Review* 36.1 (1999): 1–18.

———. *The Party of Order: The Conservatives, the State, and Slavery in the Brazilian Monarchy, 1831–1871.* Stanford, Calif.: Stanford University Press, 2006.

———. "Provincial Origins of the Brazilian State: Rio de Janeiro, the Monarchy and National Political Organization, 1808–1853." *Latin American Research Review* 36.3 (2001): 132–53.

Negri, Antonio, and Giuseppe Cocco. *GlobAL: Biopoder y luchas en una América Latina globalizada.* Buenos Aires: Paidós, 2006.

Neto, Manoel. "Canudos na boca do povo." *Revista Canudos* 2.2 (1997): 56–67.

———. "Canudos: Tempo de pensar, tempo de contar." In *Canudos (Cadernos do CEAS),* edited by Alfredo Souza Dórea, 163–70. Salvador, Brazil: Centro de Estudos e Ação Social, 1997.

———. "De Juazeiro à ladeira da Barra: A inusitada trajetória da expedição Pires Ferreira." *Revista Canudos* 1.1 (1997): 55–64.

Nina Rodrigues, Raimundo. *As coletividades anormais.* Brasília: Edições do Senado Federal, 2006.

Olavo, Antônio, dir. *Paixão e guerra no sertão de Canudos.* VHS. Portfolium Laboratório de Imagens, 1993.

Oliveira, Franklin de. *Euclydes: A espada e a letra: Uma biografia intelectual.* Rio de Janeiro: Editora Paz e Terra, 1983.

Oliveira Mello, Antônio. *De volta ao sertão: Afonso Arinos e o regionalismo Brasileiro.* Rio de Janeiro: Livraria Editora Cátedra, 1981.

Ortiz, Fernando. *Contrapunteo cubano del tabaco y el azúcar.* Madrid: Edito CubaEspaña, 1999.

Otten, Alexandre. "A influência do ideário religioso na construção da comunidade de Belo Monte." *Luso-Brazilian Review* 30.2 (1993): 71–95.

Piedade, Lélis. *Histórico e relatório do Comitê Patriótico da Bahia (1897–1901).* 2d ed., edited by Antônio Olavo. Salvador, Brazil: Portfolium, 2002.

Pinheiro, José Carlos da Costa. "Rede de intrigas/falas incendiárias." *Revista Canudos* 2.2 (1997): 149–59.

Pinho, Patricia de Santana. "Revistando Canudos hoje no imaginário popular." *Revista Canudos* 1.1 (1997): 173–203.

Poncio, Denise dos Santos. "Canudos—uma construção oligárquica." In *Canudos (Cadernos do CEAS),* edited by Alfredo Souza Dórea, 47–53. Salvador, Brazil: Centro de Estudos e Ação Social, 1997.

Prakash, Gyan. "Can the 'Subaltern' Ride? A Reply to O'Hanlon and Washbrook." In *Mapping Subaltern Studies and the Postcolonial,* edited by Vinayak Chaturvedi, 220–38. New York: Verso, 2000.

———. "The Impossibility of Subaltern History." *Nepantla* 1.2 (2001): 287–94.

———. "Subaltern Studies as Postcolonial Criticism." *American Historical Review* 99 (Dec. 1994): 1475–90.

———. "Writing Post-Orientalist Histories of the Third World: Perspectives from Indian Historiography." *Comparative Studies in Society and History* 32.2 (1990): 383–408.

Queiroz, Maria Isaura Pereira de. *O messianismo no Brasil e no mundo*. São Paulo: Dominus Editôra, 1965.

Rabello, Sylvio. *Euclides da Cunha*. Rio de Janeiro: Civilização Brasileira, 1966.

Radcliffe-Brown, Alfred. Preface. In *African Political Systems*, edited by Meyers Fortes and Edward Evans-Pritchard, xi–xxiv. London: Kegan Paul International, 1987.

Rama, Angel. "El 'Boom' en perspectiva." *Mas allá del boom: Literatura y mercado*, 51–110. Mexico City: Marcha Editores, 1981.

———. *La ciudad letrada*. Hanover, N.H.: Ediciones del Norte, 1984.

———. *Transculturación narrativa en América Latina*. Mexico City: Siglo Veintiuno Editores, 1982.

Ramos, Julio. *Desencuentros de la modernidad en América Latina*. Mexico City: Fondo de Cultura Económica, 1989.

———. "'Saber Decir': Literatura y modernización en Andrés Bello." *Nueva Revista de Filología Hispánica* (Mexico) 35.2 (1987): 675–94.

Reesink, Edwin. "A tomada do coração da aldeia: A participação dos índios de Massacará na Guerra de Canudos." In *Canudos (Cadernos do CEAS)*, edited by Alfredo Souza Dórea, 73–95. Salvador, Brazil: Centro de Estudos e Ação Social, 1997.

Rezende, Sérgio, dir. *Guerra de Canudos*. VHS. Colombia Tristar Video, 1997.

Ribeiro, Renato Janine. "O sertão virou mar ou o rebaixamento do que se eleva." In *Canudos: Palavra de Deus, sonho da terra*, edited by Benjamin Abdala Jr. and Isabel M. M. Alexandre, 11–20. São Paulo: Editora Serviço Nacional de Aprendizajem Comercial São Paulo / Boitempo Editorial, 1997.

Ricoer, Paul. *Time and Narrative*. Chicago: University of Chicago Press, 1984.

Rodríguez, Ileana, ed. *The Latin American Subaltern Studies Reader*. Durham: Duke University Press, 2001.

Roseberry, William. "The Language of Contention." In *Everyday Forms of State Formation: Revolution and the Negotiation of Rule in Modern Mexico*, edited by Gilbert Joseph and Daniel Nugent, 355–66. Durham: Duke University Press, 1994.

Rousseau, Jean-Jacques. "Of the Social Contract." *The Social Contract and Other Later Political Writings*, 39–120. Cambridge: Cambridge University Press, 1997.

Sampaio, Consuelo Novais, ed. *Canudos: Cartas para o barão*. São Paulo: Editora da Universidade de São Paulo, 2001.

———. "Repensando Canudos: O jogo das oligarquias." *Luso-Brazilian Review* 30.2 (1993): 97–113.

Sampaio Neto, José Augusto Vaz, ed. *Canudos: Subsídio para a sua reavaliação histórica*. Rio de Janeiro: Fundação Casa de Rui Barbosa, 1986.

Santiago, Silviano. *Nas malhas da letra*. Rio de Janeiro: Editora Rocco, 2002.

Santos, Eurides de Souza. *A música de Canudos*. Salvador, Brazil: Secretaria da Cultura e Turismo do Estado da Bahia / Empresa Gráfica da Bahia, 1998.

Sayer, Derek. "Everyday Forms of State Formation: Some Dissident Remarks on 'Hegemony.'" *Everyday Forms of State Formation: Revolution and the Negotiation of Rule in Mexico*, 367–78. Durham: Duke University Press, 1994.

Schultz, Kirsten. *Tropical Versailles: Empire, Monarchy, and the Portuguese Royal Court in Rio de Janeiro, 1808–1821*. New York: Routledge, 2001.

Schwarz, Roberto. *Misplaced Ideas: Essays on Brazilian Culture*. London: Verso, 1992.

Seel, Antoine. "Por trás das palavras: Fluxos e ritmos en *Os sertões*." In *"Os sertões" de Euclides da Cunha: Releituras e diálogos*, edited by José Leonardo do Nascimento, 149–72. São Paulo: Editora Universidade Estadual Paulista, 2002.

Sevcenko, Nicolau. *Literatura como missão: Tensões sociais e criação cultural na Primeira República*. São Paulo: Editora Brasiliense, 1983.

———. "Peregrinations, Visions, and the City: From Canudos to Brasília, the Backlands Become the City and the City Becomes the Backlands." In *Through the Kaleidescope*, edited by Vivian Schelling, 75–106. New York: Verso, 2000.

Silva, José Paulino da. "Breve roteiro para se chegar a Canudos." In *Canudos (Cadernos do CEAS)*, edited by Alfredo Souza Dórea, 27–34. Salvador, Brazil: Centro de Estudos e Ação Social, 1997.

Skidmore, Thomas. "Toward a Comparative Analysis of Race Relations since Abolition in Brazil and the United States." *Journal of Latin American Studies* 4 (1972): 1–28.

Skidmore, Thomas E., and Peter H. Smith. *Modern Latin America*. New York: Oxford University Press, 1992.

Slater, Candace. *Stories on a String: The Brazilian Literatura de Cordel*. Berkeley: University of California Press, 1982.

Soares de Souza, Licia. "Canudos e o rei do gado." *Canudos* 2.2 (1997): 14–33.

Sodré, Nelson Werneck. *História da imprensa no Brasil*. Rio de Janeiro: Editora Mauad, 1998.

Sommer, Doris. *Foundational Fictions: The National Romances of Latin America*. Berkeley: University of California Press, 1991.

———. *Proceed with Caution, When Engaged by Minority Writing in the Americas*. Cambridge, Mass.: Harvard University Press, 1999.

Souto Maior, Armando. *Quebra-Quilos: Lutas socais no outono do Império*. São Paulo: Companhia Editora Nacional, 1978.

Spivak, Gayatri Chakravorty. *A Critique of Postcolonial Reason*. Boston: Harvard University Press, 1999.

———. "Subaltern Studies: Deconstructing Historiography." In *Subaltern Studies*, vol. 4, edited by Ranajit Guha, 330–63. London: Oxford University Press, 1985.

Tarde, Gabriel. "The Public and the Crowd." *On Communication and Social Influence (Selected Papers)*, 277–94. Chicago: University of Chicago Press, 1969.

Taussig, Michael. "Maleficium: State Fetishism." In *Fetishism as Cultural Discourse*, edited by F. Apter and W. Pietz, 217–47. Ithaca, N.Y.: Cornell University Press, 1993.

Tavares, Odórico. *Canudos: 50 anos depois*. Salvador, Brazil: Fundação de Cultura do Estado, 1947.

Taylor, Charles. *Altarity*. Chicago: University of Chicago Press, 1987.

Theodoro, Janice. "Canudos 100 anos depois: Da vida comunitária ao surgimento dos movimentos fundamentalistas." In *Canudos: Palavra de Deus, sonho da terra*, edited Benjamin Abdala Jr. and Isabel M. M. Alexandre, 119–33. São Paulo: Editora Serviço Nacional de Aprendizajem Comercial São Paulo / Boitempo Editorial, 1997.

Toledo, Roberto Pompeu. "Caderneta de campo: Viagem aos domínios do Conselheiro." *Cadernos de Literatura Brasileira: Euclides da Cunha*, special issue, 13–14 (Dec. 2002): 74–115.

Trouillot, Michel-Rolph. *Silencing the Past: Power and the Production of History*. Boston: Beacon, 1995.

Vargas Llosa, Mario. *Contra viento y marea*. 2d ed. Vol. 2. Barcelona: Seix Barral, 1986.

———. *The War of the End of the World*. New York: Avon, 1981.

Veiga, José J. *A casca da serpente*. Rio de Janeiro: Bertrand Brasil, 2001.

Ventura, Roberto. "Canudos como cidade iletrada: Euclides da Cunha e a urbs monstruosa." *Revista Canudos* 1.1 (1997): 81–90.

———. "A Nossa Vendéia: Canudos, o mito da Revolução Francesa e a constituição de identidade nacional-cultural no Brasil." *Revista de Critica Literaria Latinoamericana* 24 (1986): 109–25.

Viana Filho, Luiz. *Mensagem do dr. Governador da Bahia ao Sr. Presidente da Republica sobre os antecedentes e ocurrencias das expedições contra Antonio Conselheiro e seus sequazes*. Salvador, Brazil: Correio de Notícias, 1897.

Vilanova, Honório (and Nertan Macedo). *Memorial de Vilanova: Depoimento do último sobrevivente da Guerra de Canudos*. Rio de Janeiro: Edições O Cruzeiro, 1964.

Villa, Marco Antonio. *Canudos: O povo da terra*. São Paulo: Editora Atica, 1995.

———. "Em busca de um mundo novo." *Revista Canudos* 1.1 (1997): 25–35.

Villela Júnior, Marcos Evangelista da Costa. *Canudos: Memórias de um combatente*. São Paulo: Editora Marco Zero, 1988.

Viotti da Costa, Emília. *Da monarquia à república: Momentos decisivos*. São Paulo: Editora Universidade Estadual Paulista, 1998.

———. "1870–1889." In *Brazil: Empire and Republic 1822–1930*, edited by Leslie Bethell, 161–213. Cambridge: Cambridge University Press, 1989.

Virno, Paolo. *A Grammar of the Multitude*. New York: Semiotext(e), 2004.

Weinstein, Barbara. "Postcolonial Brazil." In *The Oxford Handbook of Latin American History*, edited by José C. Moya. London: Oxford University Press, forthcoming.

Williams, Gareth. "La deconstrucción y los estudios subalternos, o, una llave de tuerca en la línea de montaje latinoamericanista." In *Treinta años de estudios literarios/culturales Latinoamericanistas en Estados Unidos: Memorias, testimonios, reflexiones críticas*, edited by Hernán Vidal, 221–56. Pittsburgh: International Institute of Iberoamerican Literature, 2008.

———. *The Other Side of the Popular: Neoliberalism and Subalternity in Latin America*. Durham: Duke University Press, 2002.

Williams, Raymond. *Marxism and Literature*. Oxford: Oxford University Press, 1977.

———. *Resources of Hope: Culture, Democracy, Socialism*. New York: Verso, 1989.

Zama, César. *Libelo republicano acompanhado de comentários sobre a guerra de Canudos*. Centro de Estudos Baianos da Universidade Federal da Bahia, vol. 139. Salvador, Brazil: Universidade Federal da Bahia, 1989.

Žižek, Slavoj. *The Sublime Object of Ideology*. London: Verso, 1989.

INDEX